The Seven Points of a Mother's Spiritual Growth

1. A mother learns the value of courage:

   Through taking on the challenge of raising her child.

   As she faces her need and desire to protect that child.

   As she learns to rise to the challenges of each new stage in her child's development.

2. A mother learns the value of tolerance:

   As she respects her child's right to take risks.

   As she respects her child's right to make mistakes.

   As she respects her child's right to determine his or her own personal values.

3. A mother learns the value of self protection:

   As she sets appropriate limits and boundaries for her children and for herself.

4. A mother learns self-love:

   As she comes to understand her value to her child and her family.

   As she discovers her strengths as a parent to her child.

5. A mother learns to tame her ego:

   By discovering her limits and learning to ask for help when she needs it.

   By learning to let go of the controlling reins on her child's life.

6. A mother learns to love humanity:

   When she recognizes that all children are equally deserving of love and care.

7. A mother learns of God-love:

   As she recognizes that the unconditional love she feels for her child is offered to her by God.

alpha
books

The 10 Stages of Momhood

1. We're having a baby
2. Dealing with diapers
3. Toddler-ing along
4. Preschool playtime
5. Growing through the grade school years
6. Surviving dorkdom with your preteen
7. Teen-years angst
8. Growing closer to your young adult
9. Surviving the empty nest
10. Waxing wise as a grandma

Mother's Mantras

"A mother's ultimate bittersweet goal is to succeed in making her child independent."

"Complacency is impossible for mothers: as soon as you've mastered raising a toddler, your child transforms into a whole new being: preschooler. And so it goes through every stage of your child's life."

"If you hold on to your child too tightly, you'll force him to push you away."

"Adolescents aren't really demon spawn—it just feels that way sometimes. In 8 years, they'll revert to human once again."

"Believe it or not, the day will come when you and your child become true friends."

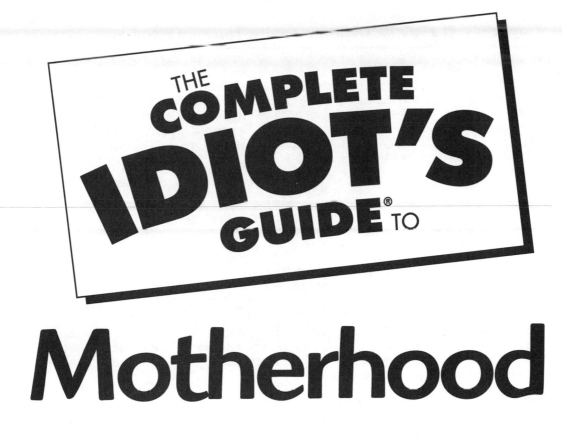

THE COMPLETE IDIOT'S GUIDE® TO

Motherhood

by Deborah Levine Herman

alpha
books

A Division of Macmillan General Reference
A Pearson Education Macmillan Company
1633 Broadway, New York, NY 10019-6785

Alpha Development Team

Publisher
Kathy Nebenhaus

Editorial Director
Gary M. Krebs

Managing Editor
Bob Shuman

Marketing Brand Manager
Felice Primeau

Acquisitions Editor
Jessica Faust

Development Editors
Phil Kitchel
Amy Zavatto

Assistant Editor
Georgette Blau

Production Team

Development Editor
Nancy E. Gratton

Production Editor
Suzanne Snyder

Copy Editor
Gail Burlakoff

Cover Designer
Mike Freeland

Photo Editor
Richard H. Fox

Illustrator
Brian Mac Moyer

Book Designers
Scott Cook and Amy Adams of DesignLab

Indexer
Aamir Burki

Layout/Proofreading
Angela Calvert
Mary Hunt
Julie Trippetti

Contents at a Glance

Contents

Appendix

Foreword

When I found out I was going to become a mother, I was hit with all sorts of conflicting emotions. Like other mothers-to-be, I felt thrilled at the thought of having a child, terror at the prospect of pain during labor and delivery, anxiety over the health of the fetus, and even a bit of sadness that my free-as-a-bird childless days were ending. In other words, I was in shock.

And that was just the pregnancy! Once I realized I had actually survived childbirth and was now the mother of this healthy, perfect newborn, I was unbelievably overwhelmed with the responsibility of mothering another human being. I remember lying there in the maternity ward after my husband had left, staring down at my brand new daughter in my arms—for what seemed like hours—unaware of my roommate's arrival, the nurse taking my temperature, or the beautiful yellow roses my sister had sent.

That was almost twelve years ago. Since then my daughter—and my son, born eighteen months later—have taught me a great deal about the fulfilling, exhilarating, exhausting and frustrating job of being a mother. And I'm still learning.

I've concluded that motherhood, for most of us, is like one long out-of-control roller coaster ride—filled with terrifying descents and painstaking climbs, hairpin turns and perilous peaks where we pause to catch our breath, knowing we'll soon be taking another dive into the unknown.

As exciting as motherhood is, it is terribly unfamiliar—with on the job training only. As mothers quickly find out, there is seldom a "right" or "wrong" way of mothering, but sometimes there is an *easy* way. What Deborah Herman has done in this wonderfully practical book is guide us—step by step, inch by inch, through this harrowing journey of motherhood. She shows us the methods that make a mom's life easiest by giving us a blueprint of sorts—a map for moms. Never have I seen such a thorough guide for mothers. Her book gives down-to-earth advice on everything from pregnancy and childbirth, through toddlerhood, preschool, adolescence, and young adulthood— all the way to adjusting to the empty nest syndrome. She has also included a helpful section called "Special Issues on the Motherhood Trail" where she tackles such difficult topics as the special-needs child, divorce, and blended families. Through it all, Deborah's wise words encourage us to keep our own identity as well as our sense of humor—a quality desperately important to surviving motherhood.

Since my own two children—age 10 and 12—are beginning to cross over into that scary phase called adolescence, I was particularly interested in Part 4, which covers such hilarious but vital chapters as "Becoming a Dork: Your Preteen and You"— whereby moms learn to take it in stride when their child suddenly refuses to be seen in public with you and "Loosening the Reins Without Letting Go," which addresses the touchy subject of maintaining discipline during the teen years.

Deborah teaches us to take the time to celebrate being mothers—without pretending it is an easy journey. Like getting on a roller coaster, motherhood means nose diving into the great unknown. The climb is painstaking, and those hairpin turns are very stressful.

Oh, but what a glorious ride it is.

—Joan Leonard

Joan Leonard, mother of two, is the author of several books, including *Tales From Toddler Hell: My Life as Mom, What to Do to Improve Your Child's Manners,* a *Reader's Digest Parenting Guide,* and *Twice Blessed: Having a Second Child.* Her articles have appeared in *Parents, Woman's Day, Good Housekeeping, Glamour, Ladies Home Journal, Redbook, The New York Times,* and *Newsday.* Ms. Leonard, who has a Masters Degree in English Literature from SUNY Stony Brook, lives in Northport, New York and teaches English at Northport High School.

Introduction

Becoming a Mom! It's just about the most exciting, overwhelming, wonderful, intimidating, amazing thing you could possibly imagine. But we're all pretty hazy about the actual details of the job when we first take it on. Babys just don't come with operating instructions, and besides, figuring out the mechanics of childcare is only a small part of our brand new job.

If you're like most of us, the problem is that you're getting your on-the-job training in a vacuum—convinced that you're the *only* Mom's who ever felt unsure of yourself. You look around and see all those *other* Moms looking self-assured, confident, and competent, and you can start to feel isolated, even a little scared.

But the fact is that today's Moms are all feeling just like you do. After all, things have changed dramatically since your own mother's generation. Unlike the Moms of the 1950s and 1960s, you've no doubt spent most of your life as a successful student and career woman—not focusing on learning the intricacies of the domestic arts. Now, suddenly, you're facing the most challenging job you'll ever take on, without any clear guidance on how to do it!

And that's why I wrote this book.

In *The Complete Idiot's Guide to Motherhood*, I share with you the experiences and (I hope) wisdom I've gained while raising my own three children. You'll learn about all the joys—and sometimes tears and fears—that you'll encounter as you navigate through the many different stages of your child's life.

Because, you see, being a mother means many different things. You're the center of your infant's universe; the wisest and wittiest person in the world during the preschool years; a hopeless dork when they hit the preteens; and an authority figure to rebel against when they're in their teens. And, after all that, if you're lucky, you have the opportunity to become a friend and mentor to the marvelous young adult your child ultimately becomes.

As you grow with your child, the changes you'll face come thick and fast. You'll sometimes feel as if the years are rushing by at a bewildering pace. But I'll be with you every step of the way, with tales from my own odyssey through the motherhood years. Think of this book as your friend and guide, offering you support and suggestions along the way.

The most important thing to realize is that there is no single, right way to be a mother. Each one of us has to discover the style best suited to us and to the unique relationship we build with our children. If this book has any single, most important message, it would be this:

> You have within you all the wisdom and potential you need to be a wonderful mother—if only you can learn to trust in your intuitive knowledge.

This is not a step-by-step how-to book on parenting. Instead, I have tried to address the much more subtle, personal issues of what it takes to negotiate the wonderful transformations that every mother experiences. The suggestions and guidance provided in these pages are intended to help you learn to trust your own natural, maternal wisdom. When you learn to do that, you'll learn why mothers the world over have found this role—unpaid, often under-appreciated, always challenging—to be the most fulfilling thing they've every done in their lives.

How to Use This Book

In **Part 1, "The Making of a Mom,"** we'll talk about all the confusing, conflicting, and definitely exciting emotions that come with your first realization that you're soon going to join that special sisterhood: the world of mothers. You'll learn what to expect as you go through the physical and emotional changes of pregnancy. And we'll pull back the curtain on the mysteries of labor and childbirth—not in terms of a medical textbook, but in the more personal idiom of a Mom's subjective experience.

In **Part 2, "From Nursery to Preschool,"** you'll cover a lot of ground. After all, becoming a Mom is not just taking on a new job—it's assuming a new role that you have to integrate into all the others you must play. So we'll look at the adjustments you'll have to make now that your comfortable couple-dom has become a threesome. But we'll also look at the bewildering array of decisions you must make as you strive to fulfill your child's needs. Here is where you'll begin to learn the essential truth: there are many, many different ways to be a great Mom—all you need to do is find the way that most suits you and your child.

Part 3, "Calling All Super Moms!" is, in many ways, the heart of this book. It strips away all the intimidating over-expectations we carry with us into our role as Moms. No, you don't have to "do it all," but yes, you *can* "have it all." All it takes is some organization (I'll help you on that by giving you some scheduling guidelines), a willingness to accept a little support once and awhile, and a well-developed sense of humor!

In this section you'll also learn how to bring some of that old magic back into your relationship with your partner. Too often, as we focus in on our new role as mothers, we forget that we're somebody's wife or partner as well. In the midst of full diapers and formula bottles, it's easy to forget that, not so long ago, we really *did* have a sensual side. Here, you'll learn how to rediscover that sensual you, and that it's possible to have a sex life after the kids are born.

Finally, Chapter 11, "Intuitive Mothering," provides you with a full, explicit statement of what real mothering is all about: the full engagement of your unique personality with that of your child. You'll learn how to respect your own internal wisdom, and how to tap into it to become the best mother you can be.

Part 4, "You, Your Kids, and Your Changing Relationship," is also important. Here you learn that motherhood is not just one role but many, and you learn how that role modifies over time as your child matures and his or her needs change. Coping with the ever-changing nature of our motherhood role is perhaps the hardest part of being a Mom. Just when you're finally accustomed to dealing with a dependent infant who thinks you're the center of the universe, she transforms herself into a very vocal, contrarian toddler whose favorite word is "NO!"

These changes are hard to handle because they hit us in the ego. But that's only to be expected. After all, it is a fundamental part of mothering to be working towards our own obsolescence—we've done our job right if we've raised our kids not to need us. We want to help them become independent, after all. But remember, no matter how independent your child becomes, he or she will always need you for nurturing and love—the mother-child bond must always stretch, but it never breaks.

In **Part 5, "Special Issues on the Motherhood Trail"** shifts the focus a little. It would be wonderful if we all lived in the 1950s world of *Happy Days*, with 2.5 perfectly healthy children and rock-solid marriages. But that's TV sitcom-land and this is real life. Sometimes motherhood means dealing with some difficult issues.

Some children have special needs, and this can be an awesomely intimidating thing to face. You have to become your child's advocate, on top of everything else that a good mom does. Every mother's heart is wounded when she sees her child in pain—whether that pain is physical, mental, or emotional. But raising a special-needs child bears within it many wondrous rewards. You'll learn here how to see, and appreciate, them.

You'll also learn how to navigate, if necessary, that other negative aspect of modern parenting life: divorce. In Chapter 18 you'll learn how to negotiate this difficult passage while keeping your children emotionally safe and secure. Chapters 19 and 20 talk you through the challenges every single mom faces, from running a household solo to re-entering the world of dating. And Chapter 21 takes up the often difficult subject of merging households—a modern take on that old Lucille Ball classic movie, *Yours, Mine, and Ours*.

The last section of the book, **Part 6: "Getting to Know You,"** brings the story to a close. When your children are grown, you have so many wonderful opportunities, not least of which is the chance to become true friends with your adult child. The close bond that can be forged between mother and adult child is perhaps the most intimate and rewarding relationship you can ever enjoy. Here you'll learn how to build, and appreciate, that relationship.

But this is also the time in your life when you can finally turn the spotlight back onto yourself: on your own, personal dreams and goals. We'll talk here about how you can get back in touch with all those parts of you that were subsumed in the responsibility of raising your children, and about how you can unleash your personal potential in ways you never dreamed you could.

Finally, it's time to "Celebrate a Job Well Done." The last chapter of this book is time to pause and reflect over all the growth and gain, the joys and sorrows, you've experienced throughout the course of your life as a mother. It's a time for contemplation and self-congratulation. You've accomplished what is perhaps the single most important job anyone could ever attempt: You are a Mom!

Extras

As you've come to expect with every other *Complete Idiot's Guide*, I've scattered some special notes and insights throughout this book to help clarify a point, share a bit of information, or pass along a personal anecdote. Here's a key that explains these little tidbits:

Momma Said There'd be Days Like This

Look here for longer anecdotes (many of them drawn from my personal experience) and quotes about common motherhood themes.

Mom Alert!

These are warnings of obstacles or problems you might run into along the way.

Womanly Wisdom

Whenever I've got a particularly useful tip to pass along, you'll find it here.

Mom-isms

These are definitions that will pop up in the text whenever a new or unusual term is introduced.

Acknowledgments

How can I possibly acknowledge and show gratitude to all the people who have enabled me to write this book? This book is my life and my journey. Whoever has crossed my path has also sparked my flame.

First and foremost I want to thank my husband and best friend, Jeff Herman, for sharing my life, believing in me, and for signing up for the great adventure. It is truly a special man who would so lovingly give up bachelorhood for a ready-made family of three hooligans and their frazzled mom.

Thank you to my three unique and resilient children who have taught me how to be a mother when I had no idea what to do. I love you all very much.

I want to acknowledge my big sister, Brenda, my idol of domestic goddesshood, and my brilliantly creative brother, Larry, for sharing a fun, mischievous childhood—and for still being my friends.

I want to thank my Grandmother, Mildred Shaff, for blazing a path for modern womanhood; and my mother, Paula Levine, for blasting that path into a superhighway. And my father, Stuart Levine, who never missed an opportunity to brag about me no matter what I did. Every writer should have a father like that.

Of course I want to acknowledge my editor, Jessica Faust, for giving me a lot of room; my development editor and wonderful motivator, Nancy Gratton; my production editor, Suzanne Snyder; and all the staff at Alpha Books who made this book possible.

Part 1
The Making of a Mom

When I first found out I was pregnant in 1984, I was thrilled. I couldn't wait for everybody to know—I even started pooching out my tummy and looking at all the clothes in the maternity shops, eager for the day when my own bulge would be big enough for me to start wearing high-waisted dresses or those pants with the elastic panels in the front.

But there's a whole lot more to incipient momhood than the proverbial glow. And some of it—like morning sickness—can be less than thrilling. Part 1 tells you all about the ups and downs of momhood-to-be, from that first positive EPT result to that last big puuuush. Get ready for the toughest job you'll ever love: You're gonna be a mom!

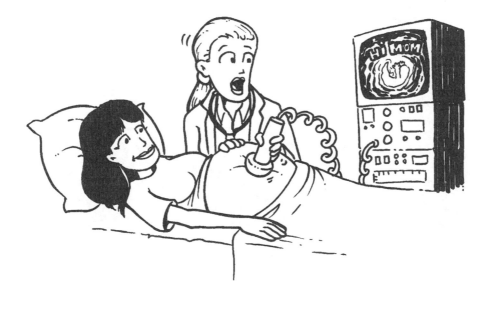

Chapter 1

So, You're Going to Be a Mom!

In This Chapter

➤ What pregnancy is really like

➤ How you are changing, inside and out

➤ Taking care of yourself

If you are pregnant, or thinking about becoming pregnant, you are going to experience changes you've never known before. With the exception of your first French kiss or the experience that got you into this condition in the first place, having a baby is the kind of thing that can really only be understood by doing it. It is, however, a common experience shared by women from every culture, walk of life, and ethnic background. It does have some common elements, however, and in this chapter you're going to learn about them, and how to make the most of these first stages of your transformation into a *Mom*!

So You Are Pregnant...Now What?

Well, you know that sooner or later you're going to give birth because what goes in must come out. But there's a lot that's going to happen in the time *between* conception and the blessed event. And whether you're a first-timer or an old hand at pregnancy, the type of pregnancy you have, barring any medical complications, will depend largely on how you feel about being pregnant.

Your Mind-Set Matters

As you know, the mind and the body are very much connected. If you strongly view pregnancy as some type of disability, you are going to treat yourself differently than if you see it as a natural process that you are well equipped to handle. It is very easy during a first pregnancy to choose to completely baby yourself—as if you have a chronic illness, however temporary. It *is* wonderful to be good to yourself, but if you focus your attention on every little new ache, pain, or physical change as if it were fatal, you will magnify your discomfort tremendously.

Your Body Has a Mind of Its Own

Pregnancy is not without very real—and sometimes very annoying—symptoms. Particularly during a first pregnancy, your hormones will very likely treat you to such wonderful experiences as the legendary *morning sickness*. Your body is preparing itself for the process of gestation. Each person has a different threshold for tolerating nausea but for some it can be quite debilitating. It usually settles down after a few weeks but sometimes can plague you throughout the entire pregnancy.

Momma Said There'd Be Days Like This

During my first pregnancy certain odors were triggers for potential barfing. For example, I love to cook with sesame oil but could not be in the room with it while I was pregnant with my oldest daughter. Instead, I pretty much lived on bland soda crackers—they're all I could keep down.

Mom-isms

Morning sickness refers to periodic episodes of nausea common during the early months of pregnancy. It can happen at any time of day (or night), but generally ends around the third or fourth month.

And by the way, although it's commonly called *morning* sickness, you can experience nausea at any time of day or night. A good way to ward off the queasies is to stick to bland foods like soda crackers or dry toast. Fluids also help. If you are actually vomiting, make sure you replace your fluids and electrolytes with drinks designed for that purpose. Gatorade or other sports drinks can help.

Restricting your diet to accommodate your morning sickness can be tough—especially if old favorites of your prepregnancy days are now triggering the nausea response. Just keep in mind that this, too, shall pass. And promise yourself a great post-pregnancy reward of all the foods you're denying yourself now.

Sleepy-Time Gal

So many physical changes happen when you are pregnant that it sometimes feels as though you're only renting your body and are at the mercy of an absentee landlord. During your first *trimester* you will very likely feel greater fatigue than you have ever felt before.

Listen to what your body is telling you. When you are tired do your best to catch a nap. If you're working during your pregnancy, even a few minutes with your head down on your desk can make a big difference—you might want to put a co-worker on "snore alert," just in case. Don't try to overcome the drowsiness with caffeine; it is not good for you or your baby.

Mom-isms

A nine-month pregnancy is usually divided into three 3-month-long periods, called **trimesters.** Certain changes or symptoms—like morning sickness—are commonly experienced in particular trimesters but not in others.

Food Fancies

Even if you're one of the many lucky ones who don't have to deal with morning sickness, you'll probably still find your food preferences changing. For some reason, foods you might not have been crazy about before can start to taste incredibly delicious. (For me it was Japanese food, but you should skip the sushi—it's not recommended during pregnancy.)

You may even experience that old stereotype of pregnancy: food cravings. Don't feel guilty! Although there's no hard-and-fast scientific proof, many doctors believe that some cravings are actually your body's way of telling you what you need. For example, a craving for very salty foods may indicate that your body is in a stage of doubling the volume of blood in your uterus to accommodate the needs of the baby—a process that depletes your system of its normal complement of salt.

Momma Said There'd Be Days Like This

At one point in my pregnancy I became lightheaded whenever I rose quickly from a chair or bed. Of course, I panicked. But my doctor said not to worry. He told me to drink extra fluids and eat something salty like potato chips so that I could balance out the fluid my body was using for the baby.

Womanly Wisdom

If your partner's empathy for your pregnancy symptoms isn't all you'd like it to be, drop him a reminder of his role in this whole process. A little creatively applied guilt works wonders, since men are generally baffled by this whole "woman" thing.

Mom Alert!

I personally think pregnancy makes women beautiful—and so do most people, if you ask them. But that can be hard to remember in your ninth month, when it seems you need a forklift to carry your expanding tummy and you can't get out of a chair without help. Keep your cool—remember, this is only temporary.

Spacing Out—My Hormones Made Me Do It

Your hormones guide the changes that occur in your body during pregnancy. Once the fertilized egg attaches to the uterus, your body's off and running with changes designed to provide everything your baby needs—and everything *you* need to ultimately give birth.

But while your hormones are making these changes, you might find yourself more absentminded than usual. Do not worry about this too much—it's a *very* common occurrence during pregnancy. Just accept that you may need some extra sets of keys. The worst of it is the teasing you may end up taking when you space out every once in a while.

Figuring on a New Figure

As your pregnancy progresses your body is going to fill out. For some women this means more cleavage than ever. And, for some women, this is a welcome change— it can make you feel very womanly. But for other women it can be an unwelcome change—the extra weight in the chest changes both posture and carriage, and can be uncomfortable.

While you are gaining cleavage you are also filling out in the hips—and certainly in the stomach. This was nothing new to me, a lifetime weight watcher, but for some women the change in shape can be depressing.

And it certainly takes some getting used to: As you begin to *show* you lose your waist and fill out in all kinds of directions. This is a very good thing for your baby and your skeletal system, but initially it can interfere with your sense of balance. Never fear—your body will find its equilibrium eventually, so you won't topple over with the weight of the baby.

Again, your attitude will determine how well you accept the physical changes that occur during the course of your pregnancy. Remember that your bodily changes are all natural aspects of preparing for the birth of your child. You will not always be built as though you are carrying a basketball under your ribcage. And with a little effort, once the baby's born you can completely regain your prepregnancy shape.

If you are eating reasonably healthy foods, don't freak out when you see the scale creep up with each monthly visit to your OB GYN. You are *supposed* to gain weight during pregnancy. Your baby is growing, and you have increased fluids and have changing nutritional needs. The thing to keep in mind is that if you're not taking care of yourself nutritionally, your body will fill your baby's needs at *your* expense.

Momma Said There'd Be Days Like This

I didn't eat for two during my first pregnancy—I ate for 23! So I took a little longer than most to regain my prepregnancy shape. When I got around to it, however, I lost the weight and was in great shape for the deliveries of both my second and third children. So don't obsess over your weight during pregnancy. Use good sense in your food choices but do not allow concern about your changing figure to make you feel down about yourself. Tell yourself how beautiful you are, because you *are* beautiful.

Make sure that you take a good prenatal vitamin and that you eat well. Do not even *consider* restrictive diets or excessive exercise. Your doctor will advise you if your weight gain or loss is healthy or not.

Most of all, don't let yourself obsess about your changing figure. You have many more important and rewarding things to think about when you're having a baby—why waste time worrying about how your shape has changed?

Picture-Perfect Pregnancy

Rather than focus on your changing girth, concentrate on the *positive* physical changes of pregnancy. For one thing, during pregnancy your hair thickens and becomes shinier. You may also find that your nails are stronger and grow faster than usual. During a first pregnancy, why not indulge yourself with manicures? If you're worried about toxins and chemicals, there are toluene-free nailpolishes available to keep baby free from chemical exposure. You might not be able to wear your rings if you retain fluids, but at least your nails will be nice.

And don't forget that well-known glow—it's real! Your body is working overtime to keep all your internal systems working at peak efficiency—your blood circulation and hormonal system in particular. You really do end up with rosier cheeks and clearer skin during pregnancy.

Swinging with Your Moods

Many of the changes that occur during pregnancy are not visible. In fact, you may be the only one completely aware of what is going on inside you. You may find that during pregnancy you become what I call *hormotional*—experiencing those bouts of unexplainable weepies or grouchies that every pregnant woman seems to get.

Don't let the mood swings get you down—hormotionalism is a perfectly natural aspect of being pregnant and it is your right as a woman to be as hormotional as you please. Indulge your moods if you can, but remember that your partner won't always understand what's going on. If he protests about your unpredictable moods, just remind him that you are pregnant—and leave it at that.

Womanly Wisdom

If your partner pesters you to explain your periodic descents into unpredictable moodiness, try responding with an incredulous look. It works wonders. Let your partner think you are in full control of your faculties (even though you have no idea why you are crying during your favorite sitcom).

Your emotions *will* balance out, once your hormones settle down. But until that happens, be careful: If you get the weepies you may have a tendency to allow all your fears to surface. You may even have scary, pregnancy-related dreams (a common one is that you have had your baby but you keep leaving it places). While it's normal to have a few fears when you are adjusting to the concept of being responsible for another living thing, don't let yourself obsess.

Most people need time to adjust to the idea of taking on the responsibility of a baby—someone who'll be completely dependent on you, at least for a while. And nine months of pregnancy seems to be just long enough to allow you to become utterly terrified, if you let that happen. But you're not the first to feel those fears, and you won't be the last. What you *will* do, eventually, is work through your fears.

Momma Said There'd Be Days Like This

As my baby grew inside me, I can remember feeling a sense of impending maturity. I had never had any real experience with infants, apart from a few baby-sitting jobs as a teenager. While waiting for my baby to be born, I found myself really thinking about what I wanted for both myself and my child. With motherhood on the way, I found the exhilarating sense of finally *growing up*.

One way to work past any fears you have is to turn them on their heads. Instead of focusing on your doubts ("It's such a big responsibility...how can I live up to it?"), concentrate on the opportunity that pregnancy offers: Your role as a mother is really one of the most precious and important things you can do with your life. It will have far-reaching impact and could influence future generations.

Momhood in the Modern World

If you're like many new moms today, you've probably concentrated more on school and career than on developing the traditional domestic skills. Mrs. Cleaver just wasn't the role model to our generation that she and other 1960s sitcom moms were to earlier generations.

Many of us grew up with no great interest in home economics, and that's not a bad thing. But it does mean that the prospect of motherhood can suddenly challenge your sense of personal adequacy—you can find yourself thinking "I'm not ready for this!"

Working Through the Doubts

Right from the start, remember that you're not alone—*most* women face the question of whether they have what it takes to be a good mother. Even if you're coming into motherhood with no experience at all, there are things you can do to alleviate your fears.

Motherhood by the Book

Some women (like me) find it most comfortable to approach new motherhood in much the same way they would approach a research paper. They buy all the books and analyze all the child-rearing theories. And that is not a bad way to start—but watch out! You can drive yourself crazy with all those theories.

It seems as though everybody has a pet approach to raising children. Some books stress environmental dangers, others provide a list of hard-and-fast rules for everything from feeding schedules to toilet training techniques. If you go the book route, read with a critical eye.

Mom Alert!

You can paralyze yourself if you go overboard on following every theory that comes down the pike—and you really don't want to spend your nine months of pregnancy walking on the proverbial eggshells. Whatever you read, question the *why* of the warnings, not just the *what*.

Making the Motherhood Transition

You really can overintellectualize pregnancy and motherhood. And as a first time mom, even though you want your baby with all your heart, you may not yet be mature enough to understand how becoming a mother will change your life and the impact it may have on your relationship with your partner. If the two of you have spent most of your lives planning for careers, motherhood (and fatherhood) may have been almost an afterthought. In that case, now—*before* the baby is born—is the time to try to work out how your childless lifestyle will necessarily change.

Avoiding the Superwoman Trap

Many women of the current generation have grown up believing the *superwoman* propaganda—you know, the line that says we can have it all. So we're not prepared for the adjustments we'll have to make in the way we live our daily lives when pregnancy—and ultimately a baby—is added to the mix. But those changes are real. Your time is not only your own. You have someone else's needs to consider, not just your own preferences. And so the word responsibility takes on a whole new meaning.

Pregnancy, Motherhood, and Relationships

Couples have babies for all kinds of reasons—some of which are wiser than others. But *all* couples find that pregnancy has a profound effect on their relationship with each other. If there are preexisting stresses in the relationship, they can be exacerbated by the responsibility of parenthood.

Momma Said There'd Be Days Like This

When my first child was born, I was in a marriage that was less than solid. My first husband and I had never learned to resolve conflict or work out our problems. Having a baby masked those problems for a time but couldn't fix them, and ultimately the marriage ended. If you're facing a troubled marriage, a baby will not resolve your issues—try to iron out your relationship difficulties *before* you become parents.

It Takes Two...

One way to maintain a good relationship with your partner during pregnancy is to involve him in the process as much as possible. Bring him to some or all of your visits to the doctor so he can hear the baby's heartbeat and feel the reality of the growing life inside you.

Too many families still define child rearing as women's work, while the father goes out into the world and slays dragons. Even career women find this stereotype operating in their lives once it is time to divide tasks. Dads are seen as helpers and baby-sitters while mothers are seen as the real parents. Although there needs to be a logical division of tasks, and science has not yet found a way for men to give birth, you can involve your partner in ways that will give him an almost equal experience.

One easy way to bring your partner into your pregnancy is to have him shop for nursery items. You'll be surprised at how frivolous even the most serious man can be when faced with teddy bears and cute miniature outfits. Even the most committed antishopping male is likely to change his mind when the shopping trip is for his own baby-to-be.

And consider taking parenting classes together. Lamaze and other childbirth-preparation workshops take both the mother *and* the father through the processes of pregnancy and delivery. When your partner understands what you're going through, he can provide much more effective support. And with this deeper understanding, pregnancy and childbirth will be a mutual experience.

Taking Care of Yourself During Pregnancy

Since you're taking the time to read a book about motherhood, you're likely to make good prenatal care a priority. You'll have regular doctor visits and will ask many questions about your own health and that of the baby.

But few doctors have the time and the insight to focus on how you *feel* about your pregnancy and about becoming a mother, so you're likely to have to take charge of dealing with that for yourself. Here are a few tips to make the task easier:

➤ Pay as much attention to your emotional state as to your physical condition.

➤ Keep some time for yourself. If you are tired, rest; if you need help, ask for it. Be aware of your needs and do not be afraid to meet them.

➤ Stay active! If you have a career, keep at it if your health allows. And if you don't work outside the home, be sure to keep something interesting going on in your life—take a class, take up a hobby.

Mom Alert!

The temptation to make all your activities baby-related can be strong, but remember—there are only so many times you can change the wallpaper or furniture in the nursery. Soon enough your new baby will need most of your time and attention, so now's the time to come up with some things that you do *just for you!*

There's good reason for paying attention to your emotional state. If you do nothing but think about your pregnancy you are going to focus on all the little aches, pains, and discomforts, and the time until delivery will seem an eternity. By keeping busy you avoid all the obsessions that pregnant women are prone to, and those nine months go by much faster.

First Trimester: Business as Usual (More or Less)

For most of your first month of pregnancy, you're unlikely to notice much of a change in your body or your feelings. In fact, many women (especially women who have somewhat irregular periods) don't begin to suspect they're pregnant until close to the end of that first month. Soon enough, however, the physical changes make themselves felt. This can be a time of wonder and excitement—but it's also the time of your most raging hormone-based symptoms (particularly morning sickness).

The Second Trimester's Activity Spurt

The second trimester, which runs from the fourth to the sixth month of pregnancy, is always a time of increased energy. This is when you run the risk of boredom if you have nothing to do—and is a great time to have some fun before nature stops you in your tracks.

Momma Said There'd Be Days Like This

With my first child, I worked as a lawyer until delivery but I was really a sight to behold. On one occasion I tried a case with another female attorney who was also in her ninth month. We looked like Humpty and Dumpty! It was good for me to work until delivery because inactivity really makes me nuts, but toward the end my energy level dropped, and I would have been better off if I had used the time to rest up for delivery.

Third Trimester—Time Out

For most of the third trimester you usually can keep pretty active, but you really do slow down in the last few weeks before delivery. You could do worse than to treat yourself like a cat during this time before delivery: Have you ever noticed how cats do nothing they do not want to do. They luxuriate in their laziness and always seem to know something we humans have yet to figure out.

Here are a few cat-like self-indulgences that can make the final weeks more comfortable:

➤ Take baths with wonderful-smelling oils. Just watch the water temperature—you don't want to get overheated.

➤ Get plenty of rest and insist that your partner support your need to be pampered.

➤ Avoid frustration. If you really want to test your partner's supportiveness, insist that you be in control of the TV remote at all times. After all, his channel surfing could disturb your equanimity.

➤ Lighten up on yourself about housework. Now's the time for your partner to pitch in and take over some—if not all—of the daily chores. This is, after all, the last chance you're going to have—for a long time to come—to just put your feet up and relax.

Womanly Wisdom

Use your pregnancy as a time to revel in your womanhood and to try to mature into the role you will soon accept. Get to know yourself as a separate entity, so you can bring all your strength and wisdom to being a mother. You will be better equipped to handle all the situations that come your way.

That last point is really true: If you think you will have the luxury to do what you want when you want after the baby is born, think again. Once you have a baby, you realize that for the next 18 years—and well beyond—you will never again have the luxury of thinking only of yourself. This is not the same as suggesting that you lose your personal identity—it's just a recognition that, in ways different from any other relationship you've ever had, the mother-child tie is lifelong and profound.

Spiritually Speaking

Your pregnancy is a good time to develop a self-dialogue—to ask yourself what kind of mother you want to be. Keep a journal with all of your thoughts and feelings. Some women use this time to write letters to their unborn children, telling them about their hopes and dreams. It is a good way to explore your own feelings and to build a sense of communication, and connection, to the baby you're carrying.

Although you want to have a good relationship with your partner during your pregnancy, remember that this time is really for *you*. You are doing something wonderful and miraculous. You are making a commitment to guide a human soul into adulthood. As the great poet, Kahlil Gibran, puts it, children are like arrows from their parents' bows. They come through us but we do not own them. Essentially, we guide them but they have souls of their own. When you find yourself impatient with the physical inconveniences of pregnancy, think of what a great privilege it is to be assigned a soul to love and nurture into its own maturity. Then, when your child grows up, you have the blessing of a relationship with a whole person who will always have a special bond with you.

So don't feel guilty if you want to treat yourself as someone special during the process of growing a baby. You *are* special. You are a woman, and only a woman can bring life into this world.

Here are some things you might want to do for yourself:

➤ Take a yoga class if your doctor says its okay.

➤ Take nature walks so you can feel your connection with Mother Earth.

➤ Treat yourself to massages, especially if you are prone to muscle aches.

➤ Fix yourself up with cute maternity outfits.

➤ Make sure to groom yourself so that you feel like part of the world.

➤ Keep a dream journal; preggies have vivid dreams.

➤ Keep a pregnancy journal of thoughts and feelings.

➤ Write a letter to your unborn child, sharing your thoughts.

➤ Laugh a lot.

➤ Do something you have always wanted to do, within reason.

➤ Bathe with fragrant oils.

➤ Listen to soothing music.

➤ Meditate.

➤ Eat good food.

➤ Tell yourself how wonderful you are.

➤ Be good to yourself.

➤ Learn good conflict-resolution skills.

➤ Avoid unnecessary conflict.

➤ Avoid negative people.

➤ Listen to your soul.

➤ Love yourself.

The Least You Need to Know

➤ Pregnancy is a perfectly natural physical condition for which you are well equipped—it is *not* a disability or a disease.

➤ Your attitude will influence the comfort of your pregnancy.

➤ During your pregnancy you will experience a series of profound physical and emotional changes.

➤ The best way to take care of the child you are carrying is to take good physical, emotional, and spiritual care of yourself.

Chapter 2

It's Showtime! Hospitalization and Labor

In This Chapter

➤ Getting ready for the big event

➤ Packing for the two of you

➤ How do you know you are in labor?

➤ The final push

Let's face it, the thing that makes women the most nervous about the birth process is the prospect of labor and delivery. We have seen it depicted on television and in movies, which only increases our anxiety about it. It is certainly the least fun part of becoming a mom, but in many ways it can be the most rewarding. You really know what it means to be a woman after you experience the unique pain of childbirth. You enter a sisterhood that men can never understand.

Getting Ready

Picture this: It won't be long now. You are in your final few days. Your doctor says your body is getting ready to give birth. It should happen any time now—and all you can think about is how you can get out of having to go through with it.

When you are a few days—or even just a few hours—from the moment of truth, you will no doubt find yourself thinking about some crazy things. You may feel as though you're entering a time of free fall—standing at the door of an airplane waiting to dive into the open air. Even though you have a parachute (your delivery team), you won't trust it until you are safely back on the ground.

At a time like this, all you really want to do, perhaps, is hang on to the door of the plane for dear life and refuse to make the jump. But there's no going back now—the baby's on its way.

Womanly Wisdom

Attitude alone won't make your labor and childbirth easy and uneventful. But, whether your labor is difficult or relatively easy, nature has given you the tools to handle the experience.

Fears, Faith, and Fantasies

We all go into labor for the first time with no real idea of what lies ahead. No one can really tell you what labor is all about. You'll no doubt hear horror stories from some of the veteran mothers you know, and from others you'll hear fairy stories—about someone's perfect little angel child who was so considerate as to pop out almost unnoticed. Although the process is basically the same for everyone, each woman's experience is uniquely her own. And unlike that metaphorical skydiver, you can make some choices that put you in charge of your birth experience—you *can* empower yourself beyond your fear.

To Medicate or Not to Medicate

Labor does hurt, and everyone has a different threshold for pain. Fortunately, many pain-management options are available to you—you're not restricted to the standbys of traditional Western medicine. Take, for example, the alternative approaches to childbirth that have been drawn from the folk medicine of non-Western cultures. Herbal remedies are commonly used during pregnancy and delivery among Native American groups, and herbs and techniques from traditional Chinese medicine provide alternatives to western medical practice. If you are open-minded and curious, these options are well worth researching. But use good sense in checking out the credentials of any person who offers alternative treatment. Anything you do during pregnancy and delivery will have an impact on your baby and on you.

Mom-isms

Giving birth is a natural process, but what's called **natural childbirth** is the experience of labor and delivery without the use of any medication or anesthesia. Instead, you rely on natural methods of pain relief achieved through breathing and visualization.

Making It Easier on Yourself

The most important thing to do is to relax and worry less about the process. Childbirth is something that's been going on for eons and will continue to occur long after your childbearing years are over. Your mind and your body are totally connected, and if you are worried and anxious when it is time to give birth, you will make your body tense and your contractions will be that much more painful. You are capable of talking to your body and telling it to use its natural pain relievers to ease your process.

Natural versus Nurturant Labor Styles

There are some very good reasons for wanting to prepare yourself to give birth naturally, without the use of pain relief or local anesthesia. These are the two reasons most commonly cited by women who choose natural childbirth:

➤ By skipping pain medication you can be more aware of the birth process.

➤ Babies delivered without medication are more alert, since there are no drugs to get into the bloodstream.

This sounds great in theory, but natural childbirth is not for everyone. You could have an exceptionally long labor, or a low threshold for pain. Both are perfectly valid reasons for wanting some pain relief. You are not going to win any good-mommy awards and your child is not going to be admitted to Harvard simply because you experienced the full sensation of labor pain.

Momma Said There'd Be Days Like This

My first labor lasted 14 hours. I wasn't in what they call **active** labor the entire time, with the contractions coming fast and furious, but I was in labor. It was tiring and frustrating and I wanted to kill my husband. I was given some pain medication that made me fall asleep between contractions. The nurses woke me up in time to push when the baby was ready to be born and I must say, even though I accepted pain relief, I have never experienced such an amazing natural process.

The Choice Is All Yours!

Many women like the idea of natural childbirth—they see it as very empowering. But it is not easy. Because so much anxiety is brought on by the fear of labor, you need to make a plan you're comfortable with, so that you can stop worrying. If you are nervous about delivery there are options for you, such as pain medication or an *epidural block*. Your doctor can explain these options to you so that you can make your own decision.

All you *really* need to remember is that this is *your* childbirth experience. No one, not even the father

Mom-isms

An **epidural block** is a form of local anesthetic that numbs your body from the waist down but leaves you completely awake and aware of what's going on around you.

of your child, can tell you what is best for you. Discuss your options with your doctor, and then choose the approach to handling the pain of delivery that best suits *you*.

Dealing with the Real Deal

Think of it this way: You have been carrying this fetus for nine months. It now weighs about seven pounds or more, and your body needs to provide an opening large enough for this baby to slide through when the time comes for its permanent eviction. How your body does this is truly miraculous. It happens so naturally that you can feel unimportant in the scheme of things. When your baby is ready to be born, your body gets to work, and it is so well designed for the task that you can set your self and ego aside and just let your body take over.

Mom-isms

Your cervix is fully **dilated** when it has stretched open to the maximum. This provides the opening through which your child will pass. During the late stages of dilation, you may hear the doctor say that the baby's **crowning**—the baby's head *is* visible at the cervical opening.

Contractions, or *labor pains*, serve a very important purpose. Each contraction opens the cervix, one step at a time. When the cervix is fully *dilated*, the baby's head normally *crowns*, and it is time for him or her to be born. (Crowning, of course, only occurs when the baby is positioned normally for birth—traveling head first into the cervical opening.)

But all the clinical information in the world can't really capture the experience of labor. Sometimes, it helps to hear about the real-life experience of others. Here are a few of my own encounters with labor:

Going Natural, Part I

My second child was born without benefit of even minimal anesthesia. I was in my total earth mother phase back then, and was really ready to go back to nature—I was even on the verge of choosing a home birth. In the end, however, I compromised with my doctor on a hospital birthing room and he supported my decision to go natural.

I am not a masochist by any means and I do not like labor pain. During this birth, I was in active "holy-Toledo-it-hurts" labor for three hours. It was certainly an easier overall experience than the birth of my first child had been, but it was also more difficult. I still contemplated husband-homicide.

Birthing "Big Head"

The biggest part of the problem was that this child, my son, had a very big head. So, while my labor in delivering him was shorter (11 hours shorter!) it was far more memorable. Sort of like giving birth to a pumpkin.

Now, when you're dealing with something like this, you go for whatever relief you can get—and if you're not taking medication, you find yourself some alternatives.

Helping Hands?

I remember grabbing my husband's hand and squeezing it during contractions. And when *he* had to leave the room, I grabbed my doctor's hand instead. It seemed like a good idea at the time, but I later learned that it is actually better *not* to squeeze someone's hand—squeezing makes you tense up, while relaxing actually makes the contraction less painful.

Going Natural, Part II

I found out I was pregnant again only a few months after giving birth to my son. I was understandably not ready to go through all *that* again. The memory of my last delivery was just too fresh to allow me to enjoy what was otherwise a wonderful and uneventful pregnancy. Still, I intended to deliver this one naturally as well.

Mom Alert!

Be careful about the whole hand-squeezing business—women in labor have been known to grip and squeeze so powerfully that they can break their partner's (or doctor's) hand.

Check-in and Count-Down to Birth

When I went into labor *this* time, my contractions were only five minutes apart—a detail I refrained from sharing with my husband. At the time, we lived on a farm about thirty minutes from our hospital, and even *I* was concerned that we might not make it in time. While my husband is usually not the hysterical type, under extreme duress he's been known to get a little crazy. Since he was driving and I wanted to make it to the hospital in one piece, I bit my lower lip, crossed my legs, and hoped for the best.

At the hospital we learned that I had about one hour more of *transitional labor* ahead of me. This is the phase where you hate everyone and use the most obscenities. The labor was intense, but this time out I finally caught on to what the birth experience was all about—I finally figured out how to influence my own pain experience.

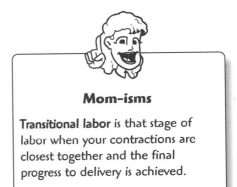

Mom-isms

Transitional labor is that stage of labor when your contractions are closest together and the final progress to delivery is achieved.

Going with the Flow

All my natural childbirth training had told me to use two special pain-management techniques: to *visualize* and to *breathe into the contractions*. I had tried these techniques in labors past, but this time they *worked*. I was finally able to relax enough during labor to see that breathing a certain way really *does* reduce the pain.

Momma Said There'd Be Days Like This

During labor it's easy to lose patience with your **birth coach** (the partner or friend who goes through the training classes and comes with you to the hospital). When your coach starts telling you how to breath, you're likely to snap back with something X-rated—after all, *you're* the one doing all the work, right? But your coach is really trying to help, by reminding you to breathe properly when the busy-ness of birthing might make you forget.

Using the Tools

During this delivery I was able to listen to my higher self, the angels, God, or maybe just my own good sense and work *with* my unborn child to make the birth experience positive for both of us. So, for once, I really put the tools I'd learned in childbirth classes to good use:

➤ **Visualization.** During this labor I visualized my baby and talked to her. I thought about what she would look like and who she might be. Each time I felt a contraction coming on I would say, "Come on little one. Soon you will be born."

I also spoke to myself, saying, "I am strong and I will not object to pain that brings on new life." I relaxed my body as completely as I could and imagined waves of water each time a contraction would begin, reach crescendo, and then recede. I gave myself affirmations, told my baby how much I loved her, and soon my darling 7 pound, 2 ounce baby girl was born. It was a very happy moment when the doctor put her in my arms and I realized that that was all there was to it.

➤ **Breathing Techniques.** This time, too, I managed to remember my breathing training (and listened to my coach when I forgot). I took deep, cleansing breaths when necessary, and remembered to take the rapid, shallow, panting breaths that help move contractions along.

Understanding the Pain

In a normal delivery, your body really *will* tell you what to do. This is important, because you can draw upon your faith in something higher than yourself, whatever you believe, to relax and conquer your fears. Fear, after all, is the enemy of childbirth. It causes the laboring mother to tense her body, breathe erratically, and work against her own progress.

We are not used to pain—we see it as a negative thing—but in childbirth, pain is your friend. It is the result of your body's efforts to profoundly change the internal configuration of your womb so that the infant can be expelled. The important thing to keep in mind is that your *response* to the pain—tensing up against it or relaxing into it—can make a big difference in the *amount* of pain you feel.

Packing for Two

When you are close to delivery you may have some time on your hands. You will be thinking about the big moment, playing it over and over in your mind. If this is your first baby, you're likely to over-prepare, because you really have no idea what to expect. One thing you can do during this time is pack your hospital and baby bags. You know that this is not something you'll want to worry about once labor begins—your organizational skills might very well be a little challenged at that time.

> **Womanly Wisdom**
>
> When you are going through labor, particularly natural childbirth, visualize your baby, talk to it, and breathe into the contractions. Go through it *with* your baby and try to overcome your fear. You will be amazed at what a difference it makes.

> **Momma Said There'd Be Days Like This**
>
> You'd be amused at what people pack when they do it under duress. One woman left the job to her husband (who left it to the last minute). She ended up at the hospital with a pair of high-heels, two already-read novels, and toddler-sized clothing. Her husband explained this last choice by saying, "I thought you were kidding me when you said they came out that small...."

Your Overnight Bag Basics

Although you'll be wearing one of those handy dandy everyone-can-see-your-butt gowns during delivery, you'll want to bring some comfortable sleepwear of your own. If you're planning to breast-feed, you can buy adorable, feminine, comfortable night-gowns designed specifically for that purpose at any store that sells maternity wear. (You'll probably want to bring several, even for a short hospital stay—you'll be surprised how many you'll need as you learn to maneuver around your infant and your lactating breasts.

You may want to pack a robe to throw on when people come to visit you at inopportune times. You'll also want to bring one or more nursing bras with nursing pads. You will not believe how heavy your breasts will feel when your milk comes in. A good nursing bra helps your back and also supposedly helps prevent your breasts from sagging.

For actual delivery you will want some very warm socks. Your feet will get cold and socks will make you feel much more comfortable. You can wear them all through delivery. It may not seem important, but every little bit helps.

You'll want to pack a coming-home outfit, but don't expect to fit into your prepregnancy jeans right after the baby comes. You'll be happier—and much more comfortable—with something you were able to wear in your fourth month of pregnancy. It's also traditional to pack an outfit to bring baby home in, along with some receiving blankets. Your newborn will have his or her first snapshot taken in the hospital nursery and will be haunted by that picture for the rest of his or her life. Choose that first photo outfit wisely.

And don't forget to pack personal items like shampoo, makeup, hairbrush, and toothbrush. It is no big deal if you forget—these items are available at any hospital—but you may be more comfortable using your own things.

Excellent Extras

When you are in early labor, a massage is particularly welcome. One good, inexpensive massage tool you can make for yourself is to put tennis balls in a sock—your partner or birth coach can use them to rub your lower back. They create just the right amount of soothing friction. There are also wonderful massage tools available at stores like The Body Shop.

You'll want to tuck some lollipops into your bag, too. You will not be permitted to eat or drink during delivery, so your mouth is going to get very dry. Your birth coach will be allowed to give you ice chips (with your nurse's permission) and you will likely be permitted to suck on a lollipop, so you'll want a few on hand. They're simple things, but you'll soon see how important such simple things become.

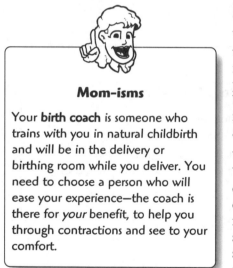

Mom-isms

Your **birth coach** is someone who trains with you in natural childbirth and will be in the delivery or birthing room while you deliver. You need to choose a person who will ease your experience—the coach is there for *your* benefit, to help you through contractions and see to your comfort.

Other Packing Options

Some people like to bring CDs or cassettes of soft music to play while they're in the delivery room. Only bring something you *really* like. You want to surround yourself with things that relax you and give you some element of pleasure, in contrast to the pain.

Remember to bring a still or video camera if you want to capture precious first moments for posterity, but I recommend that you decide ahead of time just how personal you want your baby's birth documentary to be. Childbirth does not have a great deal of dignity associated with it, and I, personally, would not want my you-know-what captured on film.

Some people like to bring note cards so that they can send baby announcements or work on thank yous for gifts while in the hospital. But remember that while you're in the hospital, you want to concentrate on resting and spending time with your newborn. You need this time to take care of yourself and to adjust emotionally and physically to your new role. If you enjoy filling out announcements or writing thank you cards, then by all means bring them with you. If they are a pressure or a chore, leave them at home.

Pulling It All Together

Pack all your essentials in an average-sized overnight bag and have it ready and waiting for the big moment. Leave it in plain view so that even the most freaked-out partner, friend, or birth coach can find it with ease. Your goal is to eliminate as much stress as possible. Your partner can pack his own bag with snacks, books, magazines, or other amusements—and maybe a bottle of sparkling juice for your after-baby toast.

Post–Packing Preparation

Now that you've taken care of the essential tasks, use your time before birth to gather your thoughts and rest. If you work until delivery, make sure you still take the time to rest whenever you feel the need. Let your body tell you what you need and be sure to listen. If possible, take a week or more off from work before delivery. Clearly, this is a personal decision that only you can make. Many employers have limits on maternity leave, and some working moms prefer to keep as much of that time as possible for *after* the birth.

If, however, you have the luxury to choose and have no solid indication that the baby will be late, try to plan on some time alone *before* delivery. You will really want to capture some moments for yourself before you become Mom. It will be a long time before you see yourself as yourself again. You will want some time to reflect and to embrace this new part of your path.

So...Is This Really It?

First-time moms all have one big question on their minds during those last few weeks before delivery: How do you know you are in labor?

Labor is not like anything you have experienced before. And your body sometimes gives you confusing cues—many women experience minor contractions, often called *false labor*, starting about a week before the baby actually comes. But believe me, when you're really in labor, you'll probably know it. And don't worry about feeling stupid if you think you are in labor and it turns out that you're not.

Momma Said There'd Be Days Like This

I almost worried myself out of having my doctor with me for my first delivery. I started having minor contractions in the evening and got all excited. The minor contractions were far apart, so when I called my doctor he jokingly said not to worry and to call him when I was really in labor. He told me later that he never expected me to take him seriously, but that's just what I did. Not wanting to bother him, I waited until the contractions were fast and furious before I called him again.

Early Warning Signals

Early labor can take many forms. Sometimes it doesn't feel like a contraction, but rather like pressure in your lower back, along your sides, or in front. The best thing to remember is that if you feel any strange physical sensations and it is about time for you to deliver, you should pay attention to those feelings.

Does the pain or pressure come and go with any regularity? If you are able to see a pattern that can be timed, you probably are in full labor. This doesn't mean you need to rush to the hospital right away—if the sensations come and go at fairly long intervals (more than 10 minutes apart), you can go through some of your early labor at home until the contractions are closer together and more productive. You can walk around your house and lie on your bed in a familiar setting before you move to the next level.

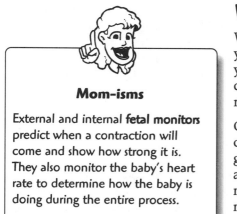

Mom-isms

External and internal **fetal monitors** predict when a contraction will come and show how strong it is. They also monitor the baby's heart rate to determine how the baby is doing during the entire process.

What's Going on Here!

When your contractions are *ten* minutes apart, notify your doctor. When they are *five* minutes apart, get into your car. Every delivery is different but you can be pretty certain that contractions coming five minutes apart mean that your body is working toward the final push.

Of course, the idea of "final push" is a relative one. You can have labor like this for a long time. Some women get stuck at the five-minutes-between-contractions point and may even need medication to bring on stronger, more efficient contractions. This is why your nurse will monitor your contractions with a contraption called a fetal monitor, and will do internal exams to determine how you are coming along.

The Final Push

At some point your doctor or nurse will do an internal exam and say you are "dilated to 10." This means you are getting ready to push the baby out—it does *not* mean the baby now pops out like a piece of toast. The act of pushing the baby through the birth canal can take quite a while and can be very tiring. Listen carefully to your delivery nurse: She'll tell you when to push and when not to push. You may find it hard to do as she says—sometimes your body fights against you. But do your best—if you push in a planned way, each push is more productive. This makes your labor more efficient, which is better for you *and* for the baby.

When it comes time for that final push, you will bear down and feel something similar to the sensation of having a bowel movement. You may feel a complete loss of dignity at this point, but this is no time to be self-conscious.

When baby's head crowns it will most likely be time for the final push. Unless the baby is turned around, its head will come out, then its shoulder, and then you will feel the most amazing sensation as the baby is born. It is one of the most glorious moments of life.

Meeting Baby

With delivery over, you'll be moved to a recovery room. After the baby has been cleaned up, she'll be brought to you, and your nurse will tell you that your newborn is ready for her first meal.

Momma Said There'd Be Days Like This

I remember *my* first time—and not knowing what to do. The nurse tried to explain breast-feeding to me and said, "Let the baby show you." Sure enough, I held her close to my breast and she wiggled her little mouth to the nipple and started to suckle. It was as simple as that. The baby knew what to do and all I had to do was follow nature.

When it's time to go to your room and the nurses take the baby to the nursery, you may feel sad. This is normal. You and the baby have been attached for a long time, and you may find that *any* separation is hard to take. But the periods of separation will be short—the nurses will bring your baby in to nurse or to bottle feed, and you'll be able then to marvel at her and snuggle with her. You'll also probably enjoy the most peaceful sleep you've had in months.

The first hours and days of motherhood are yours and are very important. You may feel very protective of your bonding time and prefer not to share this time with visitors. Do not be shy about setting boundaries for the amount of time you're willing to spend with well-meaning relatives and friends. If you are direct about your feelings, people will understand.

On the other hand, you may welcome support and company. Having a new baby is a mental adjustment and first-time moms, especially, may be feeling a little inadequate right now. There's no real need to fear—the nurses at your hospital will teach you everything you need to know about early infant care—but there is nothing like friends and family to show you the way.

Womanly Wisdom

Because hospitals compete strongly for maternity business, sterile and uninviting hospital-like environments are a thing of the past. The entire process of giving birth is now treated more as something natural and less as an affliction. And you are recognized as the consumer, free to choose the kind of birth experience you want.

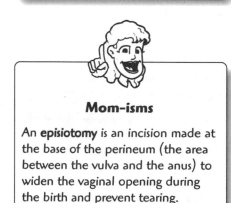

Mom-isms

An **episiotomy** is an incision made at the base of the perineum (the area between the vulva and the anus) to widen the vaginal opening during the birth and prevent tearing.

Hospital Hospitality Options

Hospitals generally offer two rooming options:

➤ **Rooming-in**: Baby stays in Mom's room and is not taken to the nursery between feedings.

➤ **Conventional**: Baby stays in the nursery and is brought to Mom only during feeding times.

Many mothers prefer the rooming-in option, especially if they have other children. Rooming-in gives you free access to your newborn, so you don't find yourself splitting your attention between baby and visitors. But first-time moms often appreciate the more conventional nursery option, because it gives them time to adjust to the baby and to new-momhood, and it's nice to be fussed over by the hospital staff.

Some hospitals offer birthing rooms so you do not need to leave the place where you deliver to go to another room for the rest of your stay. Birthing rooms are private, and they're usually decorated like something you would find at home.

Post-Delivery Details

During your hospital stay you probably are not going to feel like going dancing. You've just gone through some pretty heavy work (there's a *reason* they call it labor) and there is a strong possibility that you will have stitches from an *episiotomy*, an incision made to widen the vaginal opening.

A Stitch (or Two or Three) in Time

Don't cringe. Episiotomies are routinely done during labor, and since the incision is made at the moment of the final push when so much is going on, you won't care *what* the doctor does to get the baby out. An episiotomy is a good thing to have done if there is a danger that the baby will tear your vaginal tissue during birth.

The only problem with an episiotomy is that the stitches will need some special care after the birth. You need to keep the area clean, and you'll probably find it uncomfortable to sit in a normal position. Consider buying a special cushion (often called a "donut" because that's what it's shaped like) to sit on.

Bringing Back the Body Beautiful

In all honesty, the minor discomfort of episiotomy stitches probably won't bother you too much, because your body may feel as though you've been trampled by wild elephants. Right after you give birth some wonderful nurse named Brunhilda will come into your room at regular intervals to press on your uterus. You may be tempted to think that she's an escapee from the local asylum, getting her kicks out of causing you pain, but what she does helps to return your uterus to its original shape.

Unmentionables

Guess what. Shhhhhh. You may have hemorrhoids after giving birth. That is what happens when you push so hard. It is not as embarrassing as it sounds. But when your nurse tells you to take your sitz baths, follow her instructions. They really work to reduce your discomfort. You'll get back to normal soon enough. In the meantime, take advantage of any help anyone gives you at the hospital, and rest as much as you can.

Now that you have met Baby you have many joys and challenges ahead of you. The first, which is discussed in the next chapter, will be to integrate the baby into your life so that you (if you are on your own) or you and your partner can form a family unit.

Womanly Wisdom

Follow your nurse's bathroom instructions. If you have stitches or hemorrhoids, you will have to forgo toilet paper at first and rely on a bottle of warm water to clean your bottom. Sitz baths, where you sit in a special tub of warm water that fits over the toilet, really work.

The Least You Need to Know

➤ Take advantage of the weeks just prior to your due date to rest and prepare for the big event.

➤ The choice of pain-management options is up to you and your doctor—don't let anyone else pressure you into any choice you're uncomfortable with.

➤ Make sure you pack your overnight bag well before your due date.

➤ Don't be shy about calling the doctor when you think you're in labor—he (or she) is used to babies making their entrance at inconvenient times.

➤ Feel free to set limits on visitors after your baby's born—this is your bonding time.

➤ The hospital staff will provide you with the advice and assistance you need to take care of your newborn.

Part 2

From Nursery to Preschool

You have to have a child to qualify for membership in the Motherhood Guild, but that's only the beginning. And some would argue that, for all the physical effort of labor and delivery, it isn't even the toughest part of the job. You're in the club for life, now, and you're going to be dealing with all sorts of new challenges.

Many of the Momhood issues you'll face are directly related to the developmental stage of your child—and never more so than during the very early years. Get ready for a close-up look at those special, pre-Preschool years.

Chapter 3

And Baby Makes Three (or More)

In This Chapter

➤ Back from the hospital: the early days

➤ Adjusting to your new life

➤ Dealing with postpartum depression

Relish your time in the hospital. Get plenty of rest and allow the nurses to attend to your every need. God knows when you go home and the new-baby frenzy dies down, you will be on your own with a new little bald-headed person who expects you to know what you're doing. But don't worry—you will catch on. Babies look fragile but they are not that difficult to handle. And besides, as far as *they* know, you *are* doing it right.

Bringing Baby Home

If you can, arrange for someone to help you out when you first come home with your baby—you'll welcome the assistance. But decide ahead of time what kind of help you need. Some new moms would welcome some personal care but don't want to give up taking care of their new baby. Be clear with yourself—and with would-be helpful family members—about just what kind of help you're willing to accept.

Helpers? The Pros and Cons

If you're looking for a little help with the cooking and laundry, but want to be the one to sponge bathe and cuddle the baby, make sure that everyone knows how you feel. Otherwise, you may find yourself feeling guilty for looking a gift-nurse in the mouth, and having to fight to reclaim your nest.

Momma Said There'd Be Days Like This

When I had my first baby my mother-in-law arranged for a nurse to come help me when I first came home. I envisioned someone who would bring me trays of mystery meat and green Jell-O while I got used to being a mom. What I got, however, was a *baby* nurse who had very little interest in *my* welfare. She basically took over with my infant, and I felt very threatened.

Setting Limits

If you had a difficult delivery or a C-section and want to have help with baby care, just set the parameters for the help you need, and make sure you are compatible with your caregiver. Make it clear that you need help with housekeeping, meals, and laundry or whatever it is you need help with—and make clear those areas where you'd rather they didn't intrude. Above all, get involved with the selection and do not feel you have to accept someone's gift, no matter how gracious, if it conflicts with what you expect or need.

The Times, They've Been A-Changing

Some mothers, particularly in generations past, wanted to delegate baby care. If you examine the social climate of the 40s, 50s, and even the 60s, women didn't have the choices we have now. It was expected that a woman would marry young and have children.

Womanly Wisdom

Follow your own instincts when it comes to how you wish to care for your baby when you first come home. Becoming a mom is a difficult enough adjustment without trying to make everyone else happy first. Be gracious but keep control over your baby.

Women have options now that include career and motherhood or career without motherhood. It's great that women can add personal fulfillment to the list of things they can hope for in a lifetime. But these options also create a difference in attitude between young women today and the women of previous generations. In other words, your mom or mother-in-law may believe she's really doing you a favor by freeing you of the responsibility of baby care for a week or two. But if you want nothing more than to care for your newborn yourself, you can feel overwhelmed by the generational difference in attitude.

And remember—hired help is not the only option available to you. Friends are usually willing to help and new grandmothers can be a wonderful blessing.

Happy Homecoming!

It is great if your mate is there with you when you bring the baby home. You should celebrate your blessing together and share as much as you can. Some families have a homecoming, complete with a grandparent motorcade. If that's your style, go for it: I personally love a reason to make everything as special as possible, so for each of my back-from-the-hospital celebrations I always had picked out a special baby outfit and made it an occasion.

Remember this: It is important for your morale to have some type of transition celebration before you settle in to your new life. You spent nine months anticipating this day. You shouldn't let everything fizzle into an anticlimax—there'll be plenty of time later for day-to-day routine to set in.

Inventing Your Own Rituals

Many cultures have rituals marking the arrival of a new life into the family. Why not try creating your own bringing-baby-home-from-the-hospital ritual to show your gratitude and to mark the occasion in your database of happy memories. You won't feel like entertaining a ton of guests, so keep it simple. Lighting a candle, having a toast, and enjoying a visit from the baby's nearest relatives are more than enough. The goal is to help you feel special; to reinforce your support-system, and to postpone any anxiety you might have when you are left to your own devices.

When It All Comes Down to You

You and your mate can experience baby care together, but chances are he will have to return to work before you will. This is not sexist—it's just a practical outcome of the fact that you are the designated keeper of the womb. Your obstetrician will have recommended you take it relatively easy at first, and he'll probably suggest that you put off resuming your normal activities for about six weeks. On the other hand, it's rare for a man to be given such a generous amount of parental leave.

After a while you will find yourself the primary caregiver. As much as you might have believed this would not happen, welcome to motherhood. It is a fact of life that no matter how liberated and open-minded your partner is, you will most likely be the one primarily responsible for the care and raising of your offspring. There are always exceptions, of course—and with the high rate of divorce these days, it's even becoming common for men to take over the so-called mothering role completely. They tend to apply their own distinctive styles to the task, and they do a fabulous job. Nurturing is nurturing, after all, and fathers are fully equipped to raise a child.

Womanly Wisdom

Parental leave for fathers is a relatively new concept, so take what you can get but don't expect as much as you would like.

Nonetheless, in the division of child-rearing responsibilities, it is more than likely that you will be the one doing more than 50 percent. But this is not necessarily a bad thing—it's hard to raise a child by committee, so sometimes it's better if you are the majority partner in the deal. You may have more than 51 percent of the work to do, but it is worth it if you have more voting leverage in certain decisions.

The key is this: Negotiate your parenting responsibilities so that you have the *support* of your partner when it counts. If you've got that, it's just fine if you have to change more poopy diapers than he does. Just make sure he is changing enough of them so he can share a feeling of involvement in the job, and so he can earn his bragging rights to everyone about how much of a help he is. Most of all you want your partner to have a relationship with your children that goes beyond a baby-sitting role.

Mom Alert!

The worst thing you can do for your morale is to become isolated. Take the baby for a stroll whenever you can. A simple change of scenery will often work wonders.

Adjusting to Your New Life

At some point you are going to be on your own with your baby. Unless you have a live-in grandmother or Mary Poppins helping you out, you are going to have many days when your baby looks into your eyes and you think to yourself, "Well, *I* don't know what to do, so what are you looking at me for?"

Try to develop a support system of friends and family for advice, a good laugh, or to just hear another adult voice. You want to develop a support system independent of your mate so you won't find yourself overly dependent at a time when you feel most vulnerable.

Motherhood Is a Time for Personal Growth

First-time motherhood isn't easy, and second-, third-, or even fifth-time Moms sometimes have trouble making the adjustment to bringing a new baby home. A new baby brings changes in your self-concept in addition to changes in your role, and any unresolved issues of ego and security that you bring into your new role are going to become exacerbated.

How does this happen? Well, if you are like many of us, you might be a product of several generations in need of healing. The pain and sorrow of one generation is often brought to bear on the succeeding ones. And so you bring into your new experience— motherhood—many insecurities, doubts, and fears. But remember—you can also bring into it many hopes and renewed expectations.

Here's the great news: You really *can* create a whole new method of raising children. Just because previous generations of your (or your partner's) family had dysfunctional dynamics, you don't have to follow along the same path. With this little person you bring home from the hospital all wrapped up in receiving blankets with weak neck muscles and a cry that sounds like a kitten, you can create a *new* pattern of mothering that will change a generation. There is only one problem: To do this, you have to personally create the new rules.

Ultimately, whatever personal fears and insecurity you bring into being a mother can be converted into the source of your greatest strength if you learn to listen to your higher *mother's voice*—the part of you that knows the truth of what is best for you and for your baby.

Moving Beyond the Basics

While you're still at the hospital the nurses will teach you all you need to know about the basics of baby care. They will teach you how to diaper, feed, swaddle, and bathe your little one. By the time you leave you will feel like an expert—until you get home and have to do it on your own. Here's where a good support system comes in handy. You can rely on your supporters as you make new adjustments, but you need to remember that the best support is what you give to yourself.

Making the Shift from a Twosome to a Threesome

When it was just you and your partner, you babied each other. You played whenever you wanted to play; you stayed up and slept late whenever you wanted to. But as soon as you bring your baby home, life, as you used to know it, changes. You and your partner now have a whole new person, with his or her own needs, to accommodate.

The first night you have an infant in the house will be the strangest. First of all, you are going to keep checking on the baby to see whether she's breathing, warmly covered—and, because having a baby is so amazing and awesome, you'll even find yourself checking to make sure she's really *there*. I always kept my newborns in a bassinet in the room with me—it saved me a lot of getting up in the night when I wanted to take a quick peek.

Mom-isms

Newborns like to feel secure, so it is comforting for them to be **swaddled,** or wrapped, so that their limbs are close to their sides. To swaddle the baby, take a square blanket, fold up the edge, and place the baby's feet on top of it. Then cross one side of the blanket over the baby and tuck it under. Next, cross and tuck the other side, and then use the unfolded edge to cover baby's head.

Womanly Wisdom

If you've got a handy friend, see if he or she will build you a special cradle like the one I borrowed from a friend. It had a wood plank attached that slid under the mattress of my own bed. The cradle was open on one side so the baby could easily be lifted into my bed for a late-night feeding and put back to bed without much disruption. It was really ingenious and tremendously helpful.

Night and Day, You Are the One

Babies look so angelic when they are sleeping. The first night you have baby home you will rock her to sleep, put her to bed, and crawl into your own bed. The end of a perfect day. Then, at about 2 a.m., you'll hear "wah wah wah," and you will shoot out of your bed like a rocket. In the interests of keeping your partner involved in the child-rearing process, you will elbow him to make sure he shares your experience.

"The baby is crying," you'll moan. "What do you think is wrong?" Then you'll go through your list. Is the baby wet? Probably. You change her. Will rocking put her back to sleep? Hmmm, that's not working. Maybe you should try feeding her? Ah, yes—that works. (Don't forget to burp her.) Then you put her back to bed. Blissful sleep. Until the next time.

Womanly Wisdom

Burping a baby effectively isn't as easy as it seems. Just patting her on the back rarely gets the job done. Try starting with gentle pats at about rear-end level, and moving slowly up to just below the neck. Works like a charm.

Mom-isms

Colic is a very common gassy stomach condition that babies are prone to. When the gas pressure builds, the baby wakes up, fussing and crying. Aside from making sure that the baby isn't ingesting too much air with her milk, there's not much you can do except ride this out. It does end, eventually.

Sleep? What's Sleep?

At about 6 a.m. you hear "wah wah wah" again, so you stumble out of bed and go through the whole 2 a.m. routine all over again. Somehow at the hospital it didn't seem so tiring. You know you had to get up as many times but you seemed to be able to sleep longer in between. And, of course, that was true—in fact, in the hospital you could sleep just as much between feedings as your baby did. But those restful days are over.

By the second day, you've probably already figured out a few survival tips. You nap when the baby naps and take care of your physical needs in between baby's cries. You are still sore from childbirth and tired from lack of sleep. After you put the baby down for the night you fall asleep with the television on and have weird dreams. At approximately 2 a.m. you hear the now-familiar "wah wah wah," and the cycle starts again.

A Momma's Work Is Never Done...

Just dealing with a newborn's normal feeding schedule is exhausting enough, but you've got many other adventures in sleeplessness in store, as well. For example, babies often get *colic*, a gassy stomach condition that's liable to wake her every hour, on the hour. No matter *what* you do—feeding, burping, walking around the room in circles, rocking, singing, making stupid faces—nothing makes a difference. One thing that usually *does* work (no one knows quite why) is to drive the baby around the block in the car. Presto! This usually makes even colicky babies fall asleep.

After about a week, you may begin to feel a bit more energetic (if still a little brain dead) and start trying to do things around the house. So instead of napping when the baby naps you decide to clean. You start in one room and wander to the next but you don't seem to be getting anywhere. The house seems as messy as when you started. Then you decide you need to nap after all. You lie down, start to snore, and hear "wah wah wah."

When your partner comes home and sees the mess in each room, your disheveled hair, and the crazed look in your eyes, and says, "Hi, Hon. How was your day?" you are fully justified in throwing a tissue box at his head and bursting into tears.

Momma Said There'd Be Days Like This

I didn't have a lot of confidence before I became a mother, and in some ways I had less after the baby was born—I was facing a whole new set of responsibilities, and my first marriage was not a good or stable one. But the baby gave me a kind of strength that I believe is unique to mothers. My instincts as a mother helped me to grow strong enough to protect my child—and that helped me to be strong enough to protect myself.

Expecting the Expectable

You are bound to have days like this. It is OK. Even better, it *will* get easier, and one day you will again know what it is like to get a good night's sleep. The best thing for you to do in these early days is to lower your expectations. You are going through a physical and emotional adjustment, so set your priorities accordingly. You need your sleep more than you need a spotless home.

Shifting Your Focus

If your life before baby involved being busy and productive outside the home, learning to adjust to being at home with the baby can be difficult. Taking care of a baby can seem like an endless array of nonproductive activities, compared to what you used to do at work.

You feed the baby, she gets hungry again. You clean the baby and she poops again. You change her shirt and she spits up on the new one. You change *your* shirt and she spits up on *that*. Understandably, you get tired, and there's no one telling you "good job" as they did at your office or when you were in school.

It's unlikely that your partner is focused on telling you what a good job you are doing—he may not even be sensitive enough to tell you how beautiful you are, as he always used to (before the baby came). And even if he does tell you, you still cry because when you look in the mirror all you can see is the extra baby weight, the lack of grooming since you barely have time to shower, and the bags under your eyes from lack of sleep. You can feel pretty miserable and sorry for yourself right about now.

Tips for Self-Validation

What's a new mother to do? If she's wise, she makes a special effort to appreciate herself, and so should you. Here's how:

➤ Don't let a day go by without acknowledging what a special and wonderful job you are doing.

➤ Remind yourself that you are one of an elite group—you are a Mom! And remember that you are not alone in what you're going through.

➤ Keep in touch with other mothers—newbies and veterans of the first-baby blues. They'll help you keep your perspective.

➤ Most important, keep your sense of humor. It is very easy to become negative about the less glamorous aspects of caring for a newborn, but try to find ways to see the funny side whenever possible.

Wrangling the Wild One

Occasions for humor abound with newborns, if you keep yourself open to them. For example, if you have a baby boy you will inevitably get a shot of pee in your eye. (Now *that's funny,* really!) You have to remember to cover him at all times when you change him if you want to avoid this.

And no matter what gender baby you have, you will inevitably have to clean a messy poop that leaks out of the diaper and onto somebody's nice skirt or expensive slacks. Well, maybe that's not so funny, but it's not the stuff of high tragedy, either. You will also, occasionally, be covered with spit up and will suffer every baby-caused indignity imaginable. But on the other hand, you will fall in love in a way you have never experienced. Babies can mesmerize you with a simple smile, even if their smile is just caused by gas.

It's important during this time that you surround yourself with supportive and upbeat people. If you have a mother-in-law who makes you depressed or who is very critical, avoid contact with her during these crucial first weeks or months of motherhood. Your state of mind is more important than playing family politics.

Similarly, if you have a friend who is *always* looking for the dark side of the moon, tell her how busy you plan to be for the next 18 years. Consider this to be a time of personal and spiritual rebirth. You are a mother now and it is your duty to create an environment of love and joy for you, your partner, and your baby.

Postpartum Depression

There is always some moodiness associated with having a newborn in your life because of the simple fact that you spend the early days and weeks suffering from sleep deprivation. And, as you've already seen, having a baby can bring out a lot of underlying issues and insecurities that you've never gotten around to addressing. This can lead to a temporary bout of depression caused by the new circumstances of your life. This is a very real, well-recognized condition, known as *postpartum depression.*

Proactive Possibilities

But there is another situation that is important to consider. When a woman gives birth her body is subject to tremendous hormonal changes. These changes can disrupt her system, resulting in a postpartum depression that will not work itself out over time. It is actually a very serious matter, and can have some very serious consequences if left undiagnosed and untreated.

For example, it is not uncommon for a marriage to split up if the mother suffers from undiagnosed, and therefore, untreated, postpartum depression. When the disorder is misunderstood or unacknowledged, it can put undue stress on the relationship between husband and wife. The mood swings can become extreme, so that the woman falls victim to rages and even delusions.

Postpartum depression is *very* real. It can lead to psychosis and has been sadly implicated in the deaths of newborns. People who've never experienced the condition often find it hard to understand what the sufferer is going through, but there are support groups and well-informed practitioners who have been educating the public.

Mom-isms

Postpartum depression (PPD) is the term for any downswings in mood that women may suffer after giving birth. While a supportive partner and network of friends can help with normal depression, serious PPDs are hormonally induced and require a doctor's attention.

Mom Alert!

After weeks of sleep deprivation, it's normal to sometimes think that you could cheerfully strangle your partner for putting you in this position. But it could be a sign of a serious problem if you actually plan when and how to do it. All kidding aside, if you experience dark thoughts or fears that you can't seem to shake off, contact a psychiatrist immediately—you may have postpartum depression.

Even Old Hands Need Help, Sometimes—One Woman's Story

After my third child was born I developed what I thought was postpartum depression. I was in a stressful second marriage and noticed that all during this pregnancy (following so quickly on the heels of my second child's birth) I was more emotionally volatile, insecure, and weepy. I needed a lot of support that my husband did not know how to give me.

Descent into Rage and Weeping

After the birth, things really started to change. I would get bursts of energy and then I would crash into pitiful helplessness, barely able to crawl out of bed. I was so frustrated with my husband for not understanding that something radical was happening to me that I would throw our lawn furniture around.

I'm from a fiery Mediterranean background, so it was not totally out of the question for me to throw things out of frustration. A pot maybe, or a plate to get someone's attention. But I was feeling very out of control. I would go quickly from rage into heartsick weeping. I was unable to cope. Of course I blamed myself and decided I was just a terrible mother and an overall worthless person.

What was also frightening was that I had very dark thoughts. I would look at my baby and worry about the most horrible things happening. It is perfectly normal to worry about your newborn. It is a sign of a possible problem when you become obsessed and immobilized by irrational fears.

Dealing with Depression

My experience wasn't unique, as I quickly learned. My husband and I went to a support group where we talked to couples who were experiencing postpartum depression, and got some good ideas of how we could better cope. They encouraged us to make sure we stuck to a bedtime schedule for the children, and for ourselves. They also suggested other ways to reduce stress in our daily lives, and one of the support group members told me of her experiences with temporary medication for her postpartum depression.

All these alternatives are worth checking into if you're dealing with dramatic emotional and mood-swing problems after childbirth. For many mothers, as for me, the idea of medication poses immediate problems—drugs are not the best choice when you're nursing your newborn. But there were lots of helpful tips to learn at that support group.

For example, I examined my diet and consulted with a macrobiotics counselor. I tried alternative remedies from the health food store and consulted with all kinds of people to help me get a grip on what was happening. Thank goodness I had friends who were able to help me with the babies, because I was a wreck.

Bottoming Out and Breaking Through

Remember that I said earlier how very serious postpartum depression can be! Well, when you're in its grip, you can suffer some of the lowest of emotional lows. In my case, I finally felt so out of control and frightened that I prayed for help. I couldn't deal with my agitated, angry moods because I could blame my husband or my circumstances and explain it away.

What finally opened my eyes to the seriousness of my condition was that I became suicidal. I would sit on the floor in the bathroom with the door locked and cry. I found myself contemplating the easiest way a person could kill herself. Then I would think about my children, cry some more, and talk myself out of falling into what I can only describe as an elevator shaft. I talked to God a lot and said, "God, I may be an angry person, I may have low self-esteem at times, but I love life and I especially love my children. What is wrong with me?"

This is what can happen to you when you have some forms of postpartum depression. It is as though your mind is attacking you from the inside. Your moods go wacky and your thoughts are not what they would be under normal circumstances. It is important for you to understand that this is a *biochemical response* and should not be ignored, and it is not something to be ashamed of. It is not your fault if you become ill after childbirth. It *is* your choice whether you take it seriously enough to get help.

There Is Help for You Out There

I was very stubborn and thought my problems would work themselves out. But one day I became so frightened that I called a local mental health hotline. The woman who answered referred me to an expert in dealing with postpartum depression. After listening to my story, she took a very firm line with me and made it clear that this was not something that would just go away by itself. She was emphatic when she told me that if I didn't seek help the condition could worsen and I could become a danger to myself or to my children. She said some people need medical intervention before they can get back on their feet. When I became more frightened of not seeking help I found my way to an excellent psychiatrist.

Counseling Is Cool

Some manifestations of postpartum depression can appear more severe than others— some women's experiences are harder to identify because they may be unmasked by other underlying, chronic conditions such as bipolar disorder (also known as *manic depression*—a condition that complicated my own PPD experience). The important thing to remember is that once you *do* have a preliminary diagnosis of possible postpartum depression, you need to take action.

Work with Your Doctor

Many women share the attitude I had at the time—I was resistant to admitting the need for psychological help, and strongly resistant to using medication. My doctor took me through the logical steps of treatment. He told me to wean the baby to see whether my hormones would right themselves on their own. (Of course, you know they didn't. I wasn't so lucky.) Next, he suggested mood-stabilizing medication—only to come up against my then strongly held rejection of drugs of any kind. But he was patient with me, and after he completed my medical and family medical history and made his preliminary diagnosis he said, "Deborah, you deserve this medication. If you were diabetic you would take insulin. You need this medicine to return you to balance."

I responded so well and so thoroughly to the medical intervention that I was spared what could have been years of poor mental health. Even more important, my children were spared the loss of a mother due to a chronic mental disorder, or worse.

After six years in remission I conducted a writer's workshop and recognized on the roster the name of the woman who had so firmly guided me through the mental health hot line. At the end of the workshop I told the story of my foray into manic depressive disorder and told her how much she was responsible for my stable and happy life. There wasn't a dry eye in the room.

Womanly Wisdom

Even if your condition is mild and not chronic, any pervasive mood change after childbirth should be taken seriously and a mental health professional, preferably a psychiatrist familiar with this highly misunderstood disorder, should be consulted.

The Many Flavors of PPD

Postpartum depression comes in many forms. If you are suffering from a full-blown, chronic case, you may require medical intervention. If so, it is important that you stick with your treatment. If you are fortunate enough to have the more common form of postpartum depression, your condition will right itself over time.

It is likely that if your condition is severe enough to require intervention, you will need some kind of drug therapy. And the available medications can bring about dramatic improvements quickly. But do not become cocky and go off your medication when you start to feel better. Follow your doctor's advice on dosages and duration of treatment. For some women, drug intervention is only a temporary necessity. But for people like me, who have a more serious underlying biochemical disorder, the treatment may need to be ongoing. If you go off your medication without a doctor's supervision you may have a relapse.

Diagnosing PPD

There is no blood test, at least as yet, to determine whether a person is manic-depressive, has postpartum depression, or a myriad of other mental health issues. The diagnosis is done through taking a history, through observation, and through a knowledgeable and calculated trial-and-error process with appropriate medication. This means, unfortunately, that what works once may not work again as effectively if you have a relapse.

The Causes of PPD

Not long ago, postpartum depression was largely unrecognized as a legitimate medical condition—it was called the "baby blues" and dismissed as just another of many typical female problems. So research into the condition was rarely done. It is known that PPD, like manic depression, may have a genetic origin, and that it can be (but is not necessarily) triggered by sustained stress in one's life. And we *do* have enough information now to be good consumers of mental health resources, which can bring relief.

Babying Yourself, Too

Sometimes the circumstances of your life around the time of childbirth can make you more prone to crossing the line into the realm of postpartum depression. It is biochemical in origin, but the impact of stress on our biochemistry has long been recognized. You can take steps to minimize your risk *before* PPD strikes by making your home environment as supportive and positive as possible. Make sure you can take care of your needs.

You need to learn how to take care of *you*. This may seem to go against your mothering instincts to care for your children first, but think about it. When you fly with small children in an airplane, the flight attendants tell you to put on your oxygen mask before you put one on your child, in the event of a midair disaster. Why? Because you have to be safe and healthy before you can truly help your child. It's not selfishness to see to your own needs—it's just good mothering.

Your children depend on you to be as healthy and strong as you can be so you can be there to guide them through their lives—*not* to sacrifice yourself. So do not be self-sacrificial. Be self-*validating*. Look at the circumstances of your life and do whatever you can to make your life good and conducive to your continued confidence and mental health.

The Least You Need to Know

➤ Taking care of yourself is the best gift you can give to your children.

➤ If you get help during the first few weeks, don't be afraid to set the limits that suit your needs.

➤ Encourage your partner to share in the baby's care—it's the best beginning of a strong father/child bond.

➤ Ultimately it is up to you to develop your own, personal mothering style.

➤ The early weeks and months can be exhausting, so don't pass up any chances you get to rest—you'll need all the sleep you can get.

➤ Postpartum depression is a real problem for some new Moms—don't hesitate to get help if you need it.

Chapter 4

The Great Nursing Conundrum: Bottle or Breast?

In This Chapter

➤ Bottle or breast, which is best?

➤ What if I do not have enough milk?

➤ Nursing in public and in private: Where and how to nurse

➤ Making the break: Weaning the baby to cup and solid foods

I recently watched an old home movie of the time my parents brought my older sister home from the hospital in 1952. There were the usual scenes of the baby in the bassinet, the baby with a spit curl, the baby burping. But what was really hilarious was the scene in which my father and mother were carefully mixing the baby's formula. You would have thought they were in a chemistry lab. All the bottles were carefully sterilized and the formula meticulously measured. By the time the procedure was finished, I was surprised my sister wasn't already off to college.

The choice to breast- or bottle-feed your newborn is, for many mothers, the first decisive issue of their motherhood role. In this chapter you'll learn about the changing fads and fashions in feeding your newborn, the pros and cons of breast- and bottle-feeding, and how to make the choice that's best for you.

The Great Feeding Debate

Many doctors today recommend breast-feeding (nursing) your baby for the first year—but breast-feeding is not for everybody. And it's amazing how the tides of public opinion have shifted back and forth on this subject, in this century alone. In the early

Womanly Wisdom

I don't know about you, but I prefer to keep my breasts to myself. If you're confronted by well-meaning but nosy strangers inquiring into your baby-feeding choice, don't feel compelled to answer if you'd prefer not to. Just smile enigmatically and walk away.

decades, breast-feeding was the norm. Then, in the 1940s and 1950s, bottle-feeding with all its sterilizing and formula mixing was all the rage. And, when the 1960s brought a return-to-nature ethic, some young mothers turned to the naturalness of breast-feeding, raising their own moms' eyebrows. Breast-feeding seemed to be just another aspect of counterculture revolution. But bottle-feeding remained the norm throughout this decade and the next.

In the 1980s, breast-feeding once again was seen as something socially conscious mothers should do for their newborns. The tide had shifted so strongly that eyebrows were raised if women chose *not* to nurse their newborns. Strangers who would never discuss breasts in the course of ordinary conversation thought nothing of asking a pregnant woman, "So, are you planning to nurse?"

Choices, Choices, Choices

Breast or bottle…which is best? That all depends on you and your baby. Here's a list of some of the pros and cons of each:

Breast- versus Bottle-Feeding, a Comparison

Breast-feeding Pros	Bottle-feeding Pros
Very convenient—no preparation or cleanup required	Also convenient, especially if you use formula and disposable bottles
No need to use medication to dry up the milk you naturally produce	No need to deal with breast-milk leakage if you're away from baby during feeding times
Nursing provides a time of close personal and physical bonding between Mom and baby	Both Mom and Dad can bottle-feed the baby with equal ease
Nursing induces mild uterine contractions, helping the new mom regain her prepregnancy shape	No need to deal with the breast pump

Hitting the Bottle

Bottle-feeding these days is much easier than when my parents had to do it. Bottles can be adequately sterilized in a dishwasher, if you have one, and many bottles come with presterilized inserts that are disposable after each feeding. There are bottles of every shape, size, and material—including some that are decorated with your favorite cartoon characters (your newborn probably hasn't had time to pick her favorites yet).

There are bottles with special grips so baby has an easier time holding them when he is old enough to grab. There are bottles that almost seem capable of feeding baby without benefit of a grown up.

Bottle-feeding can mean both convenience and mobility and is a perfectly viable choice. Women who choose the bottle method often cite the impracticality of maintaining a breast-feeding schedule when they have to be away from home for work. They also like the freedom it gives them to share feeding responsibilities with their partners without having to fill bottles of expressed breast milk.

Momma's Own Milk?

For some, breast-feeding is like a religion. They can be as dogmatic as any sidewalk evangelist handing out pamphlets about salvation can be. One reason commonly cited in favor of nursing is that breast-feeding a baby, at least for the first year, provides increased immunity. Nature created humans with all that we need to survive on this planet. The baby receives her immunities and nourishment through her mother's milk. There is no food so perfectly designed for the human infant.

Another reason to consider nursing your newborn is that it allows for a special type of bonding. Mother and baby are closely connected in a way that will soon be replaced by baby's need for independence. These quiet moments are so precious and peaceful. Some of my most loving memories are of nursing my children. There is something incredibly womanly about being able to feed your child from your own body.

Of course there are many ways to bond with your baby. Women who adopt infants do not need to fear that their babies will not be as close as those who are able to nurse at their mother's breast.

A final reason for nursing is one that is purely mom-centered, but that doesn't make it any less valid a reason than any of the baby-centered ones. Breast-feeding gives a mother the feeling that this is something she can give the baby that no one else can give. New mothers typically have so many well-meaning (or not so well-meaning) people around them giving them advice that it is nice to have something no one else has—the royal breasts. When your mother or mother-in-law is being too pushy about the right way to fold a diaper or to dress the baby you can just say, "Excuse me, I have to nurse my baby now."

But nursing is not for everybody. It hurts at first. You have to get used to it, and even then it sometimes can be uncomfortable. In addition, some women are uncomfortable with their bodies and feel self-conscious or inhibited about nursing. This is no crime. Society certainly supports this mixed sense of who we are as women. Breasts are so sexualized it is sometimes difficult to see ourselves

Mom-isms

A **breast pump** is a device designed to fit over the breast and, through suction, draw mother's milk out into a connected tube or bulb. The pump *does* work, but many women find it painful and bothersome to use.

47

as mothers and not the object of sexual attention. Some women literally feel like cows when they try nursing. If you have a negative image of yourself you will not be able to relax with it and nursing will be uncomfortable.

Maintaining Mobility

After you've been home from the hospital a few weeks, you are going to want more mobility. If you have a bottle-fed baby you can have Dad or Grandma or a baby-sitter feed the baby while you leave the house. You can always leave a breast-fed baby for several hours between feedings, or you can express your milk (there's a device called a *breast pump* that helps you do this) and keep a bottle or two in the refrigerator when you need to be out during feeding time. But ultimately, bottle-feeding will give you more flexibility.

Mom-isms

Nature has a marvelous way of adjusting to your baby's needs. One natural mechanism for this is called **let down**—your milk literally descends in your breast to be available for your baby to suck. You can actually feel this happen.

Mom Alert!

When a woman misses a feeding or simply produces more milk than needed at any given time, her breasts become overfull, or en-gorged, and can feel painful and sore. The engorged breast can be relieved by expressing milk in a hot shower or by hot compresses.

Of course, if you're getting out of the house and bringing baby with you, you don't have to worry about someone else being able to feed her. Instead, you have a different set of issues to deal with—and here, sad to say, bottle-feeding tends to have an edge. It is still true that breast-feeding in public is a problem in this society. We'll get into that particular issue in greater detail a little later in this chapter.

The Dual Role of Nursing, from Baby's Point of View

Babies find the simple act of sucking to be comforting, and may cry for food when they really only want something in their mouth. You can use a pacifier, but quite often the inclination is to stick a bottle in the baby's mouth. This raises the real possibility of overfeeding, which can cause your baby to spit up more often and gain weight too quickly. If you are demand-feeding with breast milk, the baby can suck for comfort but will not get too much milk during the time between your normal *let-down* periods.

Some people choose to mix feedings of bottled breast milk or formula and breast-feeding to have the best of both worlds. This can work out well if done consistently. But keep in mind that as a new mom you need to maintain a certain level of milk flow to continue to breast-feed successfully. If the schedule of breast- and bottle-feedings is consistent, your body will adjust and produce the proper amount of milk. On the other hand, if you keep an erratic feeding schedule, you run the risk of having your breasts become engorged.

Baby versus Dad

Some women are very self-conscious about how their mate will view them if they nurse. There is an internal conflict, for most North Americans at least, when comparing women as sexual creatures and women as mothers. Don't kid yourself: Men *can* get a little weird when they see their baby suckling. They may even feel a bit resentful and confused about their feelings. On the other hand, you as a woman may be used to associating sensual pleasure with your breasts—it can be disconcerting to suddenly associate them with nurturing feelings that are potentially even more powerful.

Sensations and Sensibility

To make things even more confusing, nursing produces some kind of hormone that can make it a type of sensual pleasure. It feels good to nurse, almost like a high. And sometimes the feelings are very sexual. No one really wants to talk about this because we are afraid someone will think we are a little weird, but facts are facts. Our bodies respond to the nursing in a way that at least for now is sometimes threatening to society and to us. It may help you to realize that those sensual feelings are in fact a very normal—and very practical—physical mechanism. What you're feeling are mild contractions of the vagina and uterus which work to help these organs return to their prechildbirth shape.

If you have an open communication with your mate and you feel he might be getting a little wiggy about your focus on the baby—and the baby's focus on your breasts—you should talk about it. Nursing a baby is beautiful and natural—and temporary. Tell your mate that your baby will only need you like this for a short time in the scheme of things. You have every right to put your baby first. He will have to adjust. In other words, your breasts belong to you. You decide what to do with them. And, of course, you might remind your partner that there is nothing wrong with sharing.

Womanly Wisdom

To help Dad feel less alienated from you and the baby during the period that you are nursing, be willing to let go a little bit. Encourage him to take care of the baby, including feeding, even though you don't think he is doing things exactly as you would do them. It is better to have a helping dad than one who gives up too soon.

Pulling Pop into the Food Chain

One way to bring Dad into the process rather than making him feel more left out is to plan for him to feed the baby by himself sometimes. We women are so protective of our newborns that we sometimes forget that Dad needs to bond as well. If he's showing resentment of the baby, some of it may *not* relate to the temporary and relative unavailability of your breasts for sensual contact. Instead, it may come from a sense of alienation.

It's true that a father can't ever feel exactly the same things a mother can feel when he feeds the newborn. But if you give your mate the opportunity to find his own way to connect to the baby you will find much less resentment and a more harmonious relationship all around. It is truly a gift you can give to both father and baby. Encourage the relationship and it will last a lifetime.

Nursing Basics

Although nursing is a natural instinct for both mother and baby, it is not unusual to feel clumsy at first. If you are open-minded, your baby can actually teach you how to nurse without much prior knowledge on your part. Just put the baby's little mouth near your nipple and he or she will find a way.

Womanly Wisdom

To relax while nursing, try putting a pillow under the baby or under the arm holding the baby to achieve a more natural and comfortable position while you're sitting up.

Nature makes nursing very instinctual for both mother and child, so you don't really need too many instructions. But there are things you can do to make nursing a more comfortable and positive experience for both you and your baby. We'll take up a lot of the common issues and concerns of moms who are new to nursing, but first, here are a few helpful tips to keep in mind:

➤ Relax

➤ Find a comfortable chair (rockers do nicely) to nurse in

➤ If a little wine helps you relax, some doctors recommend it—but keep it to a small amount because what you drink, the baby drinks.

What If I Don't Have Enough Milk?

Some women do not produce enough milk flow to nurse successfully, while others seem capable of nursing 10 babies. If you're having trouble producing enough, sometimes drinking more fluids helps. Sometimes you just need time for your body to settle into this new trick it's learning to do, and as you and your baby establish a regular feeding schedule your milk will increase. But sometimes nothing seems to help. This does not mean that the woman who can't produce enough milk is a failure as a mother or that her child will be less advantaged than other children will be. Remember, it is good for a baby to be breast-fed but that is by no means the only way to go.

It is common for women to panic at the first signs of a problem with nursing. Most problems correct themselves quickly, so be patient. You will know if nursing is not for you. If you decide not to nurse, your doctor will give you some medicine to prevent your milk from coming in. If your milk has already come in and you decide not to nurse, you can just let the milk dry up on its own. You may feel a bit engorged at first but it will not take long for the hormones to note that baby is not utilizing the milk supply.

Whooo, This Feels Weird

The first time you nurse it *will* feel strange. When the baby clamps his or her mouth on the nipple it will cause the let-down reflex mentioned earlier in this chapter, when the milk fills the breasts in preparation for the feeding. It is good to have the baby nurse for only a limited time on one breast and then switch to the other. Otherwise your nipples can get sore and you will have uneven milk flow. Some women like to wear a diaper pin or other marker on their blouse or bra to indicate which side they used when they last nursed. That way they can remember to start on the other side the next time.

Still, no matter what you do, you're bound to have sore nipples. The skin is delicate and your baby's sucking reflex is very strong. But you don't have to let sore nipples cause you to give up on nursing too soon. Eventually they will toughen and nursing will not hurt a bit. It is worth taking the time to get past the initial discomfort. You can relieve some of the irritation with special creams made for lactating mothers. Hot compresses also work wonders. If you develop an infection, however, you may need medical intervention or you may wind up weaning your baby prematurely because breast-feeding is too painful for you. Further tips to avoid infection or pain: Make sure you keep the nipple area clean, and try to avoid engorgement.

You Are (and Produce) What You Eat

Watch what you eat when you are nursing. Do not forget that your nursing infant is essentially eating a predigested version of whatever you have eaten. If you want to give your baby major gas, just go ahead and eat that double chili dog or spicy burrito. On a more serious note, you must be extremely careful about which medicines you take. Do not take any over-the-counter medication without your doctor's approval, as it will pass to your baby through your breast milk.

Momma Said There'd Be Days Like This

Nursing moms should avoid some foods—like chocolate and mayonnaise—because they make the milk taste bad to baby. Other foods can just cause silly problems. One mom had a scare when she ate beets for dinner. When she changed her baby's diaper after nursing later that night, the poop was bright red. Terrified, she raced the child to the hospital, convinced that the baby was hemorrhaging at the very least. Turns out, the beets were the culprit.

Problems in Public

One of the issues of breast-feeding is the appropriate place to do it. I am a firm believer that it is appropriate to feed your baby discretely wherever you happen to be when your baby is hungry. Demand feeding is the best thing for a breast-fed baby because their little bodies know how much they need and there is no real risk of overfeeding. So if the baby gives you a hunger cry (and you *will* learn to tell the difference between the baby's cries,) you will want to stop and feed her.

Now, I'm not advocating exhibitionism here, but society really *should* show far more respect and appreciation for nursing mothers. If you use good sense and cover yourself appropriately with a clean cloth diaper or receiving blanket, you should be able to do what you need to do when you need to do it. It is unfair for nursing mothers to be banished to dirty public restrooms because hypocritical people, who think nothing of half-naked models in billboards all over town and full frontal nudity in R-rated films, are offended by this most natural of human functions.

And, if you try, you can get pretty good at nursing discretely. By the time I had my third child I could nurse while I was walking around a store—with no one the wiser. It just takes some dexterity, practice, and a little bit of nerve. Just remember that there is nothing more precious than a mother feeding her child.

So get out into the world and demand the respect you deserve. Act as though it is the most natural thing in the world, and most people won't even notice you. Many places are more child-friendly than they used to be. Check out whether there is a lounge or a quiet corner with a chair if you are more comfortable being out of the way when you nurse.

Clothing Choices

While you are lactating you will feel most comfortable wearing a nursing bra with nursing pads. Your nursing bra will be much larger than your prepregnancy (or even pregnancy-size) bra. Your back size increases, making most of whatever you were wearing uncomfortable. You can sometimes get bra extensions in case you outgrow your nursing bras. They are little pieces of material with hooks that fit right onto your bra. Milk takes up a lot of room.

Mom-isms

Lactation is the physical function of producing milk.

Milk-filled breasts leak. Isn't this dignified? Well, maybe not—but it *is* a fact of life. You have to look at the bright side. I may not have had a waist after childbirth, and I may have leaked a little milk every once in a while, but I looked voluptuous. Never in my life had I had such a well-endowed chest. Even *I* was impressed.

So what's a little spillage when you've got a figure like Sophia Loren? If you wear nursing pads with your bra and change them frequently you should feel more comfortable—*and* you'll stay relatively dry. Nursing pads are round cotton pads that fit into your bra and absorb the leakage from your nipples. If you don't wear them you might be out at your typical baby-feeding time and notice two huge wet spots where your breasts used to be.

Some women may even need to double their pads if they are prone to an easy let-down reflex. Your body is so programmed with instinct that your milk may well come in if you even *think* about your baby or if you see or hear someone else's baby.

By the way, there are nursing shields made from materials other than cotton. I had some reusable nursing shields made out of plastic. They fit around the nipple and caught the leakage. It was actually kind of weird when I got to see the amount of milk that had accumulated. They also made my already enlarged udders look like a cross between Madonna's gold-cone breasts and Dolly Parton's.

Mom Alert!

Your baby's particular hunger cry can cause an automatic let-down of milk—as can anything that sounds like that cry. Even a squeaky door, if it squeaks in just the right pitch, can cause you to spring a leak.

Express Yourself

If you go back to work while you are still nursing—or if your lifestyle requires you to be away from your baby during one or more of her feeding times—you can express some of your milk during the day so that your breasts don't become engorged. If you are able to master the art of using a breast pump, you can do well with it.

The Pros and Cons of Pumps

I never had much luck with a breast pump. When I had my first baby and had to go away for a weekend I consulted La Leche League, the major women's organization dedicated to education and advocacy on behalf of breast-feeding. On their advice, I rented a super-duper breast pump. This thing was huge, electric, and I do not mind saying, a bit scary. Using it was kind of like using a vacuum. When used at full power you might get the feeling that you are going to be sucked right in, breast and all.

I did the best I could that weekend. I quickly gave up on the electric pump and ultimately learned the fine art of expressing milk in the shower. If you are inhibited about squeezing milk out of your nipples you will get over it quickly when faced with the alternative of an automatic cow-milking machine like the one I tried.

It is actually kind of interesting to see how the milk works. It squirts out of several openings in the nipple. Okay—I did not grow up on a farm. I thought it was pretty cool. Expressing the milk didn't help me as much as I had hoped it would. I was wearing my double-decker plastic Partons and nursing pads but still wound up with two bullseyes at a Bar Mitzvah.

After my second child was born, I went back to work for two days each week. I didn't want to wean him so I tried to pump during the day to keep the milk flowing. I had gotten a small version of the electric cow-milking machine and a cute yuppie carrying case, complete with its own refrigeration system (ice packs). It looked great, but once again I had very little luck with it. I think I had pump performance anxiety.

I was in a dilemma because this time I couldn't use the shower trick. I was uncomfortable, and by the end of the day I was rushing home to find my baby so he could nurse and relieve the pressure. I solved the problem by switching to a relatively inexpensive hand pump that relied on suction instead of on electricity. It worked just fine and helped me express enough milk to relieve the discomfort.

Womanly Wisdom

The least expensive type of breast pump looks like a little bugle, with a big plastic bulb on one end and a flared opening on the other. Squeezing the bulb sets up the suction that draws your milk. You control the strength of the suction better with the manual pumps than with the electric pumps, so there's less likelihood of pain.

Mom Alert!

If you start a baby out on a bottle you will probably not have too much nipple pickiness. If you switch a breast-fed baby to a bottle, or if you add a supplemental bottle, you will probably encounter some nipple pickiness with your child. Try to find one that most closely resembles what he has been used to. The Playtex nurser is the one my baby liked best.

Bottle Basics

With all the problems of breast-feeding, you might think bottle-feeding would be much easier. But bottles have their own drawbacks, especially if you've been breast-feeding and are ready to wean your baby to the bottle. You'll find, as I did, that a baby who's used to the breast really does like Mommy best—he's likely to fuss like crazy when you try to introduce him to a bottle. I tried all kinds of bottles with all kinds of shapes and sizes. Then I took a look at my own breast and nipple when my son nursed and decided that the bottles I was using looked nothing like me. I found a nurser nipple that looked and felt more like a mother's nipple and he liked it. He still preferred Mommy, of course—there isn't a bottle made that would provide him with warm snuggles and singing—but after a while he learned to enjoy his feedings just as well when his Dad or another caregiver gave them to him.

How Long Should I Nurse?

There is no set rule for how long you should nurse a baby. Doctors now suggest one year as a healthy start for a newborn, but that is not always possible. And some women nurse as long as they can—up to three years (although that's relatively rare). You need to look at the overall picture of your life, how many children you have, what your responsibilities are, and how you feel about it. Adding guilt about nursing is silly. You will find plenty of reasons to feel guilty while you're raising your children without looking for other reasons.

Momma Said There'd Be Days Like This

I nursed my oldest child for five months. After that she seemed to be losing interest, which I mistakenly took as a sign that she wanted to wean. (My mother-in-law was also implying that I was somehow not paying enough attention to her son's needs.) Looking back, I wish I had nursed my daughter longer, if only for the sanity and peacefulness that closeness gave us.

Weaning Wisdom

Weaning a baby can be your choice, or it can be baby's. It should not be your mother-in-law's, or even your husband's choice. I weaned my boy at eight months because he was growing so fast and nursed so much that I just got tired. Some more diligent advocates of nursing might have thought that a lame reason to wean, but it was good enough for me. He had taken an interest in solid food and we were both happy.

Of course, after I weaned him I started menstruating and ovulating again and instantly became pregnant with my youngest. (If you are not planning to have children so close together, keep in mind that even though nursing suppresses menstruation, you *can* begin to ovulate again. Take appropriate precautions.) I was happy about the new pregnancy, being the baby lover that I am, but it was a bit of a shock, and I'm still dealing with the challenges of having two children so close in age.

I knew my youngest child would likely be my last, so I held onto nursing as long as I could. I nursed her for 16 months, until she could walk over to me, lift up my shirt, and latch on. Sometimes when she wanted to nurse she would gently tap me on the chest, just under my neck. Some people raised eyebrows that I had this little appendage but we were both very happy and will always have a special bond. I would have continued to nurse her for a while longer if I had not become ill, but I had to wean quickly because the medication I had to take would have been bad for her.

Mom-isms

Weaning is the gradual reduction of feedings, and ultimately leads to the baby's independence from the breast or the bottle as a source of nourishment.

How Do I Wean My Baby?

Sometimes a baby seems to lose interest in nursing, and you can use this opportunity to begin to feed him with a cup. In most situations you need to wean gradually by stopping certain feeding times. This gives your body time to adjust the milk flow so that the milk can eventually dry up.

It's always easiest to wean a baby directly from breast or bottle to a cup—weaning from breast to bottle can be problematic because it makes the second weaning (from the bottle) extremely difficult. You don't want to be responsible for what I call the "bottle-addict syndrome." You have to be very careful with bottle addicts. They constantly walk around with a bottle of water or juice hanging from their lips.

Womanly Wisdom

When you're weaning your child, avoid letting her go to sleep with a bottle or she'll have dental problems later. Also, avoid giving too many sticky snack foods, like raisins, unless you're careful to wipe or brush the baby's teeth afterward.

I will forever feel guilty about sometimes letting my very own bottle addict fall asleep with his bottle. Even though we would remove it as quickly as we could, the liquid would pool on his teeth, making them discolored and weak. This is all too common. We had to have some repair work done on his teeth when he was two so he wouldn't be self-conscious about them until his adult teeth could grow in. Try not to allow your baby to fall asleep with a bottle, and you'll avoid this whole problem.

Have Courage—Weaning Is Survivable

To wean your baby you need to be brave and strong. Be consistent. Offer distractions, not food or candy, and be ready to withstand tears, tantrums, and other natural forms of manipulation. Some babies need to become attached to some kind of transitional object to get over their need to suck or to help them to take the first steps toward independence. A stuffed toy, a blanket, or a pacifier can work.

Just be aware that once you substitute something for the breast or bottle you had better be good at keeping track of whatever has become the new center of your child's universe. I can remember several nights when I had to search frantically, retracing my baby's steps to find her one-and-only special teddy bear.

Practicing for the Bigger Challenges That Lie Ahead

Weaning a baby is only one of the *first* things that will test your mettle as a mother. There will be many more. For now, though, you will feel terrible when you hear your baby cry for his bottle or (especially) for your breast. You will want to cry, too.

Just remember—there is an external world that your baby must eventually learn to live in. Although you want nature to give you the lead on most things, sometimes you have to be the one who is in control, guiding your child to learn new things and enjoy new experiences. It would be nice if you could nurse your child to the point at which he tells you, "Okay, Mother, I am ready to be weaned now so that I can move on to a new developmental stage," but that's not going to happen. You will always need to look for signs of when to make certain changes, but mostly you need to trust how you feel. Your instincts are the best indicator of decisions that should be made.

Trust Yourself

Most mothers have all the answers we need to handle the difficult choices of child-rearing, if we can just learn to trust ourselves. If we are able to tap into the love we have for our babies without all the fear that goes along with it, we will be clearheaded enough to make the right decisions. So if you feel it is best to wean your baby at a certain point in your life, make the decision, stick by it, allow the baby to fuss, and move on.

Making the Move to "Real Foods"

Introducing solids to the baby should be a matter between you, your baby, and your pediatrician. There are many schools of thought on the subject. Earlier generations of moms, for example, believed that starting solids early was necessary to get a child to sleep through the night. Cereal may help a child feel fuller, but many children who are not given solids early sleep through the night, too.

Some children are ready to try solids at as early as four months, others at six months or even later. The most important thing to remember is to make your own decision about it. You are not a neglectful mother if you and your pediatrician believe it is best to wait to introduce solids to your child's diet.

Once again, you've got to go with what works for *you*. Your mother or mother-in-law may disagree and tell you how different things were in their day. Acknowledge their superior wisdom if you like, be polite, and do your own thing anyway. If you can't get away from the interference, then learn to be thick-skinned and stand up for yourself. It is important that you be in control of all important decisions as they relate to your child. You'll need this kind of confidence as your child grows and continues to test his or her limits. If you don't believe in your own authority, you'll have a hard time getting your child to believe in it.

Which Baby Food Is Best?

Back in the 1960s and '70s, mothers first became aware of the nutritional content of commercial baby foods. There was newfound concern about the filler and sugar content of many of them. Some mothers even made their own baby food, grinding their own peas and beans from the garden. This is not realistic for most moms today—not with all the demands that life and work place on our time.

New Commercial Baby Food Options

One good outcome of those years of baby-food awareness is that there are many fine baby foods available today to fit every need. There are even natural baby foods, made with no added sugar and only organic ingredients. But sometimes the natural products are too expensive to use on an regular basis. You will be just fine if you choose your baby food according to what is on sale in a particular week. Just remember that it is best to use an entire jar in one feeding, or dispose of the unused portion. To avoid contamination, you want to be overcautious as far as germs and food storage are concerned.

Mom Alert!

Be very careful to toss out unused portions of baby food. A tiny amount of bacteria that might not affect an adult's system can make a baby very ill.

Making the Change

When you feed your baby for the first time, he or she is going to look at you as though you are crazy. And if you wait for the baby to make the first move you are going to find cereal or mashed peas dribbling gracefully to the floor. Here's one great technique (courtesy of my mother—this was one of the rare moments when I wasn't too stubborn to take her advice): Firmly and confidently take the baby spoon in hand, and put the food directly into the baby's mouth sideways (not tip-first). The baby will likely cooperate until she discovers how much fun it is to play the "I'll close my mouth and drive my mommy crazy" or "Lets see how far I can spit mashed peas" games.

The Least You Need to Know

➤ There are advantages and disadvantages to both bottle-feeding and breast-feeding, so the decision should be made according to what is best for you, your comfort level, and your lifestyle.

➤ You need to be firm when you make important decisions about baby's care.

➤ Nursing pumps, nursing bras, and nursing pads are all designed to make breast-feeding easier on mom.

➤ Avoid weaning from breast to bottle—it's easier on mom *and* baby to wean directly to a cup.

➤ Weaning is one of the first steps in a baby's growth to independence—and one of mom's first experiences with the long, long process of letting go.

Chapter 5

Living with a Toddler

Isn't it wonderful when your baby takes her first uncertain steps? How smart she must be as she pulls herself to a standing position, holding the edge of your coffee table—after all, the neighbor's baby is two months older and not walking yet. Your child is obviously a young Einstein in the making. "Come to mama my little angel," you say. "That's it—you can do it. Take a step. One, two, boom. Try it again—one, two, three— you've got it! You're walking."

A few months later you're singing an entirely different tune: "No, no, Baby. You shouldn't pull Mommy's papers off the coffee table. No, no—don't put that in your mouth. No, no—fingers don't belong in electric outlets. Don't grab that—crash—lamp cord. Yucky dog food is *not* for babies."

This chapter takes you through the joys—and hassles—of creating a workable life amid the chaos created by a newly ambulatory child.

When Baby Gets Vertical, Expect to Go Crazy

Infants take a great deal of care, but at least they stay where you put them. To a toddler, however, life is one big adventure. There is nothing that does not inspire their curiosity.

Think of your toddler as someone from another planet. The only way a toddler learns is by exploring and experimenting. Your task is to try to remain objective. Your child really doesn't intend to give you gray hair as he gets into everything. She really doesn't mean to upset you when she reaches for your breakable items. He doesn't connect with the concept that pulling everything out of the drawers will annoy you—not even the fifth time he does it.

Just Wait—It Gets Even Better

If you think the early days of walking are fun, just wait until your child learns how to run and climb. When my two youngest were toddlers I took all three of my children with me to the airport to drop off a friend who was visiting. Like an idiot, I did not use a stroller. After all, it was easy when we were all together. My seven-year-old was holding her three-year-old brother's hand, and I had my two-year-old's hand firmly clasped in my own. As we were leaving I stopped to get them a treat.

Well, you can guess what happened. I turned my head for a minute, and both little ones took off in opposite directions. My seven-year-old ran after her brother and tackled him fairly quickly. But my two-year-old daughter might as well have been in the Olympics. She was halfway to the next terminal before she finally stopped on her own and started giggling. I caught her before she could start up again but as my chest heaved, I knew clearly who was boss.

Staying Sane in the Land of the Little Ones

One of the main concerns when you're dealing with toddlers is maintaining your sanity. Your first, best tactic is to readjust your environment. Basically, you are going to fake them out, so that they have a hard time finding some way to injure themselves or destroy your home.

The easiest way to create a child-friendly environment is to look at it from the child's perspective. Get down to his eye level and look for anything that might possibly look interesting to your little explorer. If it can be eaten, cause him to bleed, or fall on him, you probably should anticipate the worst. Mother paranoia can be a good thing.

Childproofing Basics

Would you ever have guessed that a little piece of metal that has innocently fallen from an appliance can choke a child? Even the most immaculate housekeeper, unless she is completely compulsive, is going to have debris under the furniture—you rarely get down there to see it. But your child *lives* down at that level. You need to see whether there is anything down there that can pose a danger, and if there is, put it out of Junior's reach.

Tools of the Trade

Childproof drawer and cabinet latches are wonderful inventions. You can't blame a child for being a child, and it's the nature of the beast to want to get into stuff. You are endeavoring to create a child-friendly and mommy-friendly environment so that you can accomplish two things at once:

➤ You want to be able to live with your little terminator without constant worry and exhaustion.

➤ Your child wants the freedom to learn about the world around him.

Your child's goal is really yours as well—after all, you want to encourage your child to develop in a healthy way. Toddlerhood is the time when a child develops an initial concept of the way he or she relates to the world, so you want to encourage the exploration.

Install childproof latches on cabinets that contain things that can easily break or harm your child, and leave open cabinets with such things as pots and pans. They make a lot of noise, but they don't break easily and can keep your child busy and occupied while you are in the kitchen. They are also not known to cause injury. However, you never know what a child can accomplish if she tries hard enough.

Mama Said There'd Be Days Like This

I had a camping pot that I used to keep in the car. Such pots have handles that adjust to either be stiff or to hang down on the side of the pot. My daughter, (aged about 4 or 5), put the pot on her head, wearing it like a hat. The only problem was that the handle latched under her chin and I could not for the life of me get it off her. The more she cried the more I laughed, wondering how I would explain it to anyone. I felt terrible, but I was laughing so hard that tears came out of my eyes. When I finally got myself together, we were able to unlatch the handle and free her from a lifetime of being referred to as a pot head.

Other Basic Tips

When it comes to keeping your child safe from toxic items like cleaners or household chemicals, even latches aren't secure enough. Such substances should be kept out of reach at all times. A determined toddler can manage some pretty amazing things that would stump even a Houdini. If you were really able to read their minds you would probably find that toddlers consider your efforts at childproofing to be kind of a game.

Children love to put their little fingers into electric outlets, and some even come up with the great idea that pointy metal items like scissors would be fun to stick in there. So outlet covers are great tools for protecting your child. Electrocution is a very real threat to toddlers and young children. But be prepared to discover that anything you can do, your toddler can undo, if he really puts his mind to it. My son, Joshua, wasn't even *briefly* deterred by outlet covers. He used to gather them up and hand them to me. Of course his nickname at this stage was "The Terminator," so you've got some idea of how he operated. I had to resort to the super-deluxe outlet covers, which are available for just such situations.

Know Your Limits

You can't be perfect. Do not drive yourself crazy over every little thing. The best thing you can do is to childproof the identifiably dangerous parts of your environment as best you can and then develop a keen sense of where your child is at all times. It is tough on you, because this constant watchfulness means you are effectively tied down when your child is a toddler. But the best childproofing will always be your watchful eye and constant awareness of what your child is doing. If you don't see or hear your child, check immediately. Silence usually means that children are up to mischief.

Womanly Wisdom

Anticipate potential problems before they happen. Try to stay a few steps ahead of your toddler. If you think like a toddler and understand why he does the things he does, you will be able to figure out his next move before he figures it out.

Here are a few things to consider when you're making your environment safe:

➤ Watch the placement of hot beverages so your child can't spill them.

➤ Remove the knobs on your stove so your toddler can't accidentally turn on the burners.

➤ Only get childproof medicine bottles, no matter how careful you think you are.

➤ Never feed your toddler hard candies, hot dogs, popcorn, peanuts, or anything that can become lodged in her throat without dissolving.

➤ Keep your toddler in a child safety seat when you drive, no matter how good she is at slipping out of it.

Remember that you are bigger than he or she is and this is war.

Life in the War Zone

Toddlerhood is one of those periods in your life as a mother when you are frequently going to want to throw in the towel. Just as you get used to your infant and have gotten things reasonably under control, all hell breaks loose. You discover that your cute little baby's budding personality is not always cute.

Toddlers will exhaust you physically and emotionally, but they'll also give you some of your fondest memories. You need to keep your perspective and try to get as much sleep as you can. Repeat to yourself: You *can* endure. You *can* get past this phase in your child's life. Your child *will not* always be testing his or her limits in such an all-encompassing way. (He will, however, find other ways to torture you as he gets older.)

No, Nyet, Non, Nein, No!

One thing that typically happens during toddlerhood is that mothers feel frustrated. Toddlers love the word "No"! I don't mean they like it when *you* say it. They like it when *they* say it! They like to be little contrarians.

Toddlers insist on doing things their own way. This can result in upside-down shirts, backward pants, and all kinds of mix-ups. When you try to put things right, you'll probably hear that favorite word of theirs. "No, no, no, no." It is really important for you to put your need for perfection aside during these years and to encourage your child to experiment and learn to do things for himself. Believe me, it is a lot worse when you have a child who wants you to do everything for him long after he is perfectly capable of doing whatever it is for himself. Just ask any parent whose adult child has returned home to live with Mom and Dad.

Womanly Wisdom

One of your major jobs as a parent is to help your child develop independence. The push and pull between mother and child is perfectly normal. You just need to keep this in mind the next time you want to send them to the moon without a rocket.

"No" Is Just a Toddler-Sized Word for Growing Up

Your goal as a mother is to ultimately release your children into the world as independent and separate beings. This separation process begins with the cutting of the umbilical cord, but it is certainly obvious during the toddler phase. What you do at each age influences the ease with which your child will separate from you when the time is right.

Relating to Your Toddler

When your child becomes a toddler you may have your first suspicions that she's out to get you. That's highly unlikely. Too often we view children as little adults. As their personalities emerge we tend to impose upon them feelings that we bring to the relationship from our own lives. For example, we might be sensitive about certain issues from our own past.

When your child acts up in a certain way you may be reminded of your past in a negative way. You don't know why, but you feel angry with your children for arousing your uncomfortable feelings. When this feeling strikes, it's probably because you are attributing far too much significance to your child's behavior in the great scheme of things. Your child is just being a child, but your unresolved issues make you misinterpret her behavior, seeing in it meanings that aren't really there.

Unpack the Old Baggage When You Deal with Your New Toddler

Raising a toddler can become a miserable experience. I don't know many people who, if they are being completely honest with themselves, enjoy the limitations that raising a toddler puts on their lives. Resentment, therefore, is not only common—it's a natural reaction. When you are in charge of this bundle of energy most of the time, if you don't have hot-and-cold-running baby-sitters or regular childcare, you are just plain going to get tired.

The Truth Will Set You Free

Give yourself permission to say out loud: "I love my child but sometimes I am so tired I would like to send him back for a refund." Do not feel ashamed. The truth will set you free. Other women feel the same way. We *all* contemplate escaping the responsibilities and demands of motherhood—and that doesn't make us bad mothers. I worry more about the mothers who *refuse* to admit that there are days when they just want to quit. Any woman who does not get sick of chasing her two-year-old through the mall or does not want to crawl under a rock when her toddler throws a tantrum in the middle of the grocery store needs her head examined.

Momma Said There'd Be Days Like This

One day I took my three angels to the store. While we were standing in line, my youngest wanted something. I said the infamous "n" word and she threw herself on the floor, screaming and kicking. Then the other two started entertaining themselves with mutual torture. The next thing I knew, my older daughter gave my son a body slam while I was trying to grab my youngest. Then my son started to cry and all the blue-haired ladies in the store stopped to glare at me.

Sallying Forth—Toddlers on the Town

My experiences with toddlerhood are probably a little more extreme than most—I did it three at a time. It should be much easier to handle one toddler than a gaggle of them. I fondly recall my brief period as mom of a singleton-toddler, in the years before my second and third children were born. Back then, my older daughter could go anywhere with me without much trouble. Aside from an occasional bad case of "I want," she could behave like a little lady in restaurants, movies, or anywhere else. But the ease and simplicity of those years are being paid for now: At thirteen I can't take her to any restaurant without risking terminal embarrassment. I can't even believe the things she comes up with to say and do in public. I sometimes think she is trying to get back at me for not allowing her to remain an only child.

Double Your Pleasure (Triple, Even)

When I think about my younger children and their toddler stages, everything is almost a blur. I spent a great deal of time alone with my three children on a 20-acre farm while my husband worked long hours. This was not an easy time but I learned something very valuable that helped me survive. My most frustrating and uncontrollable times occurred when I had a different agenda than the one the children had in mind. In other words, when it was obvious that I was exhausted and wanted to lie down, they would decide to play "Let's jump on the bed and see how long it takes before we can get Mommy to scream."

If I wanted to have any peace I had to keep them busy and worn out, and I had to give them the illusion that I was paying full attention. If I sat with them while they scribbled I could sleep sitting up as long as they thought I was scribbling too. What they wanted was the sense of my being there for them if they needed me. After a while they would get involved with something and would stop trying to test how far they could push me.

Mom Alert!

Toddlerhood is a very difficult age, and one in which you are likely to become isolated from other grown-ups. Make sure you keep your network of friends and family active during this time. You'll really need to talk to someone your own size every once in a while, just to stay sane.

Finding a Mutuality of Focus

I don't recommend that you run every minute of every day around the whims of two-foot-tall tyrants. But I found that my little ones acted out less when I was more in tune with them and less focused on trying to rest or do something in spite of them.

Children are very sensitive. They can tell if you are interested in what they are doing or are just trying to avoid them. It is particularly difficult for working moms to negotiate around a toddler's desire for focused attention because the toddler is going to find a way to make Mom pay for her absence. He may be young, but your two-year-old knows instinctively how to make you feel guilty for leaving him in daycare.

Keeping the Peace

When you are with your toddler, especially when you are working, it is to your advantage to minimize the impact of your separate agendas. When you're home, let the child know you are connected, concerned, and paying attention and soon you will find him happily doing his own thing while you do yours. A reassuring voice, a smile, or a hug can help your toddler feel that special contact. If you can, involve your child in what you are doing: If you are reading, give him a book of his own. If you are cooking, let him make clay pies.

Womanly Wisdom

Make sure you claim some moments of harmony with your children in your otherwise hectic life. You'll discover that you need contact with them just as much as they need contact with you. And if your needs and theirs are satisfied, you'll all be that much happier.

Psyching Out the Wild Child

If you understand what is happening inside the mind of your toddler—aside from a compulsion to destroy everything in his or her path—you will feel more relaxed with what seems like a constant push and pull. Actually the push and pull of toddlerhood is just the first incarnation of something you will see at varying levels throughout your child's development. Your toddler is just starting to realize, for example, that when you leave a room he can make you come back. In other words your toddler is learning that he is a separate human being who can have an impact on the world around him. This is very exciting for him—but it is also scary.

The Child's-Eye View of the World

Just imagine that you are this small person without much understanding of the world. You start to see that when you cry, people react a certain way. When you say "no" you

Mom Alert!

The first pangs of separation start early and are responsible for every period of disequilibrium you will experience with your child throughout his life. If you understand this one basic law of nature you will feel better about your experience as a mother.

feel a sense of power. If you run through the airport terminal, you can get Mommy to chase you until she is out of breath. But even while you're learning all these fun, powerful things, you're learning some scary things, too. You're learning that if you run through that terminal, turn around, and find that Mommy is *not* chasing after you, you are going to be terrified.

To a toddler, Mommy is the center of the universe. Big responsibility, huh? If you are happy, your toddler will be happy. If you are sad, your toddler will be sad and may possibly think he made you sad. So, as nature gives your toddler the courage to start exploring the boundaries of his universe without you, it causes him to push away.

Now, obviously, you won't ever hear a child say, "Mommy, I am talking back to you and stomping my feet because I am testing the limits of my universe." But when you are ready to scream and you feel you must be the worst mother in the world to have spawned such demon seed, remember—the conflict that occurs between mother and toddler is nature's way of allowing your once completely dependent child to take his or her first steps to independence.

Mom, the Great Disciplinarian

So often we, as mothers, criticize ourselves unmercifully when our children do not behave perfectly. What we are really doing is evaluating our worth according to external standards. We are looking to see whether we are "doing it right," and are very likely to buckle under the pressure of outside disapproval.

We're most likely to feel this outside disapproval toward the way we discipline our children. Sometimes it seems as though everyone else is an armchair disciplinarian. If your child misbehaves in public there will be any number of people willing to give you their expert opinion. Usually, of course, their instant opinion is that your children are heathens and that you lack mothering skills.

Dealing with Society's Expectations

We do not really live in a child-friendly world. It is either overly indulgent—just check out any toy store during the holiday season—or it insists on keeping children at bay. There is almost an expectation that when you are in public, except in designated areas, your children should be absent or invisible.

Well, this is one of the great mysteries of our society's values. People express concern about family values but do not want to embrace children as a necessary and important part of our world. Very little effort seems to be made to make children feel welcome in our society. There are some exceptions to this rule: Certain grocery stores, for example, have begun creating safe play areas for children and designing shopping carts to accommodate more than one child at a time.

But these minor adjustments aren't enough. Women have enough trouble taking care of children without having to feel as though the only place they can be with their children is in their own homes. Children need to explore the world around them outside their own backyard, and mothers need the support, not the condemnation, of the community.

Mom-isms

Discipline is any means employed to teach a child right from wrong, and to help him learn to accept responsibility for his actions.

Spare the Rod?

This brings me to the issue of discipline. Most experts now agree that no form of harsh punishment should be applied to children, least of all to toddlers. But discipline does not need to involve punishment. Properly speaking, it is simply any means through which a parent is able to convey right from wrong and the consequences of a child's choices. The form discipline takes needs to be determined according to the developmental age and ability of the child, not by the parent's concern for an immediate solution.

Getting Your Point Across

You've surely seen something like this: You're standing in a checkout line and, up ahead, a two-year-old grabs for a tempting piece of candy on display. Her mom—or maybe even the cashier—responds by grabbing the candy and perhaps even yelling at the child—an unpleasant scene for everyone involved.

But do people have any idea what that candy display looks like to a child? The merchandising people plan it so that children will grab the candy and convince their parents to buy it. The child is only doing what she's been manipulated to do. But suddenly, she's "bad."

In a situation like this, your best move is to gently take the candy out of her hand and put it back in the display. To avoid her likely outburst, have some object that you've brought from home to give to her in place of the item you've taken away. Most important, look at the situation from your child's point of view. She is not trying to annoy you. She is doing what is natural to a child of that age.

Mom Alert!

You will lose your cool. You would not be human if you did not on occasion raise your voice or even scream bloody murder. Just be very careful when it comes to your child. Even nice people can use poor judgment. Avoid crossing the line by knowing your own limitations.

Hey! Who's the Grownup Here?

It breaks my heart to hear the way people speak to little children. When a child is being stubborn you may very well have a battle of wills. But you will not win if you stoop below their level to be mean and intimidating.

Make no mistake about it: if you try to scare your child into obedience at any age you will pay for it later. If your toddler persists in grabbing things from the rack you may have to keep putting those things back. The "n" word is certainly fine to use, but it should be reserved for more important matters like, "No! Don't put your hand on that hot burner." Child discipline based on this kind of understanding takes patience, but you get much better results in the long run. You love your child. You will lose your cool on occasion. Just do not use your temper or lack of patience as a disciplinary tool.

When in Doubt, Don't

If you are so frustrated that you are ready to burst, ask someone to help you. Leave wherever you are and go home, where you will have more control. Even the nicest, most loving parents can become angry enough to accidentally hurt their child—and you want to avoid that at all costs. Children are dependent and demanding. If you are not patient and accustomed to the kind of sacrifice necessary to stay on an even keel, you could take it out on your child. Be aware of your limitations. If you find yourself losing control, get yourself right out of the stress-causing situation until you've had a chance to pull yourself together.

Whatever else you do, do *not* discipline a child in anger. Take deep breaths. Count to 10. Ask yourself *why* you are angry at the behavior, and deal with the real, underlying causes. I am not completely against a well-placed swat on the rear under the right circumstances, but only if the child is old enough to understand that swat as a consequence for certain behavior—young toddlers are not able to make that connection.

Suiting Discipline to Development

For disciplining young toddlers, I recommend distraction or standing your ground. As the child gets a bit older and has better language skills you can incorporate more direct means of communicating the consequences of bad behavior, but with children between the ages of one and two-and-a-half, you're still dealing with an age that's prone to temper tantrums. The worst thing you can do during a temper tantrum is to hit a child or scream at a toddler. You will make matters much worse—and not just for the short term. As the child gets older you will have taught him exactly how to make you lose control. Once that has happened, the child has taken over the authority and the power in the situation.

Mom-isms

Temper tantrums can be triggered by the "n" word, by lack of sleep, by looking at the child the wrong way, or by the phases of the moon. Tantrums, which are characterized by a look of rabid insanity coupled with kicking feet, sobbing, and the flailing of arms, usually occur in grocery stores or other public places.

Creative Correction

Good disciplinary techniques are constructive. The best thing to do when your child decides to become temporarily psychotic (that is, when she pitches a tantrum) is to do nothing. If you happen to be in a public place and are concerned that someone is going to think *you* are the crazy one, simply pick up your child, carry her out to your car, buckle her safely into her car seat, latch the childproof door locks, put in earplugs, and drive away. You do not want to indulge your child and cave in to the tantrum. This is an endurance contest, and you're the one who has to endure it.

Taking Time for Time Out

When a toddler reaches the age of two or older and has language skills, you can use disciplinary techniques like *time out*. In this technique, you tell your errant child that he or she is in time out and has to sit in a certain place for a certain period of time. You use a timer and keep the time-out period short—it's intended as a cool-down

Mom Alert!

Watch out for disciplinary tactics that are doomed to failure. If "go to your room" means "go to the place where all your favorite toys, TV, music, books, and games are kept," it's not really going to communicate your disciplinary point.

period, not as a punishment. Other, closely related disciplinary techniques are to send your child to stand in the corner, or the well-known "Go to your room!" command.

Making Your Disciplinary Efforts Effective

The key to discipline is to understand *why* you are using it—because that is the message you're going to be communicating to your child. You are your child's universe and your child's primary teacher. You teach by example and by how you relate to your child. If your discipline is erratic, your child will never understand what brings it on, and thus won't know what behaviors he or she is expected to change.

If you teach your child through intimidation, he may question his worth and how much you actually love him. The child will not get the message that his behavior is something you want to change. He will simply assume there is something about him that you do not like. This is not the message you want to convey unless you want to set aside money for your child's later therapy.

Love—the Best Behavior Motivator of All

The best gift you can give your child is the knowledge of how much he is loved. You do this through the way you talk to him and the way you employ discipline. There is an expression in the Torah: "When you discipline a child you push away with one hand as you pull closer with the other." You want to be firm but you never want a child to question whether you love him.

This is why it's important not to discipline out of anger. It is not wrong to show your displeasure with the child as long as you make it clear that you're objecting to the behavior, and not to the child. Never call your child derogatory names when you are angry about something he has done. We all get frustrated. But you have to bite your tongue before something mean comes out that you will regret later. Your child will internalize whatever you say to him. He is not going to have the ability to evaluate what you say and conclude, "Oh, she didn't mean it."

Look for Techniques That Suit You

The many good books on discipline techniques can help you develop your style. Keep in mind the age of your child, your child's attention span, and whether you're dealing with an act of defiance or a simple excess of childhood enthusiasm. As your child ages he or she will assert his or her will in more obvious ways—and while you may not like all of these ways, they will not always call for discipline.

Dealing with Dangerous Defiance

Overt defiance in areas that can effect your child's health and safety, or the comfort and safety of others, must be addressed with discipline and limits of some sort. At other times you may want to consider your child's reasons and let him flex his muscles. You don't want complete control over your child. You are looking for authority in your home, and even though you are talking about a small child you ultimately want mutual respect. This is, after all, a *person* we are talking about here—even if he or she is only two feet tall. You want to give your child room to grow, even in ways that are not the same as the ways you grew. You want to use discipline to *help* your child achieve that growth, not to kill his spirit.

The Least You Need to Know

➤ When a child begins to walk, you need to change your plan of action.

➤ You will want to create a safe, child-friendly environment for your child's sake—and for your own sanity.

➤ As your toddler asserts independence you might become frustrated—but don't feel bad about yourself. This is a tough time for *every* mom.

➤ Discipline is a tool meant to help your child grow up healthy and well-rounded; it is not a tool for control.

Chapter 6

From Potty Training to Preschool

At some point you are going to want your child to stop using diapers and to start using the potty. If you are like I was and have two at a time in diapers you will pray for the day you are liberated from this chore. The problem is, with potty training, you're also approaching a very difficult time in your motherhood career: a potty-trained child is a child who is ready to sail out into the wide world beyond your home. When potty training time arrives, nursery school (or preschool) isn't far behind. This chapter will take you through this bittersweet period in every mother's life, when her ever-faithful (if sometimes maddeningly frustrating) sidekick takes his or her first hesitant steps into independence.

Potty Training: A Child's Rite of Passage into the World of Big People

Potty training is one of those parenting areas about which *everyone* has an opinion. We all have at least one elderly friend or relative who brags about how she had her children trained before they could walk. Such stories of motherly bravado can intimidate you, but there's a detail these ladies usually leave out. A child who uses the potty before she can walk is *not* trained—her mom is. No pre-toddler has the muscle control to be able to properly train. Instead, her *mother* was trained to drop everything and put baby on the pot whenever necessary.

Potty Training Preliminaries

To successfully use the potty, a child has to have achieved certain physical skills:

➤ She has to know she has to go.

➤ She has to associate the physical sensations of having to go with a certain result—before it happens.

➤ She has to care about that result.

➤ She has to have the physical maturity to control herself long enough to get to the pot.

All of this requires an awareness and development that infants and young toddlers do not yet possess. They go when they gotta go—it is as simple as that. They have no real inhibitions about it. You can definitely expect to be at a family gathering and have baby respond to nature in the middle of a crowded room. Everyone will politely pretend not to notice the toxic smell that has just permeated the room, but you will have approximately 60 seconds to remove your child to an appropriate changing area before someone makes their displeasure known. It is a matter of etiquette. You know: "Children should be seen and not smelled."

It's generally assumed that girls train more easily than boys do. I don't know if this is true. When my oldest was about two I had her in a home daycare situation with two other girls around the same age. The caregiver, Peggy, (I'm sure she's related to Mary Poppins), had the patience to work with each child to help them get the hang of using the toilet. I knew my daughter would eventually figure it out so I didn't sweat it. I also did not mind that someone else had the honor of taking my child through this all-important rite of passage. I was happy just to lay in a supply of "big-girl pants" and cheer her on from the sidelines.

Womanly Wisdom

Pooping is a fact of life. Everyone does it. Do not be embarrassed when your baby does it at an inopportune time. Take it in stride, clean up the mess, and go on with the party. You and your child will accomplish toilet training when you both are ready.

Diverging Agendas

All you really need to keep in mind is that potty training is an effort to encourage a child to comply with *your* desire to stop having to clean up after *him* or *her*. Meanwhile, all children want undivided attention, and yours is no exception. Potty training is one arena in which these two very different goals frequently clash. You have to be careful not to make the potty training a message to your child that you are pulling away your attention. You need to find a way to reinforce your child's independence in this one area, while reassuring him with other things you can continue to do together.

Mapping Out Your Strategy

Successful training will take some strategizing on your part. You've got two general options:

➤ Train your child by example.

➤ Invest in one of those adorable books or videotapes that explain the whole deal in terms your child can identify with.

The first option works, but lots of women find it awkward to make going to the bathroom a group event. The books and videos can really help, if that's more comfortable for you. But however you choose to go about the process, look at it from your child's perspective. Think about what a toilet must look like to him. Wouldn't you need a little encouragement to make that leap of faith and sit your unprotected tushie on that thing?

Changing Your Child's Perceptions

When you're potty training, you are asking your child to pay attention to a bodily function that, up to now, has not been of any great concern. From your child's point of view, you eat, you poop, you stink, Mommy or Daddy or some other grown-up changes you—that is the way life is. To potty train, children have to actually stop what they are doing, think about what their body wants to do, and take care of it all by themselves. This is going to take some serious persuasion.

Some people reward successful trips to the potty with a treat like a piece of candy, a small toy, or a star on a wall chart. This type of system can backfire—you want to encourage your child to use the potty because it is a good thing to do for himself, not because he'll get a reward. But the reward system has its uses: If preschool starts in three weeks and they only accept children who are out of diapers, all is fair in love and potty training.

Avoid the temptation to push your child to train until he or she shows some interest in it. Of course, with some children it could be the third millennium and you'd *still* be waiting—in that case, maybe you'll have to come up with a drastic plan of action. In most situations, however, there will come a time when the child sees other children using the toilet, connects it with being a big boy or girl, with comfort, and with a nice clean feeling, and will want to give it a try.

Womanly Wisdom

You won't believe it but it is true: no matter how difficult it seems to train your child right now, you can safely bet the family jewels that your child will not wear diapers to her wedding.

The Potty-Training Gender Gap

Although girls don't necessarily train more *easily* than boys, boys do tend to train *later*. Boys will frequently resist toilet training until they're well over three years old. This does not mean your son is the dunce of the potty-training universe. It's just that boys are busy and do not want to take the time. If you do not make a big deal about it, you will have less of a battle of the wills and will find that one day he just does it.

It doesn't hurt to get him used to sitting on the toilet after meals, even if nothing happens. You can also let him run around outside without diapers if you dare—that way he can see what happens when they go. But be forewarned: boys like to play "pee on the bushes." Again, you need to be patient. Make it a game.

Momma Said There'd Be Days Like This

My six-year-old daughter wanted to help toilet train her brother, so she would sit across from him and read him a book while he sat on the pot. One day she was reading to him and I heard a scream. He had gotten bored sitting on the potty with nothing happening so he decided to get up. He ran around the house completely naked and then decided it was time to poop—he left a racing stripe down my hallway.

The Joys of Life with the Child-in-Training

Get used to the idea: You are going to have mishaps and messes during this time. The more you fret about it, the worse it is going to be for you and your child. This is a time to avoid the battles of the wills you normally find with each new transition. If you are squeamish, wear rubber gloves and try not to breathe through your nose.

Younger children can be the easiest to train because they want to do everything like their big brother or sister. You can sit back a bit and allow things to fall into place on their own. If you have an older brother with a baby sister you should expect her to try to pee standing up and facing the pot. Just explain that boys have "outies" and girls have "innies." This should suffice until you need to have those more expansive discussions.

Living with a Preschooler

Potty training generally ushers in the preschool years. Living with a preschooler can be one of the most fun times of your mothering career. It can also be totally exhausting—

preschoolers have a seemingly *endless* supply of energy. You will never feel more out of shape, no matter what your condition, than when you're hanging out with your preschooler.

If you work outside the home you are going to have a physical reprieve during the day, but expect to get back on preschooler fast track as soon as you get home. Unless you have your children run marathons during the day they are going to be like that Energizer bunny—they'll still be going when your batteries have long since died. Here are some possible solutions:

➤ Don't come home from work until someone *else* has put them to bed.

➤ Eat a lot of chocolate.

➤ Become your local coffee shop's biggest customer.

➤ Try to prepare yourself mentally for the fact that your day does not end at 5 p.m., but may only be beginning then.

You can certainly work it out with your spouse that you *both* stay on parental duty until the children are ready for bed. Have your heated discussions about it at a time when you are not both exhausted from chasing children all evening. You can work out many compromises that can even be fun. You can take regular evening walks together as a family. One of you can take that walk with the children while the other makes dinner. Or, if you're one of the many people who need an after-work collapse, you can have quiet time to vegetate while you pretend to watch Big Bird or Barney with the kids for the 900th time.

Womanly Wisdom

A well-worked-out collaborative effort between parents will never be more important than during the preschool years. With your partner as your ally, you have a better chance of keeping up with your energetic offspring. If you're a single mom, now's the time your network of family and friends will come in the handiest.

Private Time for Grown-ups? Hardly!

The only thing you can't do with one or more preschoolers is expect to be able to have your adult evening while they're still up and moving. Ignoring them or leaving them to their own devices is simply not an option. You have to somehow stay involved with them or you will regret it. Children have ways of annoying and manipulating you until you do what they want you to do, anyway, which is to pay attention to them. They don't care whether the attention is positive or negative. They simply want to be in control, and they want to be the center of your universe.

When you think about it, this is not such a bad thing. A family thrives best when its members pay attention to each other. All members of a family should be able to feel safe and secure there, and the children should feel a sense of connection and love.

Although you need not, and should not, completely indulge the bottomless pit of your child's need for undivided attention, these are the years when your home should be pretty much child-centered. You don't have to get involved in every little thing, but it is important for your child to learn early on that you are there for her when she needs you.

Home Alone with the Energizer Bunny

If you are staying home all day with a preschooler you really need to have a positive attitude—and a *lot* of flexibility. You are going to feel very out of control if you expect to be able to live within a rigid schedule. You can structure your time, but you have to remember that every day your child is growing by leaps and bounds, both mentally and physically. Her interests and abilities will change rapidly—just as you are getting used to one routine, she's likely to surprise you with something new.

Finding Salvation in the Great Outdoors

If you are staying at home with a preschooler, make it a point to get up, get dressed, and get out of the house as much as possible. Preschoolers need a lot of stimulation. If that need is not met, they may fill it themselves by destroying the house or torturing Mommy. And getting out is good for *you*, not just for your child. If you know all the Sesame Street songs by heart but have no idea who the president is, or isn't, you *really* may want to get out a little bit more.

Momma Said There'd Be Days Like This

Watch the foods your child eats. I was careful not to give my younger children chocolate because I had read about sugar highs, but I wasn't as strict with my older child. One day I came home and found my son literally jumping from our window seat to the couch and then to all the other furniture in the room. I had never seen him like this. I investigated further and found a bag of party goodies that must have belonged to his older sister—and a little patch of chocolate candy wrappers hidden under the couch.

Be careful to avoid overstimulation. I was not the walk-in-the-park type of mom. If I was going out, I liked to be where the action was: I loved taking my children to county fairs or local events and always had fun. The only problem was that the children would get overstimulated—the exact opposite of what I wanted to achieve. When a child is overstimulated you may as well forget about bedtime or sanity until she comes down from her high.

Introduction to the Arts

Preschoolers like to keep busy, and arts and crafts activities are ideal for this age. The simpler the better, and the messier the activity, the more they like it. I was not a stickler for a neat home, so I didn't mind a little finger paint on the floor. It is really good for little ones to be able to express themselves, and messes are inevitable. If you are not comfortable with a messy home there are all kinds of products that can help keep things clean while you give your child some creative freedom.

Womanly Wisdom

Vinyl tablecloths are great to put on and under the table while your budding artist is at play. They are easy to clean and pretty much stay where you put them.

Time Out for Mommy

Try to pace your day so that *you* do not become bored or lonely. Every mother needs some time away from her child or children. If you are not working outside the home, make an effort to get away by yourself for several hours each week. If you want to shop without the hassle of having a child with you, do it. If you want to go to a park and look at the sky, do it. If you want to do nothing but drive around the block, do that. You need to keep in touch with the fact that you are a separate person *as well as* a mother.

The role of being a mother is consuming and can become an overwhelming chore if we are not given a break once in a while. Without regularly scheduled breaks, it's easy to begin to resent your children or your husband, and you probably will even get on your *own* nerves. You will be doing everyone around you a favor by getting out once in a while to regroup and regenerate.

At-Home Moms Need a Break, Too

Don't use this time alone to do something you *have* to do. Use it to do what you *want* to do. It is your right as a human being to have time to do what you want to do. If you enjoy working out, then do it. If you hate working out, schedule it when you need to but do not use your personal time for this activity. Respect yourself enough and love yourself enough to demand this time for yourself. It is not a luxury; it is a necessity for your well-being and mental health.

Working Mom—Quiet Time Necessary

Working mothers also need some time to themselves. When a woman works and raises children she often views the time at work as her alone time. *Not!* Although working moms have far less "free" time available for personal time, they need it just as much as moms who work at home do. Even if a woman loves her job more than anything, it's still an obligatory activity. A person needs time to be alone with thoughts in order to grow and develop in a healthy way.

Mom Alert!

Do not let misplaced guilt keep you from taking time for yourself away from your child or children. Use this time for something you want to do, even if this means driving around the block just to be alone. Every human being needs some time alone, without any obligation to fulfill other people's needs.

Pressure-Free Preschool Prep

Some people are overly focused on helping their preschooler excel. If your child learns to read at a very young age, great—but don't push it. The best thing you can give your child at this age is a lot of love and approval. But you don't want to impose unnecessary pressure on your child. Make your approving statements a little neutral: Instead of saying, "You are such a good boy for drawing that brilliant picture," say "You drew a picture. Isn't that nice." You don't want your child to worry about always having to be a good boy and always having to create a brilliant picture. At this early age you simply want to reinforce to your child that you love and treasure him or her, no matter what.

The Gentle Art of Encouragement

When a child feels loved and treasured just for being alive, without having to earn that love, your task of setting reasonable limits on his or her behavior is made much easier. You don't have to resort to harsh punishment or fear tactics because you have a child who is secure enough not to want to constantly act out against your wishes. You also have a child who can grow up into a confident adult, able to face life's challenges. A child who is raised with love like this can learn to love and respect himself and his own choices. It really does start this early.

The Pitfalls of Pressure to Perform

I have a friend whose teenager is totally brilliant but can't perform in school. I have known this child since before she was born and I remember that her father used to brag about how he had the child working on phonics when she was just three. He would quiz her with flash cards and was quick to show his disapproval if she did not get the right answers. It became a reflection on him if she was not perfect.

It doesn't take a rocket scientist to see the connection between this early experience of pressure and disapproval and the teenager's later performance anxiety. The lesson she learned wasn't about phonics—she learned that it was impossible to meet her father's expectations. Is it any wonder that she has performance problems today? The seeds of this anxiety were planted in her preschool mind.

The "Quality Time" Crazies

With busy schedules, the inclination is to make every precious moment count by filling it with something of quality. Although keeping a child busy is good for your own sanity, "quality time" is really just hanging around together with your children. If you overbook your time you will not get to know your child and your child will certainly not get to know you.

Children just like to be near their mothers. Quality time can be cuddling in a rocking chair or letting your child help polish the legs of the table while you dust. Quality time is having the patience to calmly answer the millions of "why?" questions that are inevitably asked at this age, and you can answer those questions and baste a turkey at the same time.

You *don't* have to put pressure on yourself to provide certain types of educational exposure at this age. There really is plenty of time for all those things. The most important thing you can do for your child at this age is set the groundwork for an emotional bond that will last a lifetime. Whether you are with your child all day, every day, or for only a few hours each day, the important thing is how well you connect.

Introducing Your Child to the World

As a child grows into preschool age he constantly tests his physical, mental, and emotional boundaries. He wants to be able to venture away from Mom, but needs to know there is some kind of invisible cable that will always lead him home again. It will be a lot more fun for you if you do not resist this lifeline because it is *your* lifeline as well.

However exhausting you may find your child's constant demands for attention, you, as a mother, need this connection as much as your child does. You have protective instincts that are stronger than I hope you will ever have to put to the test, and you have a relationship that began when you carried that child in your womb. The entire time after birth is spent separating from each other. It is important that you know your preschooler is still connected to you, even though he or she has begun venturing out from home base.

Making the Big Move into Preschool

When your child is potty trained you have the option of sending her to preschool. Most preschool programs last a half day and provide structured activities and some preliminary studies to prepare your child for kindergarten. Preschool is not required: Your child doesn't need to go to preschool to get into kindergarten. For most children, however, preschool can be great.

The Benefits of Preschool Enrollment

From your perspective, preschool can be great because you have a guilt-free way to grab some hours for yourself. You can be confident that your child is doing something beneficial while you luxuriate in a hot bubble bath. Then again, you *could* use this time for household chores, but that's just silly.

The other benefit of a good preschool program is that it helps your child make the transition into an expanded world of people and experiences. Very few mothers can consistently provide a structured program of kid-centered activities like those you will find in a preschool. You would drive yourself crazy even trying. And in your immediate neighborhood it's often hard to come up with playmates of appropriate ages for your kids.

Womanly Wisdom

A preschool does not have to be lavish or expensive to be good. You need to check references and whatever accreditation your state requires for preschool licensing. Many churches or synagogues have preschool programs, as do community centers.

Finding a Good Preschool

If you work outside the home you can sometimes find preschool programs that also offer an "aftercare." I was very lucky to find a preschool connected to another facility where my children could stay longer on some days and take swimming lessons. There *are* places like this out there—you just have to look for them.

Preschool gives children the opportunity to learn how to get along with other children. For an only child this can be a shock. These children are used to having free rein at the toy box, and in preschool they will have to learn the concept of taking turns. You will be surprised at what your child can do when in the hands of a neutral party. Your child will want to be completely babied by you but will act like a little lady or gentleman in the presence of the preschool teacher.

Coping with the Separation Blues

If your child has not spent time regularly with another caregiver before starting preschool, you may have to endure the inevitable scenes of separation anxiety. You take your cheerful child to the classroom door, say your good-byes, get ready to leave, and find the child hanging onto your legs. You slowly unglue her fingers from your kneecaps, only to discover that she has wrapped her legs around you in a scissor-like vise grip.

The best thing for you to do is to reassure her, give her another kiss...and *leave*. It's hard to do. That first day, she's likely to cry hysterically, hold her arms out to you, and stamp her feet in protest at your abandonment. The temptation is to go back and scoop her into your arms.

Don't give in to this urge. You *know* she will be safe at preschool and you *know* she will have fun. You know you want her to go. You have made plans (for yourself!) for the first time in years. But this first separation can be heartbreaking. So here's a little tip.

Once you've moved out of your child's line of sight, pause for a few moments before getting into your car and driving away. Then quietly walk back to the building and listen at the door of your child's classroom. You won't hear any screaming. In fact, you'll probably hear giggling. And if you peak through the window, you'll see your daughter happily engaged in playing house with another girl about her size.

The Bittersweet Process of Loosening the Reins

There is nothing worse than hearing your child cry and call your name. You are going to want to rush to her and comfort her. Reassurance is a good thing, but when you bring your child to preschool you are trying to help her step beyond her own comfort level, and sometimes she is going to fight you on it.

The more you linger and seem wishy-washy about your decision to leave her in the capable hands of the preschool teacher, the more difficult it will be for your child to trust being left in the care of others. And keep in mind that your child is also testing her power to influence your behavior. Unless you think there is something very wrong with the situation you have chosen for your child, you must not cave in to her demands.

When the Preschool Is a Bad Choice

You don't want to be overly paranoid about your choice of a preschool, but it is possible that your child is not receiving proper care. If your child consistently resists going to the preschool and shows fear, pay a surprise visit to see what goes on when parents are not expected. Children should not be yelled at or spanked. Nor should they be left unsupervised and ignored. You are looking for a positive environment that will be an extension of all the good things you can give your child. You are the consumer. If the preschool does not meet your standards for your child's well-being, do not second-guess your feelings on the matter. Act.

Mom Alert!

Sometimes it is appropriate to give in to your child's wishes to be taken home from a preschool situation. Children mature at different rates, and your child may not yet be ready for the big step that preschool represents. Monitor his progress for the first few days, and if he doesn't settle in, defer preschool for another few months.

Watch Your Language!

Children are so cute at this age that you can have some of your best times. They are so wide-eyed and say the cutest things. They also tend to interpret things *very* literally. When my youngest was just getting out of diapers I was running out of patience. I tried to change her one night and she kept kicking her feet at me and rolling around. I exclaimed, "You're crabby!" and thought nothing more of it. A year or so later, when my daughter was a preschooler, she was playing in the bathtub. She liked to do most of the washing up by herself and didn't like to be rushed. When I told her it was time to get out she replied, "No, Mommy. I still haven't washed my crabby."

Almost Grown, but Still Your Little One

The preschool age is tough because the children are so energetic and appear to be mature, but they're still too young to handle full independence. At this age, many serious accidents occur. It is even more risky than the terrible twos were, because at that age you *expect* the child to be into everything and to need constant supervision. When a child becomes more independent we have a tendency to let down our guard. Do not be fooled. A three- or four-year-old can devise all sorts of terrifyingly dangerous pursuits. They jump off swings, fall into holes, and can even drown in the bathtub.

So remember: This is a time when you want to loosen the rope but keep a firm grip on your end.

Safety First!

Teach your children safety as best you can, drilling them on certain things like "Don't talk to strangers," "Don't run out into the street," "Don't run in parking lots," "Dial 911 in an emergency." And be sure to teach your child your phone number and address. To increase the odds that she'll remember it, try doing what I did: I made up a song with our address and phone number in the lyrics. (I still sing the song on occasion, and I haven't lived in that house for years.)

When Your Child Is a Preschooler...

When your child is a preschooler, you, your child, and your mate can have fun together as a family. There are many child-oriented activities, and three and four are perfect ages for some wonderful experiences. You must go to a petting zoo and see your child feed pellets to a baby goat. Of course, you'll have to resist any requests that you bring the goat home....

Momma Said There'd Be Days Like This

When my oldest was three we went to a petting zoo. After that trip, she spent months trying to persuade me to keep a baby elephant in our backyard. She said she would feed it, take care of it, and love it forever. The craziest thing is...I actually thought about it. (Just kidding—even I have my limits.)

You may not have as much time as you would like for yourselves as a couple, but you will find a great deal of joy if you carve out some time for everyone to have fun together. Soon enough your children will get older and become more interested in hanging out with their friends. This is a stage in life when they really do prefer being with you to being with other people. Appreciate it while it lasts.

But although this is a great time for family outings, remember to anticipate your child's needs. If you decide to take a road trip with a preschooler, be sure to pack activities and snacks, and expect to stop many times along the way. My sister, my idol and domestic- and motherhood-goddess, came up with the idea of taking one of those baking pans with the sliding plastic lids and filling it with paper, crayons, and other stuff. Not only does the container keep all the materials together, the pans form little travel writing desks. See? If you have the right attitude, traveling with preschoolers can be a blast.

The Least You Need to Know

➤ Preschoolers are like the Energizer bunny—they just keep on going, long after you've dropped from exhaustion.

➤ Try to carve out some personal time, away from family or work responsibilities, to recharge your *own* batteries.

➤ This is a good age to introduce your child to new experiences and modes of expression—but don't pressure him or her to perform. Learning should be fun at this age.

➤ Enrolling your child in preschool will return a few hours of grown-up freedom to your life.

➤ Preschoolers can seem far more competent than they really are—don't let down your protective guard. Remember: Safety First!

Part 3
Calling All Super Moms!

In the 1970s, women had the heady belief that they could have it all: Earth-mother satisfactions at home, wildly romantic personal lives, and a high-powered career, all at the same time, and all without breaking a sweat. And we spent a decade knocking ourselves out trying to achieve that impossible dream.

The 1980s brought a reality check—there really are choices to make in this life. The thing is, the choices we have are still so much better than those that any other generation of women has ever enjoyed. We can combine home, family, and career. Or we can pick two out of three. It just takes care, compromise, and a heck of a lot of planning.

When you brought your baby home from the hospital, all your old routines got knocked for a loop for a while as you spent some time just getting to know this new little family member. In Part 3 you'll learn how to pull all the elements of your life back together again—only better, this time, because now you're sharing your life with a whole new, wonderful person. Get ready to roll up your sleeves and get to work—it's time for the new, improved Supermom to make her entrance.

Chapter 7

Setting a Schedule for Success

In This Chapter

➤ Developing a routine

➤ Getting out into the world

➤ Returning to the bedroom

Whether you are welcoming a first baby or an addition to your brood, you're going to have to make some adjustments in the way you have been living your life. It is a good idea to have a family meeting with your partner and all your children as soon as possible after introducing your new baby to the household. Even invite the dog. (The cat won't care either way, so don't even bother.) You want to use this meeting to anticipate situations and concerns before they become full-blown problems. You need to work out a division of responsibilities, and everyone should know what is expected of them.

Yeah, right. The problem is, every member of the family will react to the new baby in a different way. Your mate may be coping with his own fears and insecurities. Your other child or children may feel displaced. Your dog may even worry that there is no love left for him. (And although your cat will hide it well, even she won't like the disruption of the usual routine.)

In this chapter, you'll learn what you can do to head problems off at the pass—how to anticipate and overcome the inevitable frictions that will arise as your family adjusts and learns to welcome a whole new member into the fold.

Establishing a Secure Home Base

Not everybody is going to have the same idea of what parenthood or being a sibling is all about. You can minimize conflict by discussing things ahead of time, but don't expect miracles: Be happy with whatever small steps bring you closer to a manageable family system.

Womanly Wisdom

Remain calm and steady if your kids and pets revert to inappropriate behavior when you bring baby home from the hospital. Eventually your child will feel secure enough to return to his big-boy potty habits. And while I can't guarantee that your cat will get over it, even your dog should settle in after a while.

Mom Alert!

Moms are often overachievers and prone to guilt. We all tend to see things as a product of something we have or have not done. But, in this situation, all you have done is give birth to a new baby. You certainly can't be held responsible for everyone's reaction to this.

Be prepared for the fact that everyone is going to react to your little newcomer in his or her own way. Things will probably be emotionally chaotic at first, as each person—or creature—in the household adjusts to the new family structure.

For example, young children and animals have been known to regress in their potty habits with the introduction of a new baby. Do not be overly alarmed if your two-year-old suddenly decides to go back to diapers or your dog starts leaving stinky presents for you and chews up a few of your favorite things. (Even Fluffy the cat may decide to hide out in the linen closet for two days just to see whether you'll try to find her.) Children and animals are very sensitive—they often feel threatened by a newcomer to the family, and regressive behavior is one way they're likely to test their status in the household.

Mom: the Center of the Known Universe

You may not realize it but you are ground zero to your baby, your children, your husband, and even your pets. In many ways, they center their identity and security on you. This is common: Even in these so-called enlightened times, moms are the glue that holds families together.

This is probably why we feel so overwhelmed at times. It is a heavy emotional responsibility to bear, one that goes well beyond handling the household chores. So, when you bring the baby home, each family member may well react to the threat that this newcomer is going to dominate your attention. That is just the way it is.

Keeping the Center Strong

How can you cope? You'll need to carve out time for yourself and the baby, but you'll also need to consider the overall dynamic of your family before you can successfully establish new routines. Once again, flexibility is key: If you can be flexible you may find that the best new routine is the one that finds *you*, not one that you try to impose on everyone else.

Be patient. Everything will balance itself out if you refuse to overreact to everyone else's craziness. Even a two-year-old can learn to manipulate you for more attention, and she probably will. But if you're aware that it's happening, you can resist being manipulated and keep on an even keel.

Pulling Your Partner into the Center

Your older children and pets may need a little help from you, but your partner's adjustment to the new baby belongs to him. You need to remember that you can't fix everything for everyone. Sometimes it's enough just to give him enough space to get used to the new situation.

Keep in mind that you and your husband are individuals with different ideas and expectations. Instead of letting these differences come between you, try using them to your advantage by trying to adjust your routine to suit them. For example, you may find that your energy is higher at certain times each day, and your spouse's energy peaks at other times. If you take advantage of these different natural cycles when you divide up tasks and responsibilities, neither one of you will be totally exhausted at the end of the day.

Involving Proud Poppa in the Baby's Care

One thing to keep in mind is that Dad's involvement in day-to-day infant-care activities is a fairly new concept. Women of previous generations would not have considered asking their husbands to change a diaper or stay with the baby while they went out. We like to think all that has changed, but even though today's fathers know they are expected to be helpful and to participate in the not-so-fun aspects of baby care, there is still a lot of resistance to the concept. Sadly, there's still an underlying macho perspective about baby care that may never die away.

Breaking Down Daddy's Resistance

This is where psychology comes in. Be effusive in your praise whenever your partner does *anything* related to baby care. You may think, "This is his kid, too, and no one praises *me* when I clean a diaper," but remember: You are trying to undo *years* of male conditioning. For all we know, resisting diaper-changing is built into a man's DNA.

Sad but true: When it comes to accepting the necessity of domestic drudgery, women are more mature than men are. Men generally expect to be

Womanly Wisdom

If you want to maximize your partner's cooperation, praise him for every little thing. He will expect a reward for his efforts. Don't worry about raising his feminist consciousness right now. There are more important battles to fight.

rewarded for their efforts, and if they feel unappreciated in the baby drudgery they will be quite uncooperative. Not only will you not get the help you need, you will have to listen to a lot of whining. So it's best to build an atmosphere of appreciation.

Psyching Pop Out

If you *really* want to get the most help out of your partner, though, giving him praise is not enough. Remember the story of Tom Sawyer? He maneuvered all the kids in the neighborhood into doing his chore of painting a fence. How? By making it look like so much fun. They never figured out he wanted them to do the work all along. This psychology can work for baby care. If you make it seem as though you are having all the fun, you may find your mate actually *asking* to help out.

Different Strokes for Different Folks

If you are going to ask your partner to divide baby chores with you, you'll have to accept the fact that he'll have his own way of doing things. As was mentioned in Chapter 3, it is important that you resist the temptation to criticize. If he's not as neat at changing a diaper or during feedings, let it go—after all, you want to encourage his help. Remember, he's just as uncomfortable and unsure of himself as you were at first. The difference is, *he* thinks that *you* know what you are doing.

Momma Said There'd Be Days Like This

I remember my husband throwing our baby up in the air and catching him—something that lots of men do. (To this day I think it is a stupid thing to do.) There are a lot of things that Daddy is going to do that *you'll* be sure just can't be good for your child. But most of the time what you have is a gender-based difference of opinion. Unless your child is truly endangered, don't let little differences set up a pattern of bickering between the two of you.

You and your partner will each develop your own distinct ways to interact with the baby. And men tend to have a more roughhousing, physical style than women do. You may be tempted to try to limit such activities, but unless there's a clear danger to the child, resist the urge. You want to encourage your husband's involvement with your children, even if it means a few more skinned knees or bumps. There is never only one way of doing things and it is good for your child to have more than one way of doing things, one opinion, to choose from.

Building to a Balance

The two main reasons for establishing a routine in your family are to give everyone a sense of consistency, and to make your day-to-day life more manageable. But don't sacrifice your own needs to any schedule. I've known mothers with perfectly clean homes and schedules that would do the time-management experts proud—and some of the most unhappy children you will ever see. Family systems and routines are simply *tools* for you to use so that your life is not living you. They are not the goal. A life full of love is a much more important goal.

Reality does put certain constraints on our lives that can only be handled with proper planning, but you can never fully anticipate what life will throw in your direction. Things like consistent bedtimes and mealtimes can go a long way toward establishing order in your home and making it easier to cope when the unexpected happens.

Bedtime Basics and Beyond

When your baby is about one month old you should try to move her to her own room. (If it makes you feel more secure, you can use a baby monitor.) Babies have periods of wakefulness during the night that do not mean they need immediate attention. If she is in the room with you, either you will respond to her movements or she will hear you and wake up. Either way, you will both be more tired than necessary. Both you and your baby will be better able to sleep with this new arrangement because you won't be waking each other up.

Getting a child to sleep on her own is not an easy thing to do. You have to be strong. I did a great job with my oldest child, but to this day I have trouble with my younger children and bedtime. The trick is to outlast them. Your baby will cry her eyes out and be totally pitiful when you first try to get her to settle in to sleep on her own. If you are satisfied your baby is not wet, hungry, ill, colicky, or in immediate danger, you will need to tolerate the crying if you want to help her get into a routine.

Trust me on this. My oldest child went to bed so consistently that I was able to get work done after she was in bed. But I caved in with my two younger ones, and to this day I am exhausted by the time I get them to bed.

> **Mom-isms**
>
> A **baby monitor** is a type of intercom that lets you hear the sounds your baby makes when the two of you are in different rooms. It's a great peace-of-mind preserver, especially during the first few days after baby is moved into his or her own room.

Better Now Than Later

If one parent has a work schedule that lets him (or her) see the baby only after she's gone to sleep, consider keeping the baby up a little later. It is not going to hurt the baby to create a schedule that gives her more time awake to see Mommy or Daddy.

The key here is to remember that you are in control. No matter *what* time you set as bedtime, *you're* the one to choose it, not baby. Being in control with an infant is more feasible if you can get past the crying. Once the child is really conscious of his or her own power to manipulate you, you will find yourself in an all-out war.

Most of all, you want to establish routines early in the game. In the case of my two younger children, I didn't do that. As I said, I caved. Do I pay for it now? You bet. Now that I have figured out the game, am I better at it than I used to be? You bet. It just would have been easier to establish patterns early on rather than battle them out now.

Womanly Wisdom

Setting a standard bedtime for your kids is for *your* benefit. Grown-ups deserve some downtime of their own after spending all day with an infant, so you don't want bedtime to leave you too exhausted for anything else afterward. Work together with your partner to try to create the bedtime ritual that works best for you.

A Schedule Can Set You Free

If you can, try to get into a routine for all the baby's basic activities. If you can establish some consistency with bedtime, meals, and bathtime you are off to a very good start. But keep in mind that these schedules are merely tools for managing your life. Allow yourself the flexibility to be spontaneous once in a while. If you never go out because you do not want to ruin baby's routine, you are headed for problems. You are no longer in control—the schedule is. So, although you want to establish a basic schedule, don't be afraid to break it *once in a while*. Babies are much more resilient than you might think. If they stay up a little later than usual they will be a little more fussy. It will not be a tragedy.

Living in Mommy-Time

With a new baby, expect everything you do to take twice as long as it used to. And taking the baby on the road, routine or no routine, will require patience. It's just not as easy to get up and go with an infant. It is like having an extra leg to carry along.

Plan ahead. If you are expected at your parents' house for dinner at 7:00 p.m. and they live a half-hour's drive away, plan to leave your house at 5:00 p.m. You may make it on time if you account for crying baby, wet diapers, more wet diapers, lost pacifiers, changing baby's outfit three times so it will be clean long enough to show off to your mother, lost car keys, and lost sanity.

Unfortunately, you'll soon discover that even people who have raised children of their own will develop amnesia about the experience when it comes to you, your new baby, and the fact that you need six pairs of arms to be anywhere. They will glare at you when you show up half an hour late, relatively unkempt, baby in tow. Do not let it get you down. You'll get better at anticipating situations the more you get out and try, and until that happens, try not to worry about what other people think.

Taking Your Act on the Road

Whenever you take baby anywhere you are going to need to take along the baby gear—and babies need a *lot* of gear. If you are going on a long trip, God help you—you are very brave. If you're just going shopping or to Grandma's, however, you can usually get away with a manageable amount of stuff. You'll need diapers, baby wipes, spit-up rags, a toy or two (depending on the age of the baby), diaper rash cream, and whatever paraphernalia you need for feeding. You might want to throw in an extra pair of pants or a sleeper so you can change the baby before you head back home and then transfer him right into his own bed when you get there.

Womanly Wisdom

Dressing a baby can be frustrating. Here's a tip: It is easier to put on sleeved outfits if you put your hand through the sleeve opening and pull baby's hand through instead of trying to push the sleeve up baby's arm. It is quicker and does not give baby time to wiggle away.

Baby Baggage

The best place to stash your baby gear is in a diaper bag. If you get a diaper bag as a baby gift but it is not big enough for you or the right shape or size, make sure you get another one that suits your needs. You are going to be spending a lot of time with your handy-dandy diaper bag. You want one that is not too heavy or bulky but that will carry everything, with easy access. I liked having one with compartments in case I needed to store soiled clothes. You can also use one-gallon plastic bags that zip closed —they're great for keeping messy clothes or dirty diapers from touching other things in the bag, and when they're zipped shut, they keep the stinky smell inside.

Momma Said There'd Be Days Like This

When my first child was born I didn't know what to do with myself. I had no idea how to manage my time—with or *without* the baby—but I read that the local community center was offering an infant stimulation class, and I signed up. The class was intended for women who needed a reason to get out with other women with young babies. I don't know whether it helped my baby in the long run, but it certainly helped me.

Diapering on the Road

Some diaper bags come with attached changing pads—a "have changing pad, will travel" kind of deal. This is fine while the baby is very little—the pads are usually pretty small. When you use a changing table in a public restroom you most likely will still want to use your own changing pad, for sanitary reasons. The advantage to having a changing pad as opposed to just using a blanket under baby when you change him on the road is that a changing pad can be easily wiped down with soap and water. No matter what level of diaper dexterity you reach, you are going to have a few mishaps. You would need many blankets to equal the capacity of one reusable diaper-changing pad.

Womanly Wisdom

When you pack for the baby think of basic needs: Food, clothing, water, cleanliness, and transportation. As the child grows, add "distraction" to your list—things to keep baby occupied. Good preparation gives you the mobility that can be an emotional life preserver during your baby's first year.

Equipment Overkill

There's a lot of nifty baby gear available today, and all of it can look tempting, but there is such a thing as equipment overkill. When I had my first baby, for example, I bought a super-duper deluxe portable changing table. It was cool the first few times I used it and then it just became another cumbersome object to lug around.

As you become more experienced, you will learn that the less you have to pack and carry, the better. Monitor your own use of the items you're toting in your diaper bag. If you don't use it, stop packing it. On the other hand, if it is something you really might need, don't hesitate to take it along. If you are going shopping and assume the mall will have a stroller for rent you may be sadly mistaken. You'll regret leaving your own stroller at home when you're trying to shop and hold a baby at the same time.

The Benefits of Breaking Out of the House

When you're out of the house, you can still work with the schedule you've established for the baby. For example, if your baby usually naps at a certain time, make sure he's in his stroller or carrier at that time—that way he can catch his nap while you are out and about.

With a little planning, you can take your baby everywhere you want to go. He'll adjust. If he gets too fussy while you're out, you can always just leave wherever you happen to be. Chances are he will fall asleep in his car seat and you will find your peace that way.

Building a Social Network

Many women who become stay-at-home moms after being in the work force do not know where to begin when it comes to developing a daytime life with baby. Unless you are truly a homebody you will want to get out of the house as regularly as you can. Unless you meet women in a similar situation you are going to feel very alienated. You can always hang around the formula-and-diaper section of the local supermarket but it may be more rewarding for you to take some proactive steps on your own behalf.

Generations ago, families lived close to one another and were directly involved in each other's lives. But today, many of us lack the support of close-by relatives to teach us the ropes about child rearing. Even though we resist many of the old ways, it is a shame we do not have the built-in societal network to tell us how to handle simple situations. Instead, we're forced to turn to strangers, or to professionals such as the pediatrician, for advice that used to be passed down from one generation of moms to the next.

Play Groups: for Mom and for Baby

Today's society may be more fragmented than that of earlier generations, but there are still many opportunities for meeting people, if you are creative and open-minded. Try checking at your community center, church, synagogue, and the like to find the names of women with children around the same age as yours to form a play group. You can initiate contact and then delegate some of the responsibilities to the other women in the group. If you find some compatible people, it can be well worth the effort. You do not need to find people with exactly the same background as you. Babies are the great equalizer— no matter how educated, sophisticated, or well-dressed their mothers, all babies behave in ways that are relatively the same.

Forming a play group is something you do for yourself as well as for your child. Even though moms today are creating new rules, we all could use some consistent information and the chance to learn from the experience of others. If you have the chance to get involved in small play groups of women with children around the same age, you can make your world seem a little bit larger and can get some great tips.

Your baby is going to be a part of your world for a very long time. Get out and enjoy life together. Your only limitations are those you set for yourself.

Mom-isms

A **play group** is an informal, regular gathering of a small group of women and their children. If the children are old enough they play together. If not, the women swap information and snacks while the babies do very little. Usually the location varies from meeting to meeting.

Getting Back to the Bedroom

About six weeks after the birth of your baby you'll be scheduled for a routine follow-up visit to your obstetrician. He wants to make sure everything has gone back to where it was before you had the baby and that you are doing well, both physically

Mom Alert!

Be careful not to judge yourself too harshly while you're learning how to be a mom. It's easy to come down hard on yourself if you're accustomed to feeling competent at work and now find yourself confused or inept with the baby. Sharing your frustrations with a supportive friend or family member can cut down on the stress.

and emotionally. Of course, if you have any unexplained pains or are feeling depressed before the six-week appointment, you shouldn't wait to call your doctor.

You'll have a pelvic examination, after which your doctor is very likely to give you a wink and say, "You can now resume all normal activities." "You mean *sex*?" you ask incredulously. With all the sleepless nights recently, not to mention your still recent memory of childbirth, you just may think to yourself, "Why would I ever want to do *that* again?"

Rekindling the Spark

It is very common for women to have anxiety about returning to a normal sex life after the birth of a baby. The pain of labor is still pretty fresh, your hormones have not necessarily returned to their sensual best, and you have begun to think of yourself as a mother instead of a wife. It would be very easy to fall into a pattern of non-activity to avoid having to deal with the subject head on.

Meanwhile, your partner may have concerns of his own. Men can have anxiety about sex after several weeks or months of inactivity. And if he was in the delivery room with you, he could have a very strong fear of hurting you: It is difficult to see the one you love go through the pain of labor and childbirth and not be affected by it.

The best thing to do is to be patient with each other. It's definitely a good idea to resume your sex life as soon as possible after getting the medical green light because the sooner you start, the easier it is to bring your sex life back to normal. You don't want to rush into it too soon if you feel strongly that you need more time, but be careful not to give yourself so much time that you make it a big deal.

Of course, some women find that they can't wait to get back to the bedroom after the hiatus. This is great—but remember that it takes two. Be aware that your partner may be reluctant—many men need time to adjust to the combination of roles you now play: mother of his child *and* his sexual partner. If you are the one with the renewed friskiness you don't want to be disappointed. There is nothing worse than starting to feel like a woman again only to perceive rejection from your mate. And if your partner shows a lack of enthusiasm, you're likely to read it as rejection unless you make an effort to understand what *he* might be feeling.

Signs, Signals, and Sensuality

The best thing for you to do is try to talk about it. If you are not good at talking about sex, try to slowly feel each other out. Sometimes a little nonverbal encouragement can turn the issue of when to start up again a moot point.

If you both give signals, direct or indirect, that you want something to happen, plan a romantic evening together. Make it kind of like your wedding night. Even when you both are tired, you can be excited, too. Take the phone off the hook, lower the lights, light some candles, pour some wine or sparkling cider. And make sure you time your evening to correspond with the baby's sleep. You will not want to be interrupted.

A great way to light your pilot light is to engage in a sensual massage. Start very slowly. Remember—you are getting used to each other again. You can take turns rubbing and exploring each other's body or you can face each other as you massage. This angle requires a lot of eye contact, which can be very good for reestablishing intimacy but can also be intimidating. You may want to start with your eyes closed before you jump right into each other's soul.

No matter what, do not let your husband go anywhere near the brass ring until you are good and ready. You can drive him crazy by massaging just close enough to what he wants you to touch and then moving to another location. You don't want to create frustration; you want to build excitement that will restore your connection to one another.

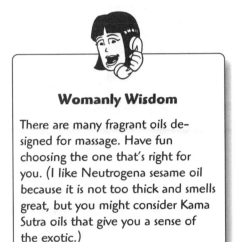

Womanly Wisdom

There are many fragrant oils designed for massage. Have fun choosing the one that's right for you. (I like Neutrogena sesame oil because it is not too thick and smells great, but you might consider Kama Sutra oils that give you a sense of the exotic.)

Easing into the Mood

Make sure you use a natural lubricant before you engage in intercourse. Every woman is different, but you may feel some discomfort. In addition to possible dryness and some minor soreness, simple anticipation can cause muscle tension. Ask your husband to rub a lubricant like KY jelly or Astroglide into your vaginal opening so that you are relaxed enough to take him in when you are both ready for intercourse.

Lubricants are very concentrated, so make sure he does not overdo it. And if you need to, do not forget to use contraception—it's best to give your body a break before considering getting pregnant again. Most of all, take your time. Treat your lovemaking as you would dining at a great restaurant. If your husband doesn't go for all the candles, soft music, and rubbing with oil, make sure you make it clear to him that you need to take it slowly until you are used to things again. It is important for your own peace of mind and the health of your marriage that you do not do something just to accommodate his needs without considering your own. Lovemaking is an equal opportunity activity, but if you do not express your needs and concerns you cannot expect your husband to read your mind.

Mom Alert!

Don't use your massage oil as a lubricant. Some of them have fruit extracts or other ingredients that could cause a yeast infection, and you do not need *that!*

Womanly Wisdom

Men are very defensive when you talk about sex and will always hear a criticism of their performance, no matter what you are saying. Be tactful: Avoid using the words "You never...." Instead, say "I feel...when we...." Praise what you like and try to encourage him to do other things you like.

Have fun with your sex life and try to keep it as active as both you and he want it to be. If you have to have him sneak home from lunch during baby's nap, it is worth it—a "quicky" now and then can be exciting.

Most of all, don't underestimate the importance of sex in your relationship. One of the best things you can do for your children is to build a solid relationship between the two of you. While sex is not the *most* important aspect of your relationship, it is something that contributes to an enduring marriage. Sex creates a bond between a man and a woman that helps them weather all the unpredictable circumstances that come up when they're raising a family. You can't put all your energy into your children. If you do, you will have nothing left for each other. By keeping your sex life active you will keep your couple life active and growing.

Keeping the Fires Burning

Now that the baby's born, you and your partner may not have the time you used to have to do things together. What used to be your leisure time is now devoted to family or perhaps to an extra job. You have to make a concerted effort to put energy into your relationship so it will grow with your family. It is more important than the fancy house and the newest toys. If you do not deposit love into your couple bank account you will see how fast life can help push you into bankruptcy.

Sex is one of many ways to keep your relationship strong. In addition, sex is important for you as a mother—an active, satisfying sexual relationship can remind you that you are a sensual woman as well. It is very easy to define yourself by your children, but you need to remember that you are vital, sexy, and capable in other areas of your life.

The Least You Need to Know

➤ When a new baby enters the household, every family member needs reassurance of his or her place in your life.

➤ Building a consistent basic routine will help you manage all the new responsibilities a baby brings into the family.

➤ When you're ready to begin venturing out of the house with your new baby, careful planning—and packing—will make your excursions easier and more enjoyable.

➤ Play groups are a great way to tap into a ready-made support group of other new moms (and veterans as well) for advice and friendship.

➤ When your doctor says you're ready, gently ease back into a sexual relationship with your partner—don't rush yourselves.

Chapter 8

Hi Ho, Hi Ho, It's Off to Work We Go

One of the hardest decisions a new mom faces, if she is fortunate enough to have the option, is when or even whether to go back to work after your child is born. We women have done so well in our efforts to enter the workplace that in many families it is what is expected of us. And we've become accustomed to lifestyles that demand two incomes. Our bills cry out for us to go back to work even before we can count on baby letting us get a full night's sleep. In other words, the economic realities of life as we know it do not go away because we decide to become mothers. In this chapter you'll work through the elements of the decision to go back to work with a baby in the house. You'll learn to identify—and overcome—needless guilt, and you'll learn how to keep your return to work from undercutting your developing relationship with your child.

The Real-World Rules of Maternity Leave

If you have a job where you work for someone else outside your home, the typical leave of absence for childbirth will be six to eight weeks. This is not necessarily a paid leave. What you are given is the opportunity to return to your job after a certain period of time. If your employer's business is too small to be covered under the Family Medical Leave Act (FMLA) you may not even have that guarantee. Basically, in that case you cannot expect much of anything unless it is given to you out of the goodness of your employer's heart.

Six to eight weeks may seem like a lot of time when your baby is not due for several months. You may plan to work until delivery and then spend your maternity leave with baby until you are ready to go back to work. However, your leave also includes any time you might need *before* you give birth. If you have a difficult pregnancy you may need to use up some of your leave before you even have your baby.

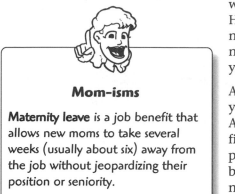

Mom-isms

Maternity leave is a job benefit that allows new moms to take several weeks (usually about six) away from the job without jeopardizing their position or seniority.

All you can do is try to plan ahead as best as possible, so you are not caught off guard, no matter what happens. As soon as you can after you discover you are pregnant, find out what your employer's policy is on maternity or pregnancy leave. The more information you have, the better you will be able to plan. If your employer does not offer maternity leave, you might want to save up your sick days and vacation time to use instead.

Can You Afford the Time Away from Work?

When you're deciding whether you'll stay home with your baby, you need to assess your financial situation. If you choose not to return to work right away after your baby is born, and you know where you stand financially, you can devise all kinds of creative solutions to suit your financial needs. All it takes is simplifying your lifestyle to fit a single income. Here are some likely places to cut costs:

➤ Consider selling that second car. Since you won't have a commute to work, you can save the insurance, upkeep, and loan payments—a significant monthly savings.

➤ Reduce your monthly clothing and dry-cleaning budget. You won't need to keep up that corporate dress code when you're home with the baby, and you'll be more comfortable in casual clothes around the house anyway (unless you're Donna Reed or the mom in *Leave It to Beaver*).

➤ Whenever you can, without cutting back on quality, consider generic brands in the grocery store and at the cosmetics counter. Rice Krispies taste the same as the generic type of rice cereal, but can cost two to three times more.

➤ If you and your partner often went out to eat before baby was born, you'll find you're saving in that department without even trying—you won't want to leave the baby with a sitter when she's really little, so you'll be eating at home a lot more now.

Dealing with the Stay-At-Home Guilts

Most middle-class families today rely on two incomes to meet their financial needs. And, as women, we have been socialized to expect to work. Don't be surprised to find that you feel guilty if you choose not to contribute financially to the household. Finances are a very touchy subject, especially when the cause of financial belt-tightening is your desire to stay home with the baby. You may find that your partner feels a little conflicted about your choice. His income alone may not be enough to maintain the household in its accustomed style, and he's also got his own cultural conditioning to deal with: He thinks he *should* be able to support his wife when she stays home to raise the children. It's a definite ego thing.

As you would in discussions of sex or anything else that touches on a man's sense of self, you want to be sensitive in approaching this subject. If it turns out that you just can't make do on a single income, make sure that your partner doesn't feel he has somehow let you down. Work together to come up with a sensible childcare plan. Or consider changing work shifts so that there's always one parent at home. Or look into alternative work situations— perhaps something that can be done from the home, so that even while you're working you're able to be there for the baby, too.

The Modern Return to Traditional Mothering

Mom Alert!

Your partner might feel resentful about having the entire economic responsibility for the family land on his shoulders. Make sure you talk your options through together so he doesn't feel ambushed into the situation. Otherwise, you may be facing a lot of avoidable tension when the baby arrives.

Womanly Wisdom

Try to solve the issue of finances and childcare as a team. Keep the discussion focused so it does not bleed into unrelated feelings and issues.

Forty years ago, when women were expected to stay home and raise children, many women felt oppressed. Women fought very hard for the freedom to choose between a career and staying home to raise children. But now the pendulum has begun to swing back the other way: Many women are discovering that, in spite of today's expectations that they hold down a job outside the home, they want the privilege of staying home with their babies, and they feel torn into little pieces over having to leave their newborn in someone else's care.

This societal shift has set up a real conflict for the new mom. Because we know how hard women had to fight to expand our opportunities, we can end up feeling guilty for deciding to devote ourselves to homemaking and child rearing when our children are young. It's easy to feel as if we're turning our backs on progress.

Professional women have a similar conflict. If they decide to drop out of their career for a while to care for their babies, they run the risk of losing their place in line for advancement. Not only will this professional woman not move up the proverbial corporate ladder, she may lose valuable years of the on-the-job training her male counterparts are receiving.

Making the Choice That's Most True to You

The question of whether to work outside the home or not is significant enough to deserve a lot of attention. Aside from economic realities, a woman's choice to stay at home or go back to her job will have a major impact on her self-concept—more so than most other decisions she faces as a new mom. Those of us born after 1950 have been profoundly influenced by the changing role of women brought about by the woman's movement. Even though no one can clearly define a consensus among women about most issues, we all know there is subtle pressure on all of us to make a life separate from our children.

Momma Said There'd Be Days Like This

When I was in law school, my female classmates all expected to have children somewhere between taking the bar exam and saving the world, but no one expected to get off the career track to raise them. Each of us handled her choices in different ways, but I do not know one woman lawyer who did not feel torn by having to choose between the professional and domestic aspects of her personality.

The important thing is to honestly consider what you want for your life. Try to isolate yourself from the "shoulds," and ignore other people's judgments. There is absolutely nothing wrong with choosing to work full-time while raising children, if that's the right choice for you. And juggling motherhood and career is not impossible: Many women succeed at it, whether they're doing it by choice or out of necessity. It is just very difficult, and requires a great deal of strength and organization if you want to avoid killing yourself in the process.

Merging the Worlds of Work and Home

If you have unresolved guilt and inner conflict over your role as a mother and your career, you're heading for problems. Sometimes we have so much fun with our jobs that we don't want to admit how much we do not like the day-to-day activities of motherhood. You need to be brutally honest with yourself. Are you the type of woman who has the patience to spend all day with a child? Are you doing your child a favor by staying home with him 24 hours a day, seven days a week, if all the time you are thinking about how miserable you are?

Some women simply are not going to be happy or fulfilled as stay-at-home moms. It's all a matter of personal style and personal needs. Guilt should not be a factor in your choice to return to your career. Making the choice to stay at home just because you think you *should* is a recipe for frustration and dissatisfaction. And it's bad for your children, too. Your dissatisfaction can lead to unhappy children who feel guilty and believe that your unhappiness is all their fault.

Womanly Wisdom

In deciding whether to return to work, be brutally honest with yourself about your personality and needs. Are you doing your child a favor by staying home, or are you going to drive both of you crazy in the process?

One Woman's Choice

After I had my firstborn I lost a lot of the fire I needed to be a tough trial lawyer. I was so in love with my little helpless baby that I became too nurturing to go into a courtroom to fight the dragons. I realized I needed to reconsider the way I lived my life, for the sake of my emotional and spiritual health and well-being. And having a child brought me back in touch with a creative side of me that I had long allowed to lie dormant: Giving birth started me on my path to writing, which was what I had always planned to do before I got sidetracked into law school.

My choice to stay home with my newborn and work part-time on my writing was not met with complete acceptance and joy. In fact, it was one of the decisions that led to the demise of my first marriage. This is why, as you take the steps to become a wife and mother, it is so important for you to investigate what is in your own heart every step of the way. If you do not know and are not aware of your own needs, you are going to send out mixed messages to the people around you. They will respond to the reality you present at the time and will not be thrilled when they think you have done a major and unexpected turnaround.

Finding the Route That's True to the Real You

The surer you are of your own feelings, the better able you will be to communicate them to the people around you. And the better your friends, family, and partner understand your choices, the more supportive they will be. This is especially important to keep in mind when you communicate with your partner. The two of you need to work together to find solutions that will make you both happy, and that's only possible if you're honest with one another.

And remember, you're not the only one facing choices. It is just as important that you examine what your partner wants as it is for you to be aware of what *you* really want. In discussing anything significant, you always want to focus on what will bring you closer together and what will meet the needs of each of you. Your relationship should not always be a power struggle. Constant tests of will waste far too much time that can better be used to work together to find creative ways to have the life you both want together.

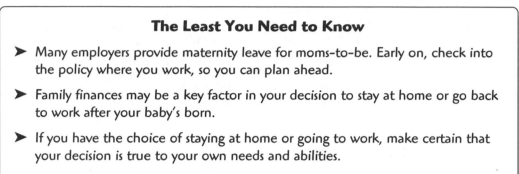

The Least You Need to Know

➤ Many employers provide maternity leave for moms-to-be. Early on, check into the policy where you work, so you can plan ahead.

➤ Family finances may be a key factor in your decision to stay at home or go back to work after your baby's born.

➤ If you have the choice of staying at home or going to work, make certain that your decision is true to your own needs and abilities.

➤ Juggling home and career can be taxing—enlisting the help of your partner can make all the difference.

Chapter 9

School Dazed

In This Chapter

➤ It's PTO Time!

➤ Keeping up with your changing child

➤ Schoolyard politics: meeting the other moms

➤ Regaining control of your daytime hours

➤ Coping when your kid is sent home sick

By the time your child is five or six he will be ready for "real" school—kindergarten. This is the beginning of an entirely new era in your life. You are now the mother of a school-aged child. With this new identity comes an entire new list of responsibilities and expectations. And often, your harshest critics will be other mothers.

In this chapter you'll learn about the changes that having a school-age child will introduce to your life. From the schoolyard politics of the PTO to excelling at carpooling, you'll find here all you need to survive your child's "school daze."

It's a Brave New World

When your child starts school you will be introduced to such things as the Parent-Teacher Organization (PTO), school parties, bake sales, and recitals. You will now be judged—the judges being your child, the teachers, and other moms—by your participation and by how well you adapt to your new role. Your life will no longer be your own.

Expect to be asked to attend every school field trip and to bake cookies for every conceivable occasion. On your child's birthday you must bring in some kind of special treat or you may be disowned. For some people this is a perfectly natural transition but the first time I baked cookies for a bake sale, my children asked who had kidnapped their real mom.

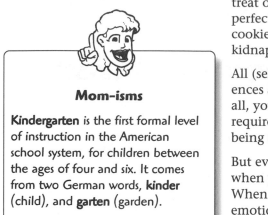

Mom-isms

Kindergarten is the first formal level of instruction in the American school system, for children between the ages of four and six. It comes from two German words, **kinder** (child), and **garten** (garden).

All (semi) kidding aside, some wonderful new experiences await the mother of a school-aged child. First of all, you have some more freedom without guilt. You are required by law to educate your child, so you are not being a bad mother by having a few hours to yourself.

But even though you may be dreamily awaiting the day when you can send your child to school, be prepared: When the day finally arrives, you will feel mixed emotions about the change. For the first time since the baby was born, you are officially turning your child over to the care and influence of another person.

Loosening the Reins

You will see many changes in your child in kindergarten. This will be your child's first exposure to structured learning, and she will be given responsibilities that you might not have considered giving her. But don't worry—the kindergarten teacher sees the child according to developmental age and knows how much to expect. You'll be proud of your child's new levels of accomplishment, but don't be surprised to find that your pride is mixed with a little resistance on your part. It is sometimes difficult for a parent to see that a child has gained the capacity to do things independently.

Keeping Up with the Changes

The truth of the matter is you can't always catch up with reality. For at least four years you have essentially defined yourself by the amount of care your child requires and how well you—and *only* you—have been able to provide that care. But now your role in your child's life goes through a major change. The child is not a baby anymore. The mother sometimes has a really difficult time adjusting to this change.

It can be especially difficult to accept these changes if it's the baby of the family who is heading off to kindergarten for the first time. I have seen mothers with tears streaming down their faces as their children happily find their places among their peers.

The Independent-Baby Blues

It's the mom, not the child, who usually has trouble coping with this change. At this age children are ready to make friends and try their wings. But Mom has probably not spent much time lately developing an identity other than that of being the mother of a dependent preschooler. You can suddenly feel as though you're not needed anymore.

Of course, your job is in no way complete, but right now it feels as though other people are more important in your child's life than you are.

Don't ignore your feelings. Give yourself a period of mourning if you need to. Grab a box of cookies, some chocolate milk, and a cozy blanket and watch those reruns of *Mister Rogers*. No one will know. It may take a week or two, but you will realize that there are many cool things left to do with your child and that you are still needed.

Going with the Flow

The process of adjusting to a child's entrance into kindergarten can be very intimidating for a parent. You're usually expected to come in for a preliminary meeting at which you're given the kindergarten's *syllabus* (an outline of what the kids will study). There you'll be with all the other parents, crammed into little chairs designed for little bottoms, listening to an explanation of phonics as compared to whole-language learning. It can seem a little overwhelming if all you remember about kindergarten is playing with clay, learning the alphabet, and making Thanksgiving turkeys out of lunch bags.

It is good to be concerned with your child and with creating a solid foundation for learning, but school introduces a new source of mother-anxiety. Where once you used to gauge your child's progress by comparing his achievements today with what he could do last week, suddenly you may experience a competitive edginess you've never had to deal with. Your little genius is now being compared to the other kids—all of whom have moms who are convinced that *their* little treasure is the best and the brightest.

Momma Said There'd Be Days Like This

I do not recall school being competitive in my own childhood. Of course, I wasn't wearing the mother hat when I went to kindergarten, so I was oblivious to any anxiety my mom might have felt. I am sure my mother's generation engaged in competitive mothering as much as we do. At least we have some options that weren't available back then. We don't have to define ourselves by how well our child ties his own shoes or how early our child learns to read.

Never before in your child's development was there a time when you could become so caught up in comparisons. Look at it this way: This is the first time your children are actually compared directly to other children. It's easy to begin to believe that how well they stack up is a reflection on you.

School Is Your Child's Business

Your adjustment might be easier if, starting from the very beginning of your child's school career, you were to view what goes on during the day as her *job*—just as you and your partner have jobs. Think of your child as the CEO of her own development corporation—and you are simply the advisory staff. Otherwise, you can become entirely *too* invested and involved in your child's education—to the extent that you actually interfere with the learning process. We want our children to meet the expectations of their teachers without relying on their parents to protect them from expanding outside their comfort zones.

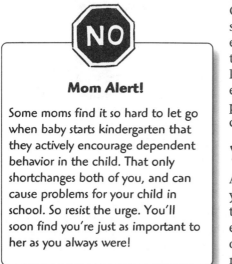

Mom Alert!

Some moms find it so hard to let go when baby starts kindergarten that they actively encourage dependent behavior in the child. That only shortchanges both of you, and can cause problems for your child in school. So resist the urge. You'll soon find you're just as important to her as you always were!

Your Child Takes Charge

Although you need to monitor what is happening to your children at school, you also have to trust that the teacher is presenting challenges your children are well-equipped to handle. Now is not the time to try to be overprotective: If you do not allow your children to reach their own levels of discomfort you can't properly assess when problems arise that really need intervention.

In other words, you need to allow your child to face the natural consequences of his or her choices. In this way, you enable the child to take the ultimate responsibility for how well he or she learns. From the very beginning a child needs to be self-motivated. There are many ways to help children love learning, but you do not want to stand in the way of their accepting the challenge.

Resist the temptation to help so much with a class project that you end up doing it yourself. Sometimes, mom's "help" can have just the opposite effect. You know you're helping *too* much when your child finally feels the need to remind you, "Hey, Mom— this is *my* project!"

But Mom Stays Informed

In the normal course of things you need to let your child find her own level of performance in school, but sometimes you have to step in. My oldest child had trouble in school and was not self-motivated. She was later determined to have *attention deficit disorder* (ADD). In situations like this you need to intervene in specific ways, but not to the extent that you allow your child to be overly dependent. Finding a good balance can be frustrating. For example, my daughter seemed to need my help but then was resistant when I went overboard. Once she was focused on her task she didn't want me to take over and deny her the experience of discovery.

Playing Nicely with Other Moms

When your children go to school you may feel a bit out of place. When you attend school functions you may feel uncomfortable if you do not know the other parents. This is a good opportunity to make new friends but it is also an artificial situation. You are thrown together with a group of people simply because your children are all in the same class at school. You can relate to each other about your children but you may not have much else in common.

Mom-to-Mom Relationships

As your children grow they are going to make friends. This throws you even more into the lives of other mothers. This can be a blessing, but do not expect too much of these acquaintances of convenience. Casual relationships are fine, but don't expect to become best friends with other moms just because your children play together.

You *will* discover that these new relationships require a great deal of tact and discretion. You would be devastated if you knew how much personal information passes from one child to the next. Do not be surprised if your neighbors suddenly seem to know a lot more about your personal habits than you would ever purposely share with them.

Finding Your Own Style

Gossip about other parents can suddenly become very risky —especially since your child can suddenly turn into the household version of the town crier. Expect what you say to get back to the mothers of your child's friends. It's best to try to keep a low profile.

At the same time, you do want to get involved in your child's school experience. That's when it becomes important to develop your own style. I am not a blend-in kind of person, myself—in fact, some people may think I am kind of eccentric. If you're like me, you may find that, when faced with group situations, you either have to take over or slink into the corner. There is no in-between. Your job will be to find a role to play that best suits your style.

Field-Trip Frolics

Some moms are reluctant to take the lead in big groups, such as PTO meetings, but can really shine in more specialized roles. I personally love chaperoning field trips—I think I like them more than my children do. I've seen how apples are picked, washed, and packaged and have gotten lost in a cornfield maze. I have seen the "Nutcracker Suite" and have been to the Center of Science and Industry.

Being a field-trip mom suits my personality. It's easier to make friends with other moms when we're all involved in a specific activity. And my children think it is really cool having their Mom in charge of watching over their friends. It is definitely a status

111

thing. And there's an unexpected bonus: All this high-visibility involvement earns you lots of mommy points—when your kids start nagging you about *other* things, you can always point to all the field trips you went on "just for them." It is always good to have such ammunition in your arsenal. Just don't let your children know how much you enjoy your role.

Developmental Dynamite

When you send your child to school you need to be prepared for the changes that occur right before your eyes. By the end of kindergarten your baby will seem like a regular kid. The maturation that occurs during that one year is amazing. And by the time your child enters first grade, you may as well fasten your seat belt—you are in for a fast and bumpy ride. Everything will blur as you learn to measure the year by back-to-school sales, Winter Break, Spring Break, and Summer Vacation.

Womanly Wisdom

Make the start of the school year a special event. Even if you have enough broken crayons in your house to start your own store, get a new box for the first day of school. That extra $5 for a new box of crayons with 94 colors will go a long way toward building up a level of enthusiasm and mental preparation in your child. You want your child to begin each year fresh.

You will see your children develop identities as they learn to interact with other children and challenge themselves. They will develop interests and, if given half a chance, will operate at a creative frenzy. This is a great thing to watch. Children do not second-guess themselves. When they are encouraged to follow through on creative ideas, they can master a skill they will use throughout their lives. By nurturing this natural creativity, you can help your child grow into a resilient adult.

Some kids are much more excited than others about starting school each fall. The more enthusiasm you can generate and the more fun you lead them to believe they will find, the fewer complaints you'll hear come September. So make back-to-school an event in itself. Make shopping for clothes and supplies fun by letting the kids pick some of their own stuff. Do something special for dinner the night before the first day of school.

Managing Your Days When Your Child Is in School

Whether you work outside the home or are a career mom, your schedule is going to change dramatically when your child starts regular school. One of the first things you'll discover is that you suddenly have a whole new approach to childcare than anything you relied on in the past.

The Working Mom's Childcare Dilemma

If you are a working mother, *your* days will not change much when your child goes to school, but your childcare needs will. You will need adequate childcare for the days your child will have off from school—and you'll be amazed by how many obscure holidays there are, once your life revolves around a school calendar. Add in some snow days and you can see you'll need strong backup. Then there are the days when your child has a fever or a cold.

In addition, when your children are in school you can expect them to come home with more colds, viruses, and mysterious illnesses than you could ever have imagined. Schools are like germ factories, and little hands are perfect vehicles for their safe transportation. No matter how well you have taught your children to wash their hands, when children play in a group they are going to be exposed to germs. And when your child has a fever, the school is going to call you to take him home—so you need a contingency plan to handle such unscheduled childcare needs.

After-School Care Alternatives

Many public schools have latchkey programs that start as early as 6:00 a.m. and run as late as 6:00 p.m. to accommodate working parents' schedules. Although the word "latchkey" presses instant guilt buttons, many of the programs are a real lifesaver. These programs involve children in structured activities and supervise them when you can't. Also, community centers often have after-school programs that offer lessons and activities. If neither of these options works for you, you can hire an in-home, after-school baby-sitter. Your children *need* supervision after school: This is a time when they are most apt to get into trouble or feel lonely.

Even older children feel lonely. When my oldest child was old enough to stay in the house by herself, I gave her the opportunity to do so. I was surprised when she told me that she wished I could be home when she got home from school. I guess the image of Mommy and milk and cookies (store-bought, of course) waiting for them when they finish a hard day dies hard. If you can set up some transitional arrangement, it is really better than leaving even an older child to his or her own devices.

Mom-isms

Latchkey programs provide childcare for a couple of hours before and after normal school hours, when many parents must be at work. They are structured programs that keep a child busy and under supervision until the parents can take over.

When Mom Stays at Home

Managing your days when you have school-age children can be just as difficult for mothers who stay home as it is for those who go out to work. The danger is that everyone will think you are available to do everything. Just because you do not leave your home every morning to go to an office does not mean that you do not have obligations and plans for your time. You are going to have to be very assertive about what you will and will not allow. If you want to be involved with the school, that is great. Schools are made so much better by the volunteer efforts of parents. In fact, many of the extras would not exist without the efforts of parents.

But do not feel that you are obligated to get involved with everything. Volunteering can be all-consuming. Learn to say "no" when you want to and "yes" when something comes along that's meaningful to you. Everyone gets recruited for a bake sale or two, but if you are very uncomfortable running certain types of activities, stay in the "call on me if you must" role. Stay-at-home moms have to be incredibly vigilant about protecting their time. Managing a family is enough work to keep most people busy without all the other obligations and expectations placed upon us.

On the other hand, if you *can* handle being involved with the school, many mothers say volunteering enhances their relationship with their children. They feel more connected to each stage of their children's development. Volunteering also gives you a close-up view of how well the school is providing for your children's education. Parents have a great impact on the way a school is run. If parents are directly involved, they can have more influence.

Mom Alert!

The most important word you can learn to say right now is *no*. If you can't use it judiciously, you may find yourself volunteered for absolutely everything the school needs to have done. Pick your volunteer projects wisely, or you'll quickly wear yourself to a frazzle.

Getting a Grip on the Guilt

If you are a working mother you are going to feel pressured by the conflicting responsibilities of work and childcare. It is difficult to work all day, come home and try to fix some kind of dinner, and then help your children stay on track with schoolwork. Depending on the demands of your job, your emotional state, and your organizational skills, you are going to be tired and stressed to one degree or another.

My evenings go so fast that I have to remind myself a million times to check my children's school bags at night. I have found trusting a child to tell you whether there is an important note or memo in his bag is as effective as waiting for him to give you accurate phone messages. It just isn't going to happen until the child is old enough to understand the hair-trigger limits of a mother on overload.

Womanly Wisdom

Keep track of school notices about illness. If your child falls ill, you'll have something to tell the doctor that may speed up a diagnosis. This can mean a much quicker recovery, and less chance of secondary infections that will keep your child out of school for a long time.

Sick Call

If you're self-employed, it doesn't always make financial sense to hire a baby-sitter to stay with a sick child. The temptation is to neglect having a backup plan—you may think you can just take off from work when the children are sick. But it's difficult to run a career with constant interruption. And there is always the guilt factor. You feel guilty about taking time off from work, and guilty if you can't be with your sick child.

You are going to get notices from school warning you of all the things your children have been exposed to. It's required by law: The school has to notify you if a child in your child's class has any type of communicable illness. Don't panic—a warning alone doesn't necessarily mean that your child has had direct exposure. If you try to anticipate problems every time you receive a notice, you are going to drive yourself crazy. You probably will see a lot of strep throat. All you can do is watch for symptoms and deal with it if it comes up.

Momma Said There'd Be Days Like This

As a self-employed mom, even though I could stay home when my kids were sick, I couldn't always stop working. I'd try to get work done at home, but *that* was usually a lost cause. I know I wasn't as nurturing as my mother's generation might have been. And I never wanted to make staying home sick seem too attractive. So I took care of my children's physical needs and comforted them when they were in really bad shape, but when they hit the I'm-just-not-feeling-too-good stage, I'd revert to "Here is your food and here is your medicine—you are on your own."

The Most Dreaded School Message of All

There is one notice you will receive that strikes fear and shame in the heart of every mother. At one point or another you will receive a notice that one or more children in your child's class have head lice. You will pray it isn't so. You will try to deny the possibilities. But if one child in your child's class has head lice, chances are your child will, too.

I really think the entire issue of head lice is intended to keep mothers humble. There is no greater equalizer than head lice—they strike the nicest, cleanest families as well as all the others. Head lice are no indication of educational or economic status or of your house-cleaning prowess. Head lice are just one of those things that happen when they happen, and you can't let them ruin your life.

Momma Said There'd Be Days Like This

When my daughter was five a dear friend of mine invited her to go along with her children to a kid's gym, where lots of kids play on a padded slide, tunnel, and monkey bar contraption. A day later my daughter said her head itched. Well, at that time I wouldn't have known a *nit* (louse egg) from the moon, so by the time I was able to figure it out the infestation had spread not only to my other two children, but also to me and my husband. Even worse, we'd just had a party—now I had to worry that I'd sent each of our guests home with an unexpected present. What can you do? You can die of embarrassment or you can declare war and go after the little suckers.

Start Spreading the News

Even though you want to crawl under your bed and hide, you *must* notify your child's school if your child has lice. One of the best defenses is for all the other parents to catch the lice before they lay too many eggs. It's mortifying to have to make the announcement, but you will be doing everyone a favor by coming clean. So quit going "Ewwww," and pay attention.

Killing Off the Critters

There is only one way to get rid of head lice—the hard way. There are home remedies like Vaseline or the chemical shampoos you can find at any pharmacy. But it's not enough to wash away the living lice—you'll just get reinfested unless you also thoroughly comb out and eliminate all the eggs. This may seem an easy task if you have boys with buzz cuts in your family, but at the time *I* had this joyous experience, two of us had waist-length hair and my youngest—who had brought our little visitors into the house—had the curliest hair you'll ever see. Try getting a small nit comb through every strand of *that* hair.

Don't stop with just treating everybody's hair! You also have to make sure to wash or bag anything that could possibly have come in contact with your children's heads. If you completely seal such items (think stuffed animals or pillows) in bags, the lice will die off after a week or so: They need a human host to survive. Reinfestation is common, so I recommend washing in hot water all bedding, hats, and anything else that might have been exposed. This is hard work, but the more you do the better your chances of killing the little suckers the first time around. If you can afford it, hire a cleaning service to completely vacuum your home and your couches. Even if this is overkill, it will make you feel a whole lot better.

After your ordeal is over, pat yourself on the back for surviving yet another rite of passage as the mother of school-age children. And if you get over your embarrassment enough to talk about your experience with friends, you'll discover just how common lice are—they've been around since time began, after all. But don't get too complacent: Plenty of character-building humiliation still lies ahead.

Inside the Little Red Schoolhouse

A teacher's world is very narrow, at least when it comes to interacting with your child. If you do not check your child's bag every night and keep on top of school issues and events you might receive what all parents dread—a personal call from the teacher. There is nothing worse than being reprimanded by your child's teacher for missing an important notice. Don't try to make excuses. The teacher has heard them all. She *knows* you forgot to check the bag.

Womanly Wisdom

When dealing with very long hair, carefully make thin, tight braids of each thoroughly combed section, clearly separating them from the hair that still needs to be treated. This way, you'll keep track of the combed and treated hair and your "patient" will have a cool new hairstyle.

Situations like this just add one more opportunity for mother guilt. But guilt is not all you get to cope with, once your children are in school. You also get great opportunities for worry. What if your child is harassed by a bully? What if your child *is* a bully? What if your child is the last one picked on the team? What if your child doesn't even want to *be* on the team?

Memories of School Daze Past

The reason school brings out so much guilt and worry is that it often forces us to relive whatever experiences we had growing up. Our children are constant reminders of every good or bad schoolyard memory we thought we had buried. We live through our children and want to make sure that whatever our life was, theirs will be better. Unfortunately, when we indulge in guilt and worry we're more likely to project our own unresolved issues onto our children's experiences than to see what *they're* really coping with in their own lives.

Getting Real

No self-respecting child is going to miss a chance to say such provocative things as, "I hate school," "The kids are mean to me," and "Homework stinks," if he or she thinks it'll get a little extra attention. You need to be able to tell when such statements are being made just for effect, and when they indicate real problems. Here's one technique: When your child complains to you about how difficult life is, just listen. Don't make suggestions or pass judgments. Simply reflect back to your child that you hear what he's saying. You can do this by simply paraphrasing what the child has said. Most of the time, you'll see that what your child is really looking for is to be acknowledged.

But if you always jump in like a knight in shining armor, ready to slay the dragons, your child is going to capitalize on this. Instead of learning to solve problems on his own, he is going to associate having problems with getting Mommy to pay attention and take care of everything. Choose your battles wisely—jump in only when your intervention can have a real impact or can teach your child something important about life. Most of the time it is important to your child's development that you allow him to work out his own fears, insecurities, and discomfort with peer relationships.

Minivan Mom

Another phenomenon occurs when your children are school-aged. It is called the after-school-activities-minivan-mom syndrome. You do not need a minivan to qualify. You just need to juggle the schedules of lots of different after-school activities and spend almost as much time in your vehicle as you spend in your home.

The Overscheduled Only Child

When you have one child, things don't get too unmanageable. However, the parents of only one child tend to have a syndrome called activity-overloaditis. This occurs when an only child is seen as having so much talent that no opportunity for enrichment is spared. We start with infant movement class, graduate to gymnastics, add piano, dance, skating, soccer, baseball, karate, and anything else that looks interesting at the time. After a while the syndrome accelerates to such a degree that the only way to know what day it is is to check the carpool schedule.

Mom Alert!

Forcing your child into an activity "because it's good for him" is rarely a good idea. Most often, all you succeed in doing is to teach the child to resent that activity, and he'll usually quit it as soon as he gets a chance.

Multitasking with Multiple Kids

When you have more than one school-age child you can find yourself severely overloaded. You can easily find yourself expected in three places at once. Activities overlap and you have no idea how your life became so unmanageable. Forget about meals—your vehicle now looks like the trash receptacle behind a fast-food joint. At least if you ever get lost you can live on the dehydrated French fries stuck under the seat.

The best cure for these rapidly spreading conditions is, to put it simply, to rediscover sanity. Choose one or two favorite activities per child and support them. Drop the rest. Spend the rest of the time together doing *unscheduled* activities. Reading. Hanging out in the backyard. Spending time together.

Sure, it's great to expose children to all kinds of new things, but only a few of those things will truly capture your child's passion. If you give children the opportunity, they will tell you what they like best. If a child begs you for dance lessons, pay attention. You want to encourage kids to stick with something they have chosen. And the lessons will mean more if enrolling in them is the child's idea.

Knowing When to Give a Little Push

You want to give your child a choice in his or her activities. But if a child rejects something out of hand, you may want to look closely at the reasons behind the rejection. When my son was younger he came up with every lame excuse in the book to get out of joining the baseball team. It turned out that he was terrified of joining because he was going to be one of the younger and less-experienced players—he was afraid he wouldn't do as well as the others on the team. We knew that deep down he really *wanted* to play baseball, so we practically dragged him there. We could see the sweat on his forehead when it was his turn at bat. His first time around was slow, but the other team members rooted for him. The second time he hit a good grounder, and from then on he begged us to keep signing him up.

And When Push Feels Like Shove

On the other hand, my oldest child was forced into piano lessons by her father and stepmother. Her stepmother was from a classical-music background and believed that piano lessons were good for young girls. Although my daughter liked music she hated the teacher and didn't want to take the lessons. Finally the teacher called my ex and pleaded with him not to continue bringing our daughter there. Evidently she was purposely playing so badly that the teacher "fired" her.

Although we want to give our children every opportunity to excel and compete against their peers, we would be better off encouraging them to explore what they love. When a child is really turned on by something there is no stopping the enthusiasm. We need to provide the opportunities and exposure, but ultimately it is up to the child to follow through.

If you want to support your children in their creative development, the best thing you can do is be consistent. If you choose activities, it is good to follow through with them and enforce a routine with your child. Just make sure that the activity is really right for your child—not something you or any other adult needs for your own fulfillment or ambition.

The Least You Need to Know

➤ When your child goes to school, take advantage of opportunities to get involved there as a volunteer.

➤ Avoid overextending yourself with school activities—it's better to do a few things well than a lot of things haphazardly.

➤ Enjoy your child's first steps into independence—but remember, he still needs you.

➤ Have a plan in place for days that your child is sick and can't go to school.

➤ Although it's good to expose your child to new pursuits, avoid overscheduling. Otherwise, you'll spend the next few years as a full-time taxi service.

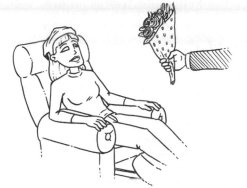

Chapter 10

Too Pooped to Pop: Romance After Children

In This Chapter

➤ Rediscovering passion after the baby arrives

➤ Scheduling yourselves into your baby's busy schedule

➤ Forging a new relationship as lovers *and* parents

Raising children together is a wonderful and romantic thing in theory. Having a child together is a cementing of your love and commitment to one another. It is the ultimate intimacy. But at times it is also the exact opposite of an aphrodisiac. It is just not sexy to be covered in baby drool and spit-up. As your children get older and the demands increase, you may not see sex as a defining aspect of your relationship with your mate. In this chapter you'll learn how to help bring your pre-baby romance back to life.

Love Among the Diapers

When you are busy and tired, your primal urges can get pretty simple: a few moments of peace and quiet may be all you want or need after the lights are turned out. Even if you make the effort to cuddle and smooch a little, your body might signal to you, "No way."

Staying Romantic Is Important

Sex can feel like work when you are tired to the bone. But it is important for you and your partner to find the time and energy to keep your pilot lights lit. It is too easy to fall into a routine that leaves no time for romantic passion. You may figure that later, when your children are a little older, you'll have plenty of time to get the old sparks flying again. But when that day comes, you may find it harder than you think to get your physical relationship back on track.

Look at Why You May Be Saying No

When you're raising a child it is common to feel overwhelmed and vulnerable. Even if you work outside the home, your partner typically has more opportunities to escape into the world while you feel tied to your children. Sometimes it seems as if you can't do anything without feeling the pull of motherhood calling you back to the baby. When this happens, avoiding sex often becomes a way of reserving something of yourself and acting out on some of your resentment. It is a perfectly natural reaction, but one that you are wise not to indulge too much.

Womanly Wisdom

If you find yourself saying "no" to your partner a lot, it may just be because you're having a hard time feeling sexy these days. Buy some bubble bath. Have a good long soak after the baby's asleep. Slip into something slinky, and see if those old passionate feelings don't start reviving just a little.

...And Maybe Pop's Pooped, Too

It is highly likely that your once studly mate is just as tired and feeling just as unsexy as you do. And he may be having just as much trouble as you are becoming adjusted to his new role as a parent. Not to mention the fact that some new dads (and some new moms, too) often have trouble letting those romantic feelings flow when they're extremely aware of the baby sleeping in the next room.

After a new baby arrives, all your old patterns of courtship and sex will probably have to be reorganized. You may have to learn to be creative—the goal of rekindling your romance is an important one, so you're wise if you do your best to make it happen. After all, sex is good for your health and longevity. It is also good for the health and longevity of your relationship.

What's a Mother to Do?

First of all, take stock of your relationship. If you can honestly say that you are having sex regularly enough to satisfy both you and your partner, don't worry if it doesn't involve having hot encounters twice a day. You've found a pace that suits you, so why fix what isn't broken. No need to look for problems when there aren't any—you've got plenty of other things to handle right now.

When a Problem *Does* Arise

Couples start having problems in their sex lives when the job of raising the children becomes so overwhelming that

Mom Alert!

Don't gauge your sex life by what you see on television or in the movies—*nobody* in the real world lives like that. There'd never be enough time to get anything else done! Find your own pace and go with that, and avoid comparing yourself with fictional characters.

there is no time to be alone and no energy, even if you find the time. Or when one of you starts avoiding sex as a (misguided) means of coping with other problems in the relationship.

Keep the Lines of Communication Open

Communication is not always the easiest thing in a relationship, and communication difficulties usually find their way into the bedroom. If you don't have time to talk about things except after the children are asleep you are going to bring your problems and conflicts to bed with you. Don't do it. Your bed is for lovemaking, not negotiations.

One way to avoid bringing conflicts into the bedroom is to set aside time to talk about things during other times and in other locations. Make appointments if you have to. Try to pick times when neither one of you is too tired or grouchy to discuss things like money matters or day-to-day problems. True, if you're having trouble finding the time to make love, you'll probably find it hard to find time for family meetings, but it's crucial that you try. Even if all you can manage are a few minutes here and a few minutes there, at least you're talking things out.

Call in the Support Troops When Necessary

You know you need to set up a childcare plan to cover you when you're off at work or running errands. Having back-up baby-sitters is equally important for the health of your relationship. If you can find relatives or friends to watch your children—even for just a few hours at a time—it can go a long way toward keeping the two of you connected on many levels. You can use this time alone to work out problems together. But best of all, you can use this time to talk about how you used to make love before the children were born and what you would like to do when you get home after the children are asleep. It can build some romantic excitement that can work wonders in your relationship.

Womanly Wisdom

When you're trying to reestablish your sexual relationship with your partner, it's important to have one place that isn't baby–oriented. Let the toys, bottles, and baby things mount up everywhere else if you must, but keep your bedroom as a place for you and your partner—you want to be able to set a sexy mood and scene when you're alone together.

Pulling Together, Not Apart

It is so important not to take your relationship for granted. Couples drift apart for what can seem like the most trivial of reasons, and the stress of a new baby in the house is hardly a trivial pressure. Even without a baby, you know that a good relationship needs constant nourishment and care, so don't let these new pressures make you forget to take that care. Keep those lines of communication open, keep expressing your feelings and lavishing love on one another as much as possible.

Cooperate, Don't Compete

Many couples get into a dangerous syndrome of emotional competition—trying to overcome each other instead of pulling together as a team. This does nothing but breed mistrust, and it can be exacerbated when a new baby enters the household with its own set of needs. But this is precisely the time when cooperation and mutual support are most needed, so it's worth your while to spend some time and energy to strengthen your bonds of love and trust as a couple.

Learning the Importance of Compromise

If you consciously try to work together, there is no reason not to find mutually satisfying solutions to most of the problems you face. What's key is that you strive to build your relationship on a solid foundation of trust, respect, and compromise. And there's an added benefit: By building a strong relationship with your partner, you are setting the best possible example for your children. The crucial lesson to learn is how to compromise—you're doing no one a favor if you go the totally self-sacrificing martyr route, and you gain nothing by forcing your will on everyone, either. The first breeds disrespect, the second is a recipe for resentment. Compromise means seeing to it that everyone's needs are at least partially met, and you can all feel like you're working together.

Making Passion a Priority

Making your sex life a priority in the scheme of things will make a positive difference in the harmony of your home. Men and women need to join with each other on a regular basis to maintain intimacy. This does not necessarily mean intercourse, but it does mean that you need time to focus on each other as lovers, and not as simply fellow travelers in the great childrearing enterprise.

Mom Alert!

Don't make your partner guess why you're too tired lately for a little romance. Tell him, even if you think it should be obvious. He's got his own insecurities now that he's a new dad, so he may not see that you're just feeling overworked—he may take your temporary lack of interest as a more permanent kind of rejection.

Now, this does not mean that every sexual encounter you have with each other must be spiritual and transcendent. If you can find the time for some fun with each other, *grab* it—sometimes, even being a little bit naughty can be pretty nice.

You can rekindle romance without risking your life in many very simple ways:

➤ Remember how much you love each other and do not forget to say it every day.

➤ Avoid criticism and give compliments as much as possible without being phony about it.

➤ Reminisce about your life as lovers before the children were born.

➤ Talk about ways you can sneak in some lovemaking time.

➤ Beg someone to take your children overnight or for a weekend, and do not leave your bed.

But most of all, remember to be loving to each other and think of one thing in your relationship to be grateful for each day.

Momma Said There'd Be Days Like This

When our kids were small, I once tried a little *too* hard to rekindle the old flames. I bought the cutest pair of red fur handcuffs at a novelty lingerie store and, while the kids were at school, I made a date with my husband to sneak home for lunch. When his car pulled into the drive, I was all set, handcuffed to the bedposts, with the key on my chest. But my husband had a surprise of his own—a rambunctious golden retriever pup pounced onto our bed and knocked the key to the floor. I had a hard time avoiding his attentions, while my husband spent some serious time on his hands and knees until he finally located the tiny key to free me.

Finding the Time for Togetherness

Finding the time does not mean finding the time for sex only. A couple also needs to find the time to allow their relationship to grow. You can't put all of your energy into raising a family and into your separate interests and expect your relationship to grow along with everything else. You need to make a special effort to know what is really going on with each other. You need to talk, or sometimes you just need to spend some time together not saying a word.

It's Not Just Children Who Need Nurturing

The relationship between you and your partner needs to be given the same kind of energy you give to your children. A relationship is headed for trouble if the energy is focused too one-sidedly: either entirely on the children or exclusively on the couple. In this, as in all things, what you seek is a balance—one that recognizes the needs of everyone in the family.

But when children are small, it's easy for a mother to bury herself so thoroughly in her children's demands that she misses the warning signs of trouble with the adult relationship. You need to carve out several different kinds of time: family time, alone time, children time, and partner time. Sounds like you need a lot of time, doesn't it? But remember that the *amount* of time spent in each area is less important than the quality of the time you put into it. If you find that things are not working well at home, chances are there is something out of balance in one or more of those relationships.

All Roads Lead Back to Mom

When you become a mom, you're taking on a bigger task than you might have guessed. You are central to the happiness and well-being of everyone in your family. It is important to them to feel close to you and to feel sure of your interest in them. Look at these relationships as plants that need lots of water and sunlight to grow. Loving your family and telling them so is like that water and sunlight—love and reassurance are the nutrients they need.

Express Yourself

You need the support of your partner. Do not be shy about demanding some time for your relationship with him, if that's what you need. Single moms may have to cope with childcare on their own, but if you've got a partner, it's simply not acceptable for you to have to do without his support in coping with your children and their needs.

When the Support Isn't There for You

If your husband is not willing to connect emotionally with you or refuses to participate in the raising of your children, you may need to get some professional counseling. Don't dismiss the idea out of hand. If you're worried about the cost, you needn't be: Many organizations offer family counseling at an affordable rate. And this is not an area in which to make false economies. It's better to do without a few extras than to let problems in your relationship escalate to unresolvable proportions.

Redefining Your Relationship

Relationships evolve over several distinct stages:

➤ The early years, when it's just the two of you

➤ The birth of the first child, when you're both learning the parenting ropes

➤ The settled years, when you've been together long enough to have created a routine

If you are a person who is used to crises or a lot of excitement, that third stage of a relationship may make you restless and frustrated. You might not know what is actually bothering you, but you know that *something* seems to be missing from your relationship and your family life. If this is the case, it's time to start an honest reappraisal of your relationship and what you expect from it. Unless you do this you will have trouble overcoming your sense of dissatisfaction, and that could very well strain your relationship.

Appreciating the Comfort of Familiarity

Familiarity and routine are not the most romantic concepts in the world. The media presents such a glamorized vision of life that it's easy to judge our own fairly "normal" existence as being somehow inadequate. But simplicity, familiarity and routine create security. And security is really what most of us want in our lives. We do not need the constant stimulation that crisis mode gives us.

Mom Alert!

When the dissatisfaction blues strike, don't just ignore them and hope they'll go away on their own. Find a way to structure rewarding things into your life. Otherwise, you risk expressing your resentments in ways that can damage your relationship with the people around you who love you the most.

Finding the Rhythm of Your Relationships

We get so used to stress that we often do not know how to sit back and enjoy our lives for exactly what they are. We always seem to want something more that we think the next woman has. Many women sabotage perfectly good relationships because they get caught up in the "is this all there is?" attitude. But the sense of dissatisfaction we feel comes from within us and is not necessarily the fault of our relationship.

It is therefore important to learn to accept your relationships with your family members for what they are, and come to terms with your own needs, instead of blindly expecting your partner or your children to fulfill your needs for you. That means getting to know who you are, and ceasing to define yourself by the roles you play. And it means recognizing the natural flow of your relationships within your family.

Each of us is ultimately responsible for our own happiness. To maximize your satisfaction with your relationships and with your life, you need to find out what you really want out of life and be willing to work at making it happen within the context of your family. After all, your family is a part of that vision—and it can provide the foundation of love and security you need to achieve the rest of your goals.

Accepting Yourself, with Love

The key to a strong relationship is for both partners to work together toward a common goal. That's best done if each of you is clear about your individual goals and can

Womanly Wisdom

The greatest satisfaction comes from the smallest things—sharing a few quiet moments with your partner, seeing the joy in your child's eyes when she learns something new. Attend to these, and you'll discover that your life is very rich.

communicate them to one another. Your task, then, is to discover your life's purpose. I'm not talking about anything big, like saving the world or earning millions of dollars. I'm talking about the day-to-day things that spell satisfaction—the things that make your life fulfilling and happy.

When you accept yourself with your limitations you will be able to accept your mate with his limitations. When you have acceptance of each other you can go about the business of enjoying your life together. You'll recognize the need to negotiate certain aspects of your life and delegate responsibilities in ways you perceive as fair, but you will stop trying to change one another to suit what you think you need in a partner and begin instead to enjoy each other for who you really are.

Laughter Is Truly the Best Medicine

The best way to redefine your relationship with your partner, when it comes to your romantic life and raising children together, is to always have a sense of humor. Your life will never be as you expect it to be—just when you're beginning to enjoy the perfect romantic evening, the baby will wake up and start crying or your toddler will decide she needs *another* drink of water. These little frustrations can seem huge at the time, but if you can laugh at the unexpected, you'll find it easier to keep them in their true perspective.

Momma Said There'd Be Days Like This

Recently I broke my heel bone and was laid up for months. I felt very sorry for myself and for all the plans that were now out the window, but when I stopped brooding I realized that there was a positive side to my injury. My children were overjoyed to have me available to color with them and just sit and talk. And because I needed their help, they learned a valuable lesson about sympathy for others. And they learned to do for themselves some things that they once expected me to do for them. My accident gave us all an opportunity to grow closer.

Savoring the Moments of Your Life

It isn't the amount of time you spend with your family, but how *present* you are when you are together. You can learn to be more present, in much the same way people learn to meditate. When you are with your children, try to separate from all the noise and the chatter and focus on just being with them.

And this is important in your relationship with your partner, as well. When you are together, especially when you are going to be intimate, savor every moment and be mentally and emotionally present. Turn off the television, light a candle if you want to, but mostly just concentrate on your love.

The relationship between you and your partner forms the foundation for your children's lives. If you are able to create a strong base for them, they will be able to go out into the world with confidence and love. So even if you are too pooped to pop, you need to make love, sex, and emotional intimacy a priority in your life. You can have beautifully folded laundry, great meals, and a spotless house but without intimacy in your relationship you'll find that all the rest is unfulfilling.

Life is to be enjoyed, and if you are fortunate enough to find love, treat it as the precious gift it truly is. Children are far more important than laundry and husbands are far more important than clean houses. So if, in all the competing demands for your attention, some things have to slide, let it be the housework, not the humans.

When you strengthen your relationship with your partner through love and compromise, you are not the only ones to benefit. Your children will be much better off as well, growing up in a home without conflict. So even when you are tired, remember to fan the flames of your love as often as you can. Make romance a priority, and your home will be a much happier place.

The Least You Need to Know

➤ Maintaining a rewarding sex life is important even when you are exhausted from other family-centered activities.

➤ If your relationship is strong and intimate, the entire family will be more secure.

➤ Compromise, cooperation, and compassion for one another will go a long way toward building a solid relationship between you and your partner.

➤ True satisfaction comes from appreciating the day-to-day joys of your family life.

Chapter 11

Intuitive Mothering

In This Chapter

➤ Learning to live without a mommy's operating manual

➤ Developing a parenting style that's right for you

➤ Discovering your intuitive self

Having a baby is such a blessing. You anticipate all the wonderful times you'll have cuddling and cooing over your little angel. You look forward to all the important milestones: first teeth, first steps, first day at school, first date. Why is it that with all the joy comes such intense emotional turmoil? Every mom seems to spend a lot of time with guilt and self-doubt. And it's hard to shake those feelings. You don't really dare talk to other women about your feelings, because you don't want anyone to know how stupid and incompetent you really feel.

This chapter will help you see that your feelings of uncertainty, of being overwhelmed, are perfectly normal. You are not alone. And it will show you that you have all the resources for being a good mother, just waiting for you to tap into them. All you need to do is learn to trust yourself.

The Natural Chaos of Motherhood

Most mothers feel incompetent and overwhelmed at least several times a day. How can we not? There is nothing about motherhood that is predictable—except how unpredictable it is. Your children will never behave exactly as you would like them to. Your partner will never manage to be the person you need him to be at all times. You can try to control what happens in your life but you can never make it work exactly as planned.

The Myth of the Perfect Mom

If you have bought into the prevailing myths of motherhood and domestic life, you are always going to be disappointed in yourself. We all have internalized images of hearth and home. But while some of us *are* able to create Martha Stewart memories, the rest of us have trouble working the microwave. Unfortunately, *all* of us tend to assume there is something wrong with us if we fall short of our image of the perfect woman. We never consider that there's more than one way to be a good mom and partner, and that there's no one standard we all have to live up to.

Mom Alert!

Don't confuse "want" with "need"—they're not at all the same thing. Of course you must place your children's needs ahead of your wishes, but when it's just a case of competing "wants," yours count as much as anybody else's.

We all have different constraints on our lives. Time is one big consideration, of course, when you have children and a job and no one to help with the housework or dinner preparation. But even if you really had all the time in the world, your own preferences and desires need to be considered as well. Do you really *want* to spend your time playing domestic goddess? If so, great! If not, well that's great too! The point is to make sure that you judge yourself according to your success in achieving your *own* goals, not according to how well you live up to someone else's.

Lost Without a Rule Book

The problem is that most of us were raised to think that we're selfish when we put our wants ahead of the wants of others. But that's likely to cause problems later on: It's only natural to feel angry about having to sacrifice our desires. And as often as not, we don't acknowledge that anger until it bubbles to the surface.

At the same time, we generally have only a vague notion of what we "should" be doing. None of us got a motherhood instruction manual: There are no actual checklists of what the perfect mother is supposed to do. All we really have is the nagging feeling that there is something we have forgotten to do.

It wasn't always this vague, however. Sometime around 1876, somebody got the bright idea to write a rule book for moms. It was called *The Complete Home*, and it outlines a woman's day from start to finish, including instructions for doing the fancywork of needlepoint.

Then, as now, women typically judged themselves not by what they felt was right, but rather by the chores they had to do—and how well they managed to do them. And this internal judgment is reinforced every time Mom-in-law sniffs dismissively at the dishes still in the sink from breakfast, or the PTO bake sale committee suggests that this year maybe you shouldn't consider contributing cookies—how about running the carpool instead. We are, all of us, convinced that we really *should* be all of the following:

➤ Smarter

➤ More domestically talented

➤ More patient

➤ More involved in our children's school

➤ Sexier for our partners

➤ More *everything*

But the only real "should" that makes any sense at all is that you should be true to yourself and recognize that you're doing the best you can.

Banishing the "Shoulds"

We all have responsibilities we need to take care of in order to function in this world. But most of us impose far more of a burden on ourselves than we expect from others. And we go on to judge ourselves as of little worth when we fail to live up to all the "shoulds" we take on. We guarantee ourselves a permanent condition of guilt and resentment, because we're always falling short of the impossible standards we, and others, set for ourselves.

Momma Said There'd Be Days Like This

One woman I know was trying to juggle a demanding career and raise her daughter. She planned on going the whole superwoman route—she was going to be so organized that neither her career nor her family relationships would ever suffer. She thought she was managing it all, until reality struck. One evening as she was dealing with some paperwork, her little daughter sat down nearby and started scribbling on some paper. "What are you doing," asked my friend. Her daughter looked up at her with a grin and replied, "I am working now. Go play quietly someplace else!"

Developing a Realistic Mom Agenda

You have to work on banishing the "shoulds." The first step is to recognize that you have a right to a life. What you need is to work out a schedule that not only covers your basic responsibilities but also leaves you some time for yourself.

Mothers are notorious for refusing to cut themselves any slack: If you're with your children, you feel guilty because you think you should be working; if you're working,

Womanly Wisdom

Only you and your partner really know the obligations you face each day—so only you can really know the best way to fulfill them. Trust your own sense of the right way to handle things, and feel free to ignore well-meaning advice if you find it inappropriate.

you feel bad because you're sure you should be with your children. But you can't be everywhere at once. Give yourself a break. Make your decisions about how to allocate your time according to your own perception of what's most important—then stick with it.

Working Out Your Own System of Values

It's not enough to sort out your schedule. You also have to make decisions about how you want to raise your children. For example, you'll soon discover that everyone has an opinion about discipline, and they're all willing to share it with you at the least opportune times.

Here's a case in point: If your child is unruly in public, total strangers will feel perfectly comfortable about piping up with their suggestions for handling the situation. At the very least, they won't be shy about expressing their disapproval with the way *you* are handling it. Objectively, you can say to yourself that you don't care what strangers say about you and your child. But, of course, you *do* care. You'll feel hurt and incompetent and embarrassed by the whole scene.

At times like these, you may sometimes wish you had a handbook of rules for coping. But those days are long past. The old rule books don't apply, so you're left with the task of coming up with your own mothering style. This can be scary—it makes us feel vulnerable to the criticism of others because we can't claim some objective authority to justify our choices. And we're never 100 percent sure that what we are doing is right.

But the lack of a standard rule book can be liberating, too. It means we're free to find better, more constructive ways to handle the problems of parenting in today's world.

A Rude Awakening

Children today are living in an entirely different world than the one we grew up in. They have the benefit of technological breakthroughs and access to information that we never even dreamed of. But they are also exposed to far more pressure and questionable influences than we ever were—from TV and movies to violent video games.

As the pressures children face have changed, parents have had to change as well. This generation of parents tends to be far more open than our parents' or grandparents' generations to including their children as active participants in family life. Children are no longer expected to be seen and not heard.

A Delicate Balancing Act

Parents today are trying to strike a workable balance between two seemingly opposite goals: They are trying to foster creative self-expression while maintaining a reasonable degree of authority. We can't go back to the days of "Father Knows Best." Instead, we're forced to adjust to the fact that our children are far more sophisticated in certain ways than we were at their age. And we have to accept the consequences of our decisions to encourage their development of self-confidence and individuality.

R-E-S-P-E-C-T, Oh What That Word Means to Me

The first step in achieving a good balance in your childrearing ways is to recognize the importance of the concept of respect. That single word provides the key to encouraging your child's self-expression without losing your parental authority. You need to convey to your children that what you think and feel matters.

Leading an Exemplary Life

The only way to effectively teach your child to respect you and others is to lead by example. You and your partner, for instance, need to show respect for one another's feelings and opinions. And you need to extend that same respect to your child—children are like little lie detectors and can spot hypocrisy a mile away.

Finding Your Parenting Style

Although there is no standard set of rules for us to work with as parents, there are lots of wonderful books that provide concrete tips on everything from managing your home to raising your child. In the end, however, you can't raise a child by the book.

You're going to have to work out a style of your very own, building it up from everything you've experienced and observed throughout your own life. You need to have the confidence to listen to your own heart when it comes to raising your children. This can be hard to do—it means risking criticism when your choices differ from what others think you should do. But it's the approach that is most likely to be successful, because it involves being true to yourself and your values. Tap into your own experiences as a child—remembering not just how your mom handled situations but how you, as a child, felt at the time.

Discipline or Punishment?

One of the central issues in childrearing today is how to instill discipline. It used to be easy: Mom

Mom Alert!

"Children should be seen and not heard" was, and is, a stifling way to raise a child. If your child has no opportunity for self-expression at home, he will find it difficult to form and defend opinions of his own in the outside world.

Womanly Wisdom

As your child becomes proficient in language, you'll find that it's easier to get her to follow your rules if you take the time to explain, in simple terms, why they're for her own good. Children want respect, too, and by explaining your rules you are showing her the kind of respect you want her to learn to give to you.

said, "Go get the stick" or Dad decided it was time to take a trip out behind the barn with a switch. There wasn't a behavioral problem around that parents couldn't solve with a few well-placed wallops.

Those days are gone. We now understand that when you strike a child you only create fear and humiliation. When you use pain and fear to break the spirit of a child, you give up any chance of earning the respect you think you deserve. What you gain in its place is a very angry child who has learned not to trust the people he loves the most.

When You Have to Say "No"

We need to find alternative ways to maintain appropriate boundaries for our children's behavior. Without these boundaries, children can be amazingly disrespectful and tyrannical. To set limits you must learn how to use the power of a well-timed "no."

A "no" can be hard to enforce. If your child is a glib talker, he's probably got a million arguments why your every "no" should turn into a "yes." And it can be exhausting to hold fast in the face of a child's concerted efforts to change your mind. But stick to your guns! Each time you reverse a "no" you chip away at your credibility.

Momma Said There'd Be Days Like This

When my daughter was little I found it hard to enforce rules. By her preteen years she'd become impossible to control. We could have gone on forever like that, but one day I had a real breakthrough. Just before a planned family trip to Disney World, she misbehaved badly. I told her she couldn't come on the trip if she didn't change her behavior. She didn't believe I'd go through with the punishment—and I must admit, it was hard. But I held firm. We went, and she stayed home. I thought she would hate me forever, but our relationship took a turn for the better from that day forward.

It's Intuitive, Not Permissive

Intuitive mothering doesn't mean that you set no rules for your child. After all, children need limits to feel that life is not hurtling out of control. Intuitive mothering just means that you must develop and apply the rules of your household according to your own internal sense of what is right and wrong. You still need to learn to set limits and stick with them.

Different Strokes for Different Folks

Parenting styles are very personal—what works for you may not be your neighbor's cup of tea. Some mothers think it's important to include their children in most aspects of their adult lives. They bring the children to adult gatherings, to restaurants, and so forth. This style has some very positive points. The child learns how to relate to adults, and the adults get to enjoy the best of both worlds: an active social life that doesn't require them to spend time away from their children.

Other parents may choose to reserve some of their social time for themselves, without children around. This, too, is a valid option. It has the benefit of allowing parents some private time to recharge their batteries after a hectic week of child-centered living, and gives them a chance to reconnect in their relationship.

Whichever style suits you, it's important to give your child the sense that she is valued by adults, and not someone who can simply be banished from the main action. So even if you choose to reserve some of your social life as for adults only, it's a good idea to include your children periodically in some of your gatherings. That way they'll learn how to interact with grown-ups, and will feel more plugged into *your* life. In addition, they'll learn an important lesson in diversity.

It Takes a Village...

The absence of a standard set of child-raising rules for all of us to consult is only one of the reasons that bringing up children today seems more difficult than it was for our parents' generation. Another, and equally problematic, trend has been the break-up of the extended family. The little nuclear group of Mom, Dad, and the children often lives far from the aunts and uncles, grandmas and grandpas who once were part of the neighborhood.

It's not hard to find playmates for your school-age child, but it *is* often difficult to expose her to a diverse range of people—diverse in age, interests, backgrounds, and styles. This exposure can be crucial: Children who learn to appreciate what is good in different types of people learn also to appreciate what's unique in themselves.

Mom Alert!

To develop adequate social skills, your child really needs to participate in the give-and-take of relationships with children her own age. If you live in an area where few children live nearby, make an effort to hook up with a play group, or take regular trips to a local park where she'll have a chance to interact with other kids.

Defining Your Parenting Goals

As this chapter has stressed all along, you need to develop your own parenting style, one that suits your personality, interests, and values. But it's equally important that you develop a firm understanding of your parenting *goals*. Earlier generations of parents focused on obedience, sometimes to the exclusion of all else. A good child was a quiet, well-behaved one.

Today, we generally set our goals a little higher. Sure, none of us want our children to terrorize everyone and run wild. But we don't want their good behavior to come at the expense of their creativity and enthusiasm. We believe that childhood is a time for a child to *be* a child—that it's unnatural to try to make them conform completely to adult standards of behavior.

Womanly Wisdom

If children are valued they will learn to value others. Set limits, stick to them, but make all decisions with love.

Combining these two desires—for reasonably well-behaved children who also feel free to express their individuality—can be difficult. And it sometimes requires effort on your part to pull it off. For example, you need to recognize that certain places are not necessarily appropriate for children. Children do, after all, get bored—and when they're bored they're likely to act up and make noise. This is understandably unwelcome at the opera, or in a romantic restaurant. On the other hand, the only way children can learn to interact with the world outside the family is through immersion in it. They should be welcome in such reasonable venues as family restaurants, grocery stores, and similar places.

Fine-Tune Your Intuition

Now that you've determined your mothering style and goals, it's time to take a close look at the most important tool you can develop as you work out your own approach to mothering. Intuition will be your greatest ally in this brave new parenting world where there are no rule books.

But what, exactly, *is* intuition? It's a type of knowing that goes beyond the objective facts and taps into all your deepest feelings, memories, and values. Intuition is *not* some kind of paranormal activity or oogly-boogly phenomenon. Rather, it's as natural as breathing, if you take the time to develop it.

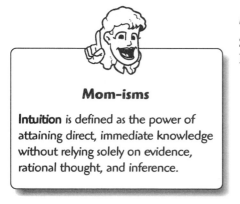

Mom-isms

Intuition is defined as the power of attaining direct, immediate knowledge without relying solely on evidence, rational thought, and inference.

Recognizing Your Intuitive Gifts

So, how do you recognize an intuitive feeling when you have one? Here are a few examples of intuitive moments:

➤ It's that nagging feeling you get in your gut when you know something is not quite right but you don't yet know what it is.

➤ It's feeling the hair rising on the back of your neck, telling you you're in some kind of danger.

➤ It's the feeling that your child is ill or hurt even though you're not with him at the time.

138

➤ It's knowing that something's bothering your child, even though he says nothing is wrong.

➤ It's that instant reading you get from a stranger—that she's a good person or perhaps someone you really need to avoid.

Coincidence? I Think Not

We've all had our intuitive moments, and sometimes we act on them. For example, you meet someone at the PTO and right away you feel a bonding of the spirit—and after you actually get a chance to talk to her, you become best friends. Or you get that funny feeling in the pit of your stomach that something's not right with your child, and then the phone rings and the school nurse tells you that your daughter's got the flu and needs to come home.

We often write off such experiences as coincidence, but that's not a very satisfying explanation. They happen too often to ignore them.

Developing the Intuitive Faculty

We may not fully understand how intuition works, but we can't pretend it doesn't exist. Maybe it's just that we're tuning in to body language, or memories, or some higher ability of our brain. Whatever it comes from, intuition *is* a skill that we can develop, tune, and improve.

Momma Said There'd Be Days Like This

Some people believe in guardian angels. It is not a scientific explanation, but I like the idea of ethereal beings from another dimension whispering important information into my ears. I look at this life as one big classroom in which our goal is to learn what we can about ourselves. It is like a process of perfecting the soul through trial and error. I like to think that spiritual beings are there to help us in our struggles to understand this world, to lovingly give us a nudge in the right direction when we need it.

Wherever the intuitive ability comes from, you might want to try to develop your own. Here are the three basic steps you need to practice:

1. Open yourself up to your own spiritual center or inner voice.
2. Actively attend to what that inner voice is telling you.

3. Act on your instincts, as they are guided by that inner voice—and try not to fit some preconceived interpretation.

Do not try to come up with answers. Ask the questions, let them go, and wait for answers to come to you. It is important to learn the distinction between what is just your mind and what is really your intuition. Intuition is a very natural process, and one that you can train yourself to recognize and employ. I also believe we can ask for help from the spiritual realm.

The stereotypical understanding of intuition is that it's a skill that is specific to women. Why might that be? Maybe we have such direct experiences with intuition because we tend to be more in touch with our nurturing side. The ability to love is what really creates the connection of one soul to another.

Although men can be great parents, only women can fulfill the spiritual aspects of being a mother. This is our millennium. Women, especially mothers, are coming into our own. We are starting to realize our importance in the scheme of things. We now realize that we can do many things with our lives, but that being a mother is perhaps our greatest opportunity to influence the world. As mothers, we pass on a legacy of love and support.

And our intuition is perhaps our greatest tool. There is no precedent for the situations we may be facing in the next 20 years. Everything changes as fast as the newest microprocessor. While the world around us is becoming more high-tech, sometimes all we have to rely on to set a course for ourselves and our families is our intuitive sense.

The Least You Need to Know

➤ The old rules that guided your parents' generation no longer apply in today's world of childrearing.

➤ Each of us must develop our own parenting style—one that suits our personalities, interests, needs, and desires.

➤ To help your child develop the skills she needs to relate to others, give her the opportunity to interact with people of diverse ages, opinions, and backgrounds.

➤ When working out your personal mothering style, your greatest tool will be a finely tuned intuition.

Part 4
You, Your Kids, and Your Changing Relationship

You've made it all the way to what may be the most difficult—and simultaneously the most rewarding—years in your career as a mother: You've made it to the teen years. From just before puberty until he heads off to college, your child will lead you a merry chase as he challenges your rules, your humor, and even your sanity.

Strap on your seat belt—your baby's growing up, and he's going to take you on an emotional roller coaster ride unlike any you've ever ridden (since your own teen years!).

Chapter 12

Communications 101: Talking About the Tough Stuff

In This Chapter

➤ Ethics 101: Teaching your child right from wrong

➤ Getting in touch with your own value system

➤ Talking to your children about sex

➤ Talking to your children about drugs

Being a mother is a daunting responsibility. You are the single most important influence in your child's life, with the exception of everything else he experiences along the way. The difference is that children look to their mothers for the subtle cues of how to behave. (Not-so-subtle cues on the rear end also tend to have a great impact.) In this chapter you'll learn about the way you, as Mom, provide those cues—and you'll also explore how your own maturity and responsibility can and will undergo transformation as you assume the role of guide and mentor to your child.

Reining in the Wild Child

When children are very young, the role of teacher can be *most* frustrating. Getting a child to sit still long enough for a reasoned lecture or lesson is almost impossible—especially when the child is only newly acquainted with language and the subject of the lesson involves the word "no"! Spanking gets your child's attention—but only for about two seconds. Your earliest task as a parent is to decide upon, and enforce, the limits your child needs in order to live well and safely.

The Necessity of Limits

The roles of mother and child can be compared to those of teacher and disciple. Your job as a mom is to guide your child toward finding a true sense of self. You create a secure sense of structure for your child by educating him or her about your own beliefs and values, but it is a wise parent who also teaches children to think on their own. This has to be done in stages, of course. You do not want an overly empowered little tyrant running your household.

And that, of course, is the challenge facing any parent, and especially moms: You want to maintain authority in your home while giving your child the knowledge and self-confidence to ultimately make wise decisions on his or her own behalf.

Teaching Right from Wrong

One of the things we are entrusted to teach our children is the difference between right and wrong. Some people believe a strong religious foundation will do this for you. For many people religion is the key to moral education. In addition to whatever structure you may provide through religion, I believe you teach right from wrong through example.

A Couple of Cautionary Tales

A generation ago, parents relied on physical punishment to maintain discipline in their children. Today we understand that this approach is not particularly effective. It doesn't provide the child with any understanding of *why* his behavior is wrong—all it teaches him is not to get caught. And it can seriously backfire. My mom learned both these lessons the hard way.

My brother was a terrible hellion when we were little—a fact I used to my own nefarious advantage lots of times. It was easy for me to make sure my brother got the blame, since he was the one with the bad reputation. For example, when we'd go for a drive with my mom, my brother and I would sit in the back seat. A favorite amusement of mine was to give him a good smack and then scream, "Larry, stop hitting me." Of course, my mother immediately assumed I was the innocent party, so she'd reach back to swat in Larry's general direction to make him stop hitting *me*.

One day, my mom took my brother and me to visit my Grandmother. There was never much kid stuff to do at Grandma's so we would spend a lot of time torturing each other. When our misbehavior finally got to be too much, Mom lost her patience and told my brother in no uncertain terms to behave himself. He answered back and ran off—something that simply wasn't tolerated in

Womanly Wisdom

There's a difference between giving your child freedom and allowing irresponsible license. The first encourages creativity and self-expression; the second can turn your child into a real little terror.

those days. So Mom had to chase him, because disrespect could not go unpunished. Unfortunately, when she swatted at his retreating hind end, she missed her mark and slammed her hand into a plaster wall, breaking one of her fingers. Definitely not the outcome she was going for.

It is good that the emphasis has shifted away from raising children to fear their parents. As a discipline tool, corporal punishment was most effective in ensuring the need for psychotherapists as children grew up trying to reconcile love and rejection. And by inflicting physical pain we undo all our efforts to teach our children self-control and confidence. Physical punishment breaks the spirit or sets the stage for rebellion later on.

Mom Alert!

Sometimes even the most anti-spanking mom is tempted to administer a little seat-of-the-pants justice. But it can be dangerous, especially for toddlers. It's too easy to miss your mark (the diaper-padded bottom), and even a seemingly light spank that lands in the wrong place can cause injury to your little one's kidneys.

How's Your Example?

Because punishment is such an ineffective and inefficient teaching tool, you want to develop something better suited to accomplishing your child-rearing goals. Teaching by example is a far more effective approach. But it's not easy: You have to put your own behavior under close scrutiny to make certain that you're setting the proper example for your child. Here's why:

➤ It is very difficult to teach a child not to be prejudiced if you make derogatory comments about all types of people who are different from you.

➤ It is difficult to teach a child not to be a snob if you talk about other people as being inferior.

➤ It is difficult to teach children to tell the truth if you show them how easy it is to tell so-called "white lies," like the time you said you didn't want to go to your aunt's because you had the Tasmanian flu.

Children are like little scientists—and you're the principle specimen under their microscope. They will model their conduct after yours in many significant ways. They are very impressionable, and they will accept the reality they are shown until they are old enough to form judgments of their own.

If you want your child to reflect your ethical standards, then look at yourself to see whether you are setting a good example. This does not mean that you need to be perfect, it just means that you need to be a responsible adult who lives the kind of life you expect your child to live. Children are highly sensitive to hypocrisy—they'll spot it immediately if you say one thing and do another.

Having the "Big Talks" with Your Child

When your kids are small, your disciplinary problems will be of the garden-variety type: Teaching them to show respect for others, helping them learn the value of cooperation, encouraging them to do their schoolwork on time. As they get older, however, the moral and ethical choices they face become more complex, and more difficult for you, as a mom, to handle. The two most daunting areas of concern are sex and drugs.

But if you haven't built up a regular habit of talking openly to your children, you're going to run into trouble when it's time to have the big Sex Talk or Drug Talk and have it taken seriously. You need to talk to your children as much as possible about the trivial, the mundane, the weather—whatever is currently on their minds. Your communication with your child needs to be nurtured all the time.

And that nurturing will pay off in major dividends when you find it necessary to deal with the big issues. If you can consciously listen to them enough of the time so you know what is on their minds and so they feel connected to you, you're teaching them that when they really need you they can come and talk to you.

Keeping the lines of communication open doesn't need to be difficult. All it takes is a willingness to be receptive to their interests. They've almost always got something to share.

Momma Said There'd Be Days Like This

I had helped my daughter with a report on global warming for her science class. That afternoon her younger brother pulled me aside and said, "Mom, I need to have a private conversation with you." I had no idea what to expect. He then said, "I want you to tell me all about global warming. Winter is my favorite season and I don't want it to go away." It cracked me up that he was spending so much time thinking about the subject, and I had a great conversation with him.

The "Birds and the Bees" Discussion, Modern Style

Talking about sex to children used to be even more embarrassing than it is today, so it was put off as long as possible. But that secrecy often caused needless confusion and worry. It certainly did for me.

When I was about nine, I saw a sanitary napkin in my mother's bathroom and asked her about it. She blushed and told me she would tell me when I was 10 years old. It seems that Mom was saving up a lot of things to tell me when I turned 10: That was her standard answer whenever I asked a certain kind of awkward question. I even wrote a poem at the time about all the secrets I would learn at that magic age.

Well I fooled her. Shortly after our nondiscussion about that napkin, I was at a girlfriend's house and didn't feel so well. I went to the bathroom and there was blood on my underpants. I panicked and thought that somehow I had cut myself and must be dying.

When I got home I kept it a secret as long as I could, but finally I got scared enough to tell my mother that I needed to go to the hospital. She started to cry and hugged me (well, she smacked me first because of some crazy cultural thing from her Russian heritage—I never did figure out what *that* was all about). Needless to say I was confused. She got out this little pink book put out by Modess and read it with me. It explained about the menstrual cycle and all the things that were now happening to my body. Then she took me to the pharmacy to buy my own napkins and even got me some perfume so I could feel like a real woman.

Womanly Wisdom

Schedule a talk with your daughter about menstruation well before she hits puberty. The age that girls start their periods has been trending younger and younger, and you want her to be informed *before* she actually begins menstruating.

Sex and the Modern Child

My mom could maintain her delicacy about the topic of sex because it was easier then to insulate children from sexual knowledge. The movies, TV, and advertisements were far less explicit than they are today. If you wait as long as my mom did before talking about sex to your children, you may find that they already know more about the subject than you do. But they'll know about sex without understanding your own values on the subject. So it's best to talk openly about it early on. The sex talk then can be seen as a series of minilectures, each one progressively more detailed. Here's the general sequence of events:

Momma Said There'd Be Days Like This

One woman really took her responsibility to treat the sex talk seriously. She was ready when her daughter got around to asking the dreaded question, "Where did I come from?" She'd even put together a cute little poster with illustrations of happy little bowtie-wearing sperm and eggs with pink ribbons. After she presented her masterful speech on the subject she asked if her daughter had any further questions. "Yes, Mom," said the long-suffering little five year old. "Susie next door comes from Montana—where did *I* come from?"

➤ Your child will begin showing signs of curiosity as early as age five, when the customary question seems to be "Where do babies come from?" Most of us don't find this too difficult—at this age children are happy with a wonderful explanation of eggs and seeds.

Mom Alert!

If you have strong views about the way the discussion of sex should be presented to your child, do make a point of watching any sex-ed videos alone first—that way you'll know just what your child is getting into. And, of course, sit with your child while the video is running, so you can clarify anything that seems to be confusing.

➤ When your child is a little older he or she will probably ask for more details. That's when you can give a fairly simple explanation of how the mommy and daddy make a baby, and it's a good time to introduce a daughter to the concept of menstruation. You're probably best off keeping it simple at this time—she's probably not ready to be anything but grossed out by the idea of blood.

➤ When you're expecting a new baby, don't be surprised if your child shows another flurry of interest in the subject of sex. Since more details are probably required, you might be most comfortable renting an animated video that explains sex at a level a child can understand. These videos can be very useful, particularly if you're not sure how to raise the issue or need a little help getting over your own embarrassment about the topic.

Dealing with Your Own Hang-ups About Sex

Talking about sex is not easy because we all have our own issues with it. But no matter how uncomfortable you may be about having these sex talks, you want your children to know about it in the context of your own beliefs and values. Children today are constantly exposed to words and images about sex, from the advertisements on TV to sexually explicit music lyrics. It is confusing for them and frustrating for parents who are trying to instill a healthy attitude about the subject. And, adding urgency to our need to have these talks, today we face the fear that what they don't know can harm and even kill them.

Setting the Tone

When you talk to your children about sex, it's best to keep the conversation matter-of-fact. It's never a good idea to try to make it sound like something dirty or horrible: This will not prevent them from experimenting, it'll only to make them need therapy later in life.

Sexual curiosity is natural as early as in the womb. But if your child is made to think that the desires he feels after puberty and into adolescence are inherently bad, he can become very confused and begin to condemn himself for having them. By giving your child the best information and by opening the communication early, you will provide an atmosphere in which your child is more likely to make wise and appropriate decisions.

Mind Your Audience

When you talk about sex, make certain that the information you're giving is appropriate to the age of your child. Younger children are mostly curious about the mechanics of the act—although it's appropriate to stress the importance of love and commitment as an integral part of sex. When you're talking to a child who's approaching puberty, you want to make the linkage between feelings and responsibility more explicit: Reinforce that the feelings are very real but make it clear that acting on them has certain real consequences.

Womanly Wisdom

Open your discussions of sex early in your child's life: Don't wait until he's already got more information than you do about the subject. In this generation, that means you should probably get started by the time your child is age five.

The Dangers of Delaying the Discussion

No matter how uncomfortable you may be with talking about sex, by the time your child hits the preteen years you'd better have at least *begun* dealing with the subject. By that time your child will certainly be learning about it from other children, from the media, and even (very possibly) from the Internet. These sources may be presenting sexual information from very distorted perspectives, and you want your own values clearly on the record so your child develops a healthy attitude about his or her own sexuality.

As with anything else you want to teach your child, it's up to you to set the parameters. This subject is too important, and the consequences of ignorance too serious, to simply hope your child can learn what he or she needs to know from school or from peers. There are fewer societal structures than ever before. While greater tolerance for people's choices is a good thing, the lack of clear rules gives your child many more choices than you could have imagined. Preteens and teenagers are getting pregnant and are contracting sexually transmitted diseases in record numbers.

Promise to Be There for Them, No Matter What

You are not going to be able to inoculate your children against bad or early sexual experiences as you were able to inoculate them against the mumps. But open communication on the subject is your best defense against your child's making the wrong choices. Talk to your children and make it easy for them to talk to you—they're going to need to know they can turn to you for help.

One of the best days of my life was the day my teenage daughter sat next to me and started to cry. She told me that a 13-year-old girl at a neighboring school had gotten

Mom Alert!

Avoid using a judgmental tone when you're talking with your child about sex—it may send her the message of rejection that will keep her from turning to you if she really needs your help.

pregnant. She said she couldn't understand how such a young girl could be so stupid as to start messing around with sex. It really shook her up. I was sorry that she was so upset but I felt thrilled that she felt comfortable telling me something so personal, and that some of the things I had told her over the years had truly reached her.

When you discuss this, and every other important issue, with your child, extend your respect for his thoughts and opinions. If you really listen to your child you will know what is on his mind and he will feel free to tell you when he is in trouble. If your child feels backed into a corner by your accusations, he'll never feel comfortable turning to you for answers when he's likely to need you the most.

Talking to Your Children About Drugs

The other "big talk" that parents frequently find difficult is the talk about drugs. Unlike the topic of sex, there's really no need to modulate your message about drugs to suit your child's age—there is nothing wrong with mentioning from day one how bad such things are for a person's health.

I might have gone a little overboard with my oldest daughter. I used to preach the evils of cigarette smoking so much that when she was barely old enough to talk she would walk up to complete strangers and chastise them. She accused them of using drugs because somewhere in our conversations I told her about nicotine.

Did You Inhale?

One of the biggest difficulties mothers have in talking to their children about drugs is guilt. If you were alive in the late 1960s through the 80s it's highly likely that you did some experimentation of your own. How can you tell your child to not do something that you yourself have done?

Womanly Wisdom

Be aware of what your own current use of nicotine or alcohol may look like to your child. If you condemn teenage drinking but indulge in a few martinis after work, your child will spot the inconsistency right away. It's wise to practice what you preach.

There are a couple of schools of thought on that question. Some say: It's easy! Lie about it. The 1960s, 1970s, and 1980s were a crazy period in the history of American society, and now that you're older you're absolved of all the stupid things you may have done back then.

On the other hand, some say that their experience taught them first-hand that experimentation with drugs can be devastating. This school of thought says that your experiences give you credibility when you speak about the dangers of drugs with your child.

In either case, what you don't want to do is glamorize or romanticize drug use. Talking about all the fun you had partying in your misspent youth is definitely not a good idea. You know that your experiments were dangerous—and you no doubt know some people who weren't lucky enough to come through the experimentation unscathed. If you choose to talk about experimenting with drugs when you were younger, *those* are the stories to relate. Above all, don't be ambiguous in your message: Your children will have enough temptation without having an indirect sanction from your former, less mature self.

Whatever your personal feelings about drug use among adults, your adolescent or preteen child is simply not equipped to handle the serious problems associated with drug use. And substance abuse impairs a young adult's physical, emotional, educational, and social development. Life is difficult enough at this age without adding drugs to the mix.

Don't Be an Ostrich

You may want to believe that your child is safe from experimenting with drugs. You live in a good neighborhood and your child goes to a good school, so you may try to convince yourself that everything's cool. But drug and alcohol use is rampant in all our schools. It is important to talk openly with your children as early as possible, without being overly preachy. You want to convey a sense of trust that they will make the right decisions when they are not under your roof.

Making It Easier for Your Child to "Just Say No"

The best thing you can do to protect your child is to help him develop a good self-image. Praise your child for the good things he does and make sure he feels part of something special. A family offers a safe haven for children during the difficult teen and young adult years when drug and alcohol abuse is most likely to occur.

Teenagers are painfully aware that they have little status. They want freedom but can't really do anything about it. It is very enticing to avoid these uncomfortable feelings by numbing them with drugs or alcohol. And teenagers sometimes think that trying alcohol, nicotine, or other drugs is a way of showing that they're grown up. In addition, teenagers tend to believe they're invincible—which is likely to make them minimize the dangers that drugs present.

Opening the Discussion

Talking about drugs with your children is not easy. If you come across as too cool about it, you'll raise questions about your own drug use, and you'll have

Mom Alert!

Watch out if your child starts to show major changes in attitude and disposition. It may just be the preteen blues, but if your child becomes moody and secretive, and schoolwork starts to suffer, you'll want to investigate the possibility of drugs or alcohol in his life.

to find a way to deal with them. If you come across as too naive about the subject, you are going to have problems with credibility: Your child may well wonder what you could possibly know about it, if you've never had a drink or seen a drug other than aspirin in your life.

The best thing you can do is just be a mom. Speak openly about your concerns. If you can find a book about drugs and your child will cooperate, look at it together. If your child complains that he already knows everything there is to know, tell him you need to have this discussion for *your* peace of mind.

Womanly Wisdom

Talk to your children about everyday stuff and really try to listen. Then when you talk about important things you are more likely to have an impact. Otherwise, you won't be taken seriously.

What you *don't* want to do is repeat the mistakes of previous generations: You want to avoid the excess of that classic 1930s antidrug movie *Reefer Madness*, for example. Teens are too sophisticated today to fall for that movie's contrived plot about young people becoming possessed and insane by the effects of marijuana.

Children do not need condescension. They need support, trust, and reliable information. Talking about drugs with your children is a difficult task because you will feel as though what you say is going to be the deciding factor in the choices your child makes out in the world. There are so many factors that enter into one child's experimenting with drugs while another child wouldn't even consider it.

The Least You Need to Know

➤ Effective communication starts with the little things—if you keep yourself available for conversation with your child, you're laying the groundwork for the big-issue talks that will come up later.

➤ Teaching your child right from wrong is better done by example than by punishment.

➤ Your child's curiosity about sex is likely to start young—take advantage of her interest by answering her questions with a level of detail appropriate to her age.

➤ No matter where you live, the problem of drug use among children is widespread—make sure you communicate your concerns and your values to your child before the problem strikes your home.

Chapter 13

Becoming a Dork: Your Preteen and You

You've settled into your children's routine. You have the carpools worked out. You know what is expected of you. You get along well with your kids. Your children come home from school and are glad to see you. They hug you and eagerly tell you about their day, their friends, and their activities. You feel pretty confident about being a mother, now.

Well, don't get too complacent. In this chapter you'll learn that some things are just too good to last.

Bursting Mommy's Bubble

It happens when you least expect it. Boom! Everything changes. One day your little girl looks at you as though you are the embodiment of a goddess, and the next day she tells you your haircut makes you look like a geezer. You'll get no warning, but one day your happy, tender mother-daughter talks will start sounding like this:

> **Appalled Daughter:** "Mom, you are not going to wear that outfit out of the house are you?"
>
> **Bewildered Mom:** "What is wrong with this outfit?"
>
> **Appalled Daughter:** "You look like a grandma."

Or if you happen to be shopping with your 10- to 12-year-old, your conversation might sound like this:

Helpful Mom: "Look at this great outfit, honey. It would look so nice on you."

Aghast Child: "Mom, (the eyes rolling) do you want me to look like a *dork*?"

Helpful Mom: "What's wrong with this outfit?"

Aghast Child: "*You* wear it if you like it so much. Don't you know anything about what's in?"

Mommies Should Be Seen and Not Heard

When children hit the double digits something transformational happens to them. And the first place it affects is their mouths. Kids at this age become all attitude. Everything they say is followed with the disclaimer "whatever," and they have a whole repertoire of comments to indicate that they have now become far too cool to have a mother telling them what to do.

When you are out in public with your preteen, don't even *think* about showing any outward signs of affection. Unless there's absolutely *no* possibility of being seen by anyone close to your child's age, do not try to hug her, do not pat her on the shoulder—in fact, it's probably best not to even acknowledge that you actually know who she is.

Momma Said There'd Be Days Like This

I knew times had changed when, while shopping at the mall, my 11-year-old daughter asked to look around without me. I figured she was getting old enough for some controlled independence, so I said OK. Before I let her go I gave her the safety lecture on mall etiquette. I furrowed my brow, looked her in the eyes, and warned her about some gangs that might hang out there. Without blinking an eye she replied, "Don't worry, Mom. I am my own gang."

The Times, They Are A-Changin'

Today's children have a very different experience in middle school than most of us parents can imagine. The good news is they exhibit a confidence and streetwise attitude that is far beyond what most of us had developed by that age. The 10- to 13-year-olds of today seem much older than we did when we were that age. This means that what used to be called a generation gap is now more like the Grand Canyon. As mothers, we are breaking new ground—dealing with problems that our own parents never even dreamed of—but we often feel less adequate than our mothers did when we became prepubescent.

We don't have the hard-and-fast rules anymore: Very few of us have trained our children to obey us blindly. Oh, how we lament this choice at times, but we know it is a much better thing to have thinking children than clueless ones, as many of us felt *we* were expected to be at that age.

Forging a New Mother-Child Relationship

Children don't necessarily become instant delinquents the minute they hit 12 years of age—although sometimes it certainly *seems* that way. Their changing behavior can be disconcerting—and even unpleasant at times.

Baby Just Needs a New Pair of Shoes

Don't immediately assume that this new behavior is *bad*. Part of the problem is *ours*. It's difficult adjusting to the fact that you have a child one week and a preteen the next. It happens almost that fast.

Remember when your kids had a growth spurt and suddenly the shoes that fit last week became way too small? If you forced them to wear the old shoes, their feet would hurt and maybe even get damaged. Far better to let them wear new shoes that fit, right? Think of the preteen years as another kind of growth spurt. Let your kids try on behaviors that suit their new, more grown-up selves.

Transitions to Teen Time

The preteen period is a very interesting time in a child's development. And it can be very funny (but don't ever let your child even imagine that you're laughing—preteens are notoriously unwilling to laugh at themselves). Imagine it: There's your preteen acting totally cool in front of his peers, and then in the privacy of his room, he'll pull out his toys and play with him as he always has.

The preteen time is a transitional one, during which your child is trying on a lot of different behaviors. He may start talking about girls but have no interest in them at all. His hormones haven't kicked in yet, so all this new talk of girls is strictly to impress his friends. In fact, he may be feeling a bit nervous because he doesn't really see what all of the excitement is about.

Womanly Wisdom

A lot of preteens find it really convenient to have younger brothers and sisters in the family. They can always use them as an excuse for fooling around with kid toys and games. This is especially handy around Halloween.

Preteen girls are curious about sex, but mostly they're prone to crushes. Even with all the messages about sex that children are exposed to, we still expect the preteen years to remain innocent. Unfortunately, many kids are becoming sexually active in the preteen years when, developmentally, they have no concept of what a relationship is or what the consequences of their actions might be.

Momma Said There'd Be Days Like This

When I was a preteen we started to have boy-girl parties with friends from our youth group. At one of those parties, I remember a boy saying he'd found some of his dad's *Playboy* magazines. He said, "If he has a wife, why would he want to look at pictures of naked women?" His innocence is typical of preteen boys who haven't been overexposed to sex. And even though the media seems to pull kids into sexual situations long before they are ready, it's best to try to help them stay innocent a while longer.

Sex and the Preteen's Mom

Sex has always been an issue that moms worry about, but it seems to be getting harder to cope with. Part of the reason for that difficulty is that we're just so much more aware—there are sexually explicit movies and magazines, sexual innuendo in many commercials, and sexually explicit songs on Pop radio. And the results of teen (and preteen) sexual experimentation are harder to ignore—the old days of discretely sending little Susie or Janie off to "visit relatives" if she got pregnant are long gone.

Womanly Wisdom

If you have more than one child, try taking your preteen off for an overnight at a local lodge or hotel every once in a while. It's the kind of grown-up thing that appeals to a preteen, and it will give you private time together for talking and for bonding during this difficult age.

When our children become preteens, sex suddenly becomes a worry—it's probably the first time you really start thinking about it, and it's certainly time for that "special talk" if you haven't already had it. Chapter 12 gives you more guidance on the subject of talking about sex with your children; in this one, it seems important to mention a couple of issues.

First, this is an age when you have to be a little wary and certainly have a sense of who your child's friends are. Reinforce your availability to answer questions or talk to your child without seeming overly suspicious. Try to schedule time alone with your preteen doing something you both enjoy.

Realizing How Uncool You Have Become

Being the mother of a preteen is not the most ego-gratifying period of a woman's life. If you thought you were clueless about what to do when the baby was brand new, think again—*this* is the time when you really begin to doubt that you know what you're doing. You have far less control over your preteen children than you've ever had, because the second they leave your house they are making all kinds of decisions you may never know about.

Betwixt and Between

Expect to worry. A preteen child combines the toughest parts of teenage-dom and childhood: He's old enough to think he can make his own decisions, but he's still too young to recognize his limitations. And, to make matters worse, preteens seem genetically hardwired to believe that all parents (and especially moms) are stupid and ignorant and that somehow they have been dropped into your family by mistake.

Teenagers, you hope, have already begun the maturation process that may ultimately lead to responsibility. Preteens, however, are still too close to being children to be able to objectively see how they are presenting themselves to the outside world. And while they may want you to see them as cool and up to the minute, inside they may still be clinging to their teddy bears or worrying about the monsters in their closets at night.

The Mom's Side of Preteen-dom

The preteen years feel like a time of loss to many mothers. If you have defined yourself in any way by your relationship with your child (and who doesn't, at least a little bit?) you're sometimes going to perceive your child's behavior as pushing you away. You'll be strongly tempted to cling and try to retain some control over your child, but that's only guaranteed to make your child need to push away even harder.

Oh My Gosh! I'm Turning into My Mother!

One day you are going to find yourself haranguing your preteen, trying to maintain some control, and you'll suddenly realize that you sound just like *your* parents did when you were that age. At first you'll probably cringe at the recollection of how uncool you used to think your own mom was—and the realization that you have now become just as uncool to your kid.

If you're wise, you'll remember what *you* were like when you were trying to break away and become your own person—and you'll remember that you weren't doing it just to be mean to your folks.

Mom Alert!

The preteen's demand for independence is at least 50 percent bluff. Don't react by giving your child more freedom than she is ready for. No matter how much she seems to be rebelling against you, she's really counting on you to hang in there for her.

Your preteen is not really rejecting you. She is just trying to find an identity separate from you at a time when she is terrified to let you go. The insults and cracks are your preteen's way of making it easier to let go of your constant protection.

Understanding—and Surviving—Preteen Angst

Preteens try to act cool, but in reality they are scared of everything. They know that they do not fit into the adult world and that they are not yet self-assured enough to fit in with the teenagers. But they also know they are no longer babies and that they can't hold on forever to the things of childhood. Nature is telling them to move on and they do not know how—except by making your life miserable.

Mom-isms

The symptoms of preteen **angst** are moodiness and downright contrariness, but deep inside it's really about insecurity. It's caused by the fact that preteens face so many conflicting desires: To grow up but still be a baby, and to make their own decisions but still be able to turn to Mom when the going gets tough.

When It's "Anchors Away, and Full Steam Ahead..."

Aren't mothers lucky? We want to be the anchor, while our child's motorboat tries to speed away. Preteens don't really *want* to be out of control, but they don't want to stand still for any length of time, either. Whether or not they admit it, they *need* us to be there for them. When they're all dressed up in the latest fashions and trying to imitate the people they admire, they may look older than their years. But if you really stop to listen to them they are still ordinary children.

And When the Old Toy Box Still Looks Pretty Good

Mom Alert!

If your child is so out of sync with his peers as to cause problems in school or at play, by all means seek a professional consultation. Just don't create problems where none exist. Consider yourself lucky if your child wants to savor childhood. She will be ready to move on when the time comes.

If you're fortunate, your preteen might stay on the younger side of the teens, behaviorally speaking. If your child is still playing with toys or behaving in silly, childlike ways, count your blessings. These transitional years are the time when children can test their limits without having to go too far into any dangerous territory. This is a time of information-gathering and self-discovery. So don't worry about encouraging any behavior that you feel is more age-appropriate, especially when it comes to the opposite sex. Each child has a kind of internal clock that, when left to its own devices, will make everything that is supposed to happen, happen in its own time.

To Everything, There Is a Season

If your daughter still likes to play with her dolls in the preteen years, don't worry. Unless your child is expressing behaviors that clearly indicate she's having problems, be content to guide her gently, while letting her grow up at her own pace. Whatever you do, try to resist the temptation to compare your child to everyone else's kids.

Hanging on While Your Child Hangs Out

Your child hates you. At least, that's what she seems to be telling you, several times each week. Preteens are just like that—there are only extremes in their universe. Don't be too concerned about this when your child spews venom at you. Realize that, in the lexicon of preteen-dom, there are *no* shades of gray.

Communication, Preteen Style

A preteen says:	A preteen means:
I hate you!	I'm not feeling particularly good about myself right now.
I hate you!	The cute guy in homeroom saw me with a zit this morning, and now he'll *never* talk to me.
I hate you!	You're treating me like a child, but I really think I *can* do this by myself now.
I hate you!	I think I'm flunking algebra class.
I hate you!	I'm really scared right now and what I want most of all is a hug but I can't ask for it because, after all, I'm almost a teenager.

Coping with Them Fightin' Words

When preteens use extreme language ("I hate...," "You never...,") it is a way of expressing anger when more sophisticated tools are unavailable. And it's bad enough when your child talks like this in private. It's even worse when she lashes out in front of others. Even though it's embarrassing when your child says she hates you in front of your dinner guests, don't add fuel to that fire. Just say, "I know you are angry. I love you. We can talk about what is bothering you when you are feeling calmer."

Your child will use anger at you to express many different things. She may use anger to manipulate you, or she may just be expressing frustration with her life. If you allow your feelings to be hurt every time you hear this phrase, you'll just be prolonging the conflict. It's better to let your child's mood work itself out.

Womanly Wisdom

Preteens and teenagers will sometimes use conflict simply to force you to interact with them, even though the interaction is negative. Insecurity runs high at this age, and they may feel that this is the only way to engage you in their feelings. Try to tune out the harsh words and listen to what your preteen is *really* saying.

Killing 'em with Kindness

When it seems that you just *must* react to your preteen's provocative behavior, remember this: There's nothing that will torture your child more than your refusal to respond to her tirades. If you do nothing while she's trying everything she can think of to rattle you, you are going to maintain complete control over the situation. Remember, however—the minute you get involved in a yelling contest, you have lost.

Riding the Preteen Roller Coaster

Preteens can be very emotional. Some of this has to do with their uncertainty about growing up, but some of it is strictly physical—they're starting to go through hormonal changes that they do not understand. Your preteen's ups and downs are there for her (or him—boys get them, too) to handle—they sure won't be very much fun for you. The best thing you can do is stand out of the way and wait until your child asks you for help.

The only real way to survive this stage in your child's life is to have begun building good communication much earlier. If you have a good basic relationship, your preteen may push you away but will still turn back to you when she needs your advice, counsel, and involvement. And make no mistake about it: A preteen needs a mother, perhaps more than she needs you at any other stage.

Mirror, Mirror on the Wall

If you have any doubt that the preteen years are a time of insecurity, just watch your child discover the mirror. In many ways, he is seeing himself for the very first time. He'll spend hours in front of the mirror, looking at every angle of his face, and all the while, he'll be comparing himself to everyone he knows. "Is my nose too big?" he'll worry. "I hate my ears," she'll moan. This is a time of extreme self-consciousness, and your acceptance is an important reassurance that everything is still fine. Even though your child feels as if he's being turned upside down with changes, you can help him see that he is still the same person, only getting better.

Dealing with Dork-dom

All the while that your child is dealing with these changes, she has definitively demoted you to dork status. What's worse yet, now's the time that you're bound to start *feeling* like a dork, as the world changes around you. Your child's entry into the preteen years is the first time you'll really have to acknowledge that you're not a kid anymore, yourself. For the first time in your life you'll find yourself looking at clothing and wondering whether it will make you look as though you're trying to be too young. Now's when your supercool daughter can come in decidedly handy: When she tells you, "I'm in junior high, so I know about these things," you'll be wise to realize she is right. Don't let it make you feel like a has-been—thank her for saving you from looking like one of those moms who always seem to be trying to be *too* cool.

Who *Is* This Child of Mine?

One of the things that will shock you deeply when your child hits the preteen years is how much her personality suddenly differs from yours. You may swear that no child of yours will ever listen to heavy metal rock and roll, and of course that's all she'll want to listen to. For years you may have forbidden him to watch horror films, and suddenly that's the only kind of movie he likes.

It is really difficult to accept that your child has an entire personality of her own and that you really can't influence it that much anymore. You can limit or forbid certain things, but you can't change what interests her.

Mom Alert!

The more you try to control a child, the more rebellion you'll have on your hands. Listen and guide (when asked-resisting the temptation to lecture) and you will have better results.

Shifting Your Mothering-Style Gears

In the preteen years, your best bet is to recognize that you can't rely on force of will, or on the blanket "do it because I told you to" approach. You're better off concentrating on reinforcing the sense that you believe in your children and trust them to make good decisions.

As the mother of a preteen today, you're going to find that you have to make new rules for coping—your own mom's way of doing things often just won't work. You can't control all the influences he's exposed to, and you can't take him out to the woodshed with a switch when he misbehaves. You want to teach him to respect you and to respect himself enough to live up to healthy standards and resist peer pressure to get into trouble. By encouraging individuality and a strong self, you will give him the courage to refuse to go along with the crowd.

Staying Close, but Not Too Close

Be around for your preteen. Even though it appears your child can have more independence and can even spend time alone at home, try to make sure he is supervised after school. Those after-school hours between three and six are the hours during which kids are more likely to get into trouble. At this age you know your child is pretty capable—you know, for example, that he can use a microwave on his own, so he won't starve if he wants a snack when you're not there. But a preteen is still a child, and it's best if you can be there when he comes home from school. If you can't, at least try to have someone a little older there for him—someone who can offer support and supervision.

Womanly Wisdom

As parents feel a child begin to pull away and form a separate personality, the temptation is to resist by imposing restraints. It's best to strike a balance: Set reasonable limits, but at the same time loosen the reins a little.

161

The preteen years are challenging but can also be the time when you do the most *real* mothering: When a child is young, hugs and kisses are enough to solve most problems—your simple loving presence is usually enough. It's when your child is a preteen that you can create a special bond that can grow over your lifetime. As your child begins to develop her own personality, separate from you, a new bond forms between you that ultimately will be transformed into mother and friend.

Your Child Is Changing, and So Are You

Just as your child is just beginning to discover his or her own identity, you also are going to go through many changes during your child's preteen years. You will be reevaluating your role as a mother as you adjust to your child's changing needs. At times you may feel very unappreciated. And, if your child is like most preteens, she's probably is driving you a little bit crazy right now. Don't worry about it—all it really means is that you're doing your job—you've given your child enough confidence to try things on her own, and enough security to dare to sometimes even challenge your judgment. Congratulate yourself for that.

You can have a good relationship with your preteen. As with any stage in your child's life, you want to stay emotionally involved. Let yourself love your child and cherish even the most difficult of days. You really will laugh at them someday. Just make sure to take pictures to use as bribes in later years. Catch a few candid mirror shots. They are worth a bundle, especially if you catch some with pimples or a bad haircut.

The Least You Need to Know

➤ The preteen years are the years when your child reaches double digits and you officially become a dork.

➤ A preteen child seems duty-bound to reject a mom's opinion on just about everything.

➤ Don't be surprised when your preteen refuses to acknowledge your existence in public places.

➤ During your child's preteen years, he or she is working hard to develop a personal identity distinct from yours.

➤ Your role as mother changes during your child's preteen years—it's the time to start loosening the parental reins and forge a new relationship.

Chapter 14

Dr. Jekyll and the Teenage Hyde

In This Chapter

➤ Welcome to planet teenager

➤ Changing your mothering style

➤ Building a new relationship

My 13 1/2-year-old daughter does not like school. In fact, in every class where she has a marginal (terrible) grade her teachers have kindly noted that she "does not work to her potential." It is nice that they have seen her potential, but not one of them has told me how to cultivate a rose from a very thorny plant. She loves to draw and has no trouble motivating herself to follow her creative pursuits, but academics just give her the heebie-jeebies. And I, of course, get the heebie-jeebies whenever I face the council of elders, her academic team leaders, who look at me like *I* know what to do.

Why do our children's teachers think we know how to get them to do better in school?

This chapter is all about surviving your child's thorny teenage years with humor and grace. In it you'll learn how to recognize the Dr. Jekyll hidden deep inside when all your teenager is willing to show you is an evil Mr. Hyde.

The Traumatic Teen Years

We all cope differently with teenage troubles. I tend toward the figurative heart attack. My husband, on the other hand, is much more calm about everything. If our daughter isn't keeping up with her homework, I clutch my heart and gasp for air. He sagely observes: "Let her fail the eighth grade. She is the only person who can change her future."

Needless to say, the gap between our styles on this issue is big enough to drive a truck through. Obviously, we were going to have to find a compromise if we wanted to cope with this early teen crisis. But finding the right way to handle a rebellious teenager is tricky. You never know when what you think is a reasonable solution will trigger a major blowout…as I soon found out with my own newly minted teenager.

Momma Said There'd Be Days Like This

It is not as though I don't try to motivate my teenager. Every day when she comes home from school I ask, "What homework do you have?" Sometimes I even look through her bag, to help her organize her assignments. She tells me she has done her work at school—and like an idiot, I believe her. Then I get a report from school that she has not turned in a bunch of assignments and that she faces failure in several subjects unless she turns in the assignments after her winter vacation.

A Typical Mom-to-Teen Scenario

In an effort to help my daughter improve her performance at school, I hit upon what I thought was a reasonable plan. On the very first day of winter vacation I decided to take charge by organizing my daughter's time. I laid out a schedule of how she was going to be able to complete her assignments while still having time for fun. It made perfect sense to me. She would do work first, play later. Nothing terrible.

Crashing into Teenage Contrariness

So after taking her to a first-evening-of-vacation movie I told her my expectations. I told her in no uncertain terms that she was going to come to work with me the next day and get started on her homework. She complained and complained that it was her vacation and she was going to have fun. She said she was not going to do the work and I couldn't make her.

I explained firmly that she had too much work to do to wait to the last minute. I took a stern line: "You will be up tomorrow morning and will go with me to the office." I was so adamant I almost saluted myself. It felt powerful. But then everything took a turn for the worse.

Staying Strong Through the Tears

My daughter knows very well how to push my buttons. She got very upset and said she was planning to do her homework, but just not so soon. Then she escalated her emotionalism into crying mode. Tears have worked against me in the past, but I felt this was too important: I was determined to stand firm. The colder I became the more upset she became until she managed to work herself up into a real rage. She said she was not going to listen to me and that she was going to run away from home. She said she was going to pack her things in a wagon, get a job, and get her own place. My continued refusal to back down finally pushed her over the edge into truly hateful language. Then she stalked off to her room.

Post-Rupture Recovery

My sense of victory at taking charge of the homework situation died right there. I had never seen her so upset, and her rage was frightening. My husband, Zen master of step-parenting, put his arm around me and stopped me from running into her room and trying to make it all better. He advised a cool-down period, and reassured me that she'd only said all those awful things in the heat of the moment. But I was reeling with doubt. What if she really did feel that way about me? What if we never managed to heal the breach between us?

No matter how bad I felt, I knew I had to follow through on taking her to work with me, but I didn't want to set off another battle. That next morning, I sneaked into her room and crawled under the covers next to her, trying to convey my wish that we repair the damage we'd done to one another. She was awake, and she didn't pull away, so I knew she was as heartbroken as I was. We both were not ready to talk directly about the fight so I started to read from one of her kid humor books. After a few minutes we both started laughing, hugged and everything was okay. Then we headed off to my office as if everything was back to normal. And, in a way, it was—when we got there she *still* avoided her work, and I went back into nagging mode. Later we were able to talk more openly about our feelings.

Mom Alert!

When you've had a major blow up with your teenager, don't try to resolve the issue then and there. Both you and your teen will need a little cool-off time, or you'll just keep pushing each other's buttons and escalating the conflict.

Intuition to the Rescue

We could have gone round and round like this forever—I nagging, she resisting, with periodic blow-ups punctuating the whole affair. But that night I had a dream that put everything in perspective. In the dream, I was telling one of my old college professors about my troubles with a course I was taking. I didn't understand a thing that was going on and when I asked the teacher for help he belittled me, so I fled the room and didn't want to go back. My dream provided me with the insight I needed to help my daughter—I realized that my daughter just might be feeling that same kind of pressure with regard to her schoolwork.

The next day I took my new insights along with us to the office. When she started her old work-avoidance tricks, I let it go until lunch, when I planned on sharing my dream with her. I never got the chance—she opened up immediately and told me that the biggest problem she was having with her homework was the pressure I was putting on her to do it. Every time I nagged, she became blocked and simply had to put it off one more time.

The Contrarian Country of Adolescence

Much of a teenager's counterproductive behavior stems from just such contrarian urges. The teen years are a time of great confusion, and your child is feeling pressure from all sides: emotional, intellectual, social, and hormonal. Sometimes the only reaction available to her is to shut down—to dig in her heels and mulishly refuse to do what she's told. When that happens, pushing your teen won't help—it just makes a bad situation worse.

I asked my daughter how I was supposed to get her to do her work without nagging? She replied, "You are not, it is my work and I am supposed to do it on my own." I felt relieved with this insight. It is easy to become so pressured by our children's issues that we forget that they have to figure things out for themselves.

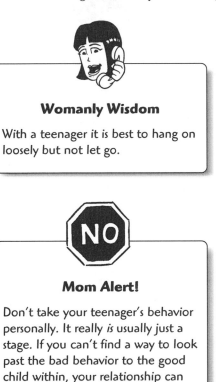

Womanly Wisdom

With a teenager it is best to hang on loosely but not let go.

Mom Alert!

Don't take your teenager's behavior personally. It really *is* usually just a stage. If you can't find a way to look past the bad behavior to the good child within, your relationship can suffer serious long-term damage.

Changing Your Mothering Style to Suit Your Teenager

Your child is having a difficult time learning to make the transition to adulthood. And you also, no doubt, are finding these years difficult. Your old ways of relating to your child are no longer appropriate—the old days when your child thought you knew everything there was to know are long past. And while you still want very much to actively guide and protect your child, such behavior comes across as controlling, not as helpful.

So what's a teenager's mom to do? She does what she has done with every other new stage in her child's developmental life: she reevaluates her style to find one that suits her child's current needs.

Being mother to a teenager means you constantly alternate between being pushed away and pulled back. Your child wants the chance to make his own decisions—and his own mistakes—but he's not ready to be pushed completely out of the nest just yet. He can indeed be a sweet and caring Dr. Jekyll one minute, and then in the next he can turn into a raging Mr. Hyde, convincing you that he's truly demon spawn. It's an emotional roller coaster ride—so hang on tight!

The Two Faces of Teendom

Much of what you see as your teen's bad behavior is really her perfectly normal response to the imperative of growing up: She's just trying to break away and assume her own adult identity. But, because she's a teen, she is ill equipped to manage this change without major drama.

Your Teen at Home: Rampage and Rejection

Teenagers are notorious for rejecting their mothers. They are also well-versed in the art of manipulation—mostly by using the threat of this rejection to get their way. The techniques we used so successfully to soothe and comfort our children when they were young just can't stand up to the constant challenge that teenagers seem to thrive on. This new teenage person in the household sometimes seems to have declared war—and we lack suitable weapons with which to defend ourselves. But never fear—there *are* strategies that you can use to survive these difficult years:

➤ Have attitude. Know you are a good mother, and don't be convinced otherwise.

➤ Remember to be a parent. Teenagers still need mothering.

➤ Reassure yourself that your teenager does not really hate you.

➤ Don't overcontrol or under-care.

➤ Reward yourself in special ways and pray for continued endurance.

Surviving Teendom, by the Numbers

Step one in surviving your child's teenage years is to have attitude. This means you know you are a good mother and no amount of harassment from your teenager is going to convince you otherwise.

Step two is to remember that you're still a parent. Don't stop mothering your teenager just because he or she have begun to closely resemble adults, only goofier.

It's easy to forget that your teenager is still a kid, when so many of the things he does seem so adult. We rely on teenagers to take adult responsibilities such as baby-sitting their younger siblings; we allow them freedom to hang with their friends; we let them get a driver's license; and some of them even hold down a paying job. But with all this adult-seeming behavior, they still need the support—and the limits—a mother can provide.

Womanly Wisdom

Adolescence is a time of great insecurity for your child. It's easy to bruise his fragile sense of self. Whenever possible, then, let your child set the pace for trading confidences. If you come across as prying, he'll just clam up on you anyway.

167

Step three is to reassure yourself that your child does not really hate you, no matter how rebellious he or she may seem at times. Your child will most likely say and do things that make you feel rejected, and you may find it hard not to take them personally.

But the extreme behavior and language stem from the teens' sense of powerless: They are too old to be treated as children and yet too young for all the privileges of adulthood. This can be very frustrating, and often the target of that frustration is Mom. You do not need to become anyone's whipping girl, but you do not want to overreact to your teen's challenges, either. Give your teenager enough space to work through his own temporary demon-possession, and keep your feelings safely out of the way.

To put this another way, when a teenager lashes out it is not typically as personal as it seems—it is really business. Your teenager is trying to break out of a highly entrenched protected environment. He is seeking the self-confidence to succeed in the world without external protection. You can compare the teenage years to the labor pains experienced before a baby is thrust into the world. The teenager is getting ready for a rebirth into adulthood, and no matter how willing he seems, he will go out kicking and screaming until he can adjust to his new environment.

So, as your teenager pushes you to the limits of your endurance, work *with* him as much as possible. If you can communicate during those rare moments of equilibrium (even teenagers do have them) open your heart and explain that you understand what he or she is going through. Fill your teenager with positive, supportive messages so that he remembers he can turn to you in a time of crisis.

Mom Alert!

Overreacting to your teen's bad behavior can easily trigger a blowup. Don't take it so seriously: It is just your child's way of hanging onto being a child while he or she is trying to become an adult. By driving you crazy your child is actually demanding a connection with you even though it is through negative attention.

A Visit from Dr. Jekyll

You may be surprised how well your teenage monster behaves outside your den. When a teenager is at home, he or she will revert to behavior that you will likely find unpleasant at best—you can only pray it's reserved for you and not shared with the populace at large.

When your child is out of the house you may hear stories or rumors about this responsible, really cool kid—and you'll gasp in amazement when you hear it's your very own homegrown monster. Do not be surprised if the rumors turn out to be true. Of course, sometimes your little monster may be a teenage scourge both inside and outside your home. Do the best you can to maintain limits, but realize your child is making choices for which there are personal consequences. You are not responsible or to blame for every choice your child makes. Sometimes, even though you guide your child perfectly, he will still take the path of most resistance.

Respecting Your Teen's Cool

Don't disregard your need to be a mother to your teenager. By now you know it isn't cool to show too much mothering in front of your child's friends. My son has not allowed any public displays of affection within one mile of his school since he was seven years old. But there are still many ways you can connect to your child without having to baby him. Now, the biggest exception to this rule arises when your teenager is ill. If your child has a cold or the flu it is perfectly fine to indulge him or her with the works. Just don't let on that you are actually fulfilling the call of your chicken-soup gene.

Building a New Relationship

Mothers of teenagers have mixed feelings about everything. On the one hand, you might reminisce longingly for the early days when your child was just a baby and things were simpler. On the other hand, make sure you have a friend throw some water on your head so you don't get caught up in the rose-colored memory of days gone by.

The mother of a teenager sometimes does not know how to do her job. At least she *thinks* she does not know. Talk about being unappreciated. She used to be able to call the shots, but now most of her suggestions and efforts are thrown back in her own face. For example, I have given up trying to buy clothes for my teenager. Even if she picks out the very same thing I would have picked for her, I am careful not to show my preferences. Her need to resist me is stronger than her tastes, and at her age she often says just the opposite of what I say, just to be contrary.

Womanly Wisdom

Keep in mind that at this age two issues are at stake. First, she is becoming older and more willful. Second, you are becoming aware that you, too, are getting older.

Confronting Modern-World Fears

Children are more sophisticated today than we were at a similar age. They have had far more exposure than we had to the concepts of drugs and alcohol. But that doesn't automatically mean they are practicing everything they've heard about. In some ways there is a backlash of very responsible young people who think drugs and other forms of experimentation are just plain nasty. In fact, as you develop your new relationship with your teenager, be sure to reinforce your trust that he or she will make good decisions for his or her life. You always want to give your child a sense of unconditional approval, not of certain behaviors, but of his existence as your child. Love is not to be won or lost. Separate the behavior from the person.

This is the best thing you can do to prepare your child for the world. You can't be everywhere at all times. Leave that job to God. At some point your child will move on to his or her own relationship with a higher purpose. You can only be there to guide.

You still have authority to set limits for your teenager. I asked my daughter if she wanted me to tell her she could do whatever she wanted and she said, "No. That would be bad." Children feel very unsafe when there is too much freedom. You should have some sense of what is going on with your child most of the time.

Momma Said There'd Be Days Like This

When your teen is out for the evening, there is nothing wrong with expecting to be told where he is going and when he is coming home. There are viable consequences for breaking the rules that will still be effective to a teenager. Even in prisons they use taking away television privileges to keep inmates in line. It actually works because of the importance television plays in the prisoner's life. Try unplugging the tube or taking away the Nintendo. It still works. Be consistent and be firm. Just avoid overemotionalism. Once you scream, you lose.

Discovering Your Teenager's Persona

The teenage years are seen as something you need to get past, but actually they can be the most wonderful of all the stages you will go through with your child. You can still do some direct mothering (have a chance to be a mother) before you need to change your child's status into being one of the adults. Teenagers can be a lot of fun to hang out with. I enjoy my daughter's company as much as or more than that of many of my adult friends. We share many common interests and love being together. We agree to disagree about certain things: I refused to see the remake of *Psycho*, but I conceded to watching the *Beavis and Butthead* marathon.

The strange thing about being the mother of a teenager is realizing how much teens really understand about life. My daughter gives very good advice. I try not to ask her questions in an obvious "I don't know the answer" sort of way. I do not want her to be under the pressure of thinking she is the mom, but I have learned to listen to what she has to say. I must admit my ego had difficulty accepting how much she has grown and how her opinions are being formed, entirely separate from anything I have told her.

The nice thing is that I sometimes catch her saying something I know I *did* say to her at some point in her life. I never realized how much she had been listening to me all those years.

When a child is a teenager a mother needs to create a new relationship. In some ways you need to give your child the room to choose how much interaction he wants from you. It is much more effective for you to let your child know you are available and to wait to be asked for your help, than for you to be too quick to supply all of the answers.

Give Your Teenager the Space to Set the Pace

This is a perfect time for us moms to pursue interests of our own. If you are a working mom this should not be a problem. But if you have been a stay-at-home mom, I might as well be telling you that you are being fired from the only job you have ever known. You can't look at it this way. This is just a time in your motherhood career path to learn some new skills so that you can adapt to the changing times ahead.

You may want to pursue a hobby or renew your education. You may want to continue to be devoted to your child's activities, but perhaps you can give yourself more permission to do some things you enjoy for yourself. This is a vulnerable time for your female identity. You have to fight the urge to feel confused and negative. This time of your life can be wonderful and full of growth.

Momma Said There'd Be Days Like This

When I recently had a floor replaced in my home the contractor used some kind of toxic glue. Although he said he would be finished before the holidays, we had to evacuate our family to a single room at the Holiday Inn for an overnight stay. There is something about putting a teenager with two younger siblings that causes him or her to regress to the level of the younger children. Needless to say, the room got chaotic. I told my husband to take care of the problem and locked myself in the bathroom.

We learned some valuable lessons that day. Either we need more than one room, we need to bring the shackles when we travel with the kids, or I need to lighten up. Of course, my husband—who actually started the pillow fight that led to my daughter being stuck between the bed and the wall—suggested the latter. Sometimes that really is the only choice.

If you have younger children in the house you will be kept busy for years to come as you guide them down the path to adulthood. You may find that having younger children and a teenager in the same domain creates a type of disequilibrium. The two age groups will inevitably try to torture each other and will want you to be the referee. After certain ages it is difficult to travel with children who are at different personality stages.

There is a lot to be said about finding a place where no one can get to you. Bathrooms are nice but taking some time to get away from kids altogether is even nicer. Perhaps more important now than at any other time, you want to create space for yourself that reunites you with who you are. Your children may demand less of your time but they will still demand as much attention as possible. You can control what is comfortable for you if you keep in mind that children do not need to have their lives run for them to your own detriment. You are not doing them any good by being everything to everyone.

As your child reaches various stages of independence, try to encourage individual interests and cultivate a few of your own. Try not to define yourself through the eyes of your family members, or you will become a shadow of a human being. You may need to go through a period of redefinition, but it is part of your growth. Raising children does not mean your development as a human being stops. You have been in a stage, just as your children have. It is now time for you to move beyond your definition as mother into person who happens to be a mother. Although this is who you have been all along, it is easier at this stage to see that you have never really been lost, you have just been otherwise occupied.

The Least You Need to Know

➤ The teenage years require yet another change in your mothering style.

➤ The thorny teenage years mean you're in for a roller-coaster ride on the emotions of your child. Don't panic—you'll survive.

➤ You need to continue mothering your children but must keep in mind that they need to be encouraged to develop independence and self-confidence.

Chapter 15

Loosening the Reins Without Letting Go

In This Chapter

➤ Getting used to your child in adult clothing

➤ Moving from the center to the sidelines (sort of)

➤ Making the break while staying connected

➤ Making the most of your newfound freedom

It is not easy to keep up with the changes that occur when your child finally makes the shift to full adulthood. It seems to happen overnight—your sunny-smiling toddler suddenly changes into a towering giant and sprouts whiskers. The little boy who used to play for hours inside a cardboard box is suddenly wearing a power suit—and looks like he'd be perfectly at ease in a corporate boardroom. Just last holiday season he was still sitting with his younger siblings at the children's table, having food fights and making disgusting noises; now he's leading grace and carving the turkey.

In this chapter you'll learn the bittersweet pleasures of seeing your child make the miraculous metamorphosis into adulthood. You'll discover how to lay the groundwork for the new relationship on your horizon—a relationship of respect, love, and friendship with that young adult you still call your child.

Ready or Not, Here Comes a New Adult!

Children grow up whether you're ready for it or not. They begin to make choices and decisions—and even have relationships—that you know nothing about. In other words, they begin to build lives that are separate from their parents. And they seem to start the process when you're not looking. While you're still relating to the traumas of teendom, they're quietly making the shift to adulthood.

You're Facing Up to the Inevitable...

Well, this is what you've been working toward all along, right? Intellectually, you always knew that your child was bound to someday leave the nest—in fact, your whole job as mother has been to prepare her for this very event. But try telling that to your heart when you suddenly realize your role is changing once again, and that your child is ready to spread her wings and fly solo.

Womanly Wisdom

Try to view this transitional period from your child's perspective—to her, adult independence appears as a great adventure. Set aside your nostalgic longing for the child that was, and celebrate with her the adult that she has come to be.

...While Your Child Sings "I Gotta Be Me"

While you're feeling nostalgic for those good old days when your child was still depending on you for guidance, that very same child is likely to be counting the days until he's free to start his independent adult life. It seems harsh to think that this transition that seems so sad to you is so avidly anticipated by your child. But it's up to you to make the effort to look ahead and rejoice in the changes and challenges now facing your child.

Coping with Your Child's Coming of Age

When your child becomes an adult, you are once again faced with a transitional time in his life and in your relationship with him as his mother. He very well may know a great deal more about the world than you—perhaps he's had more schooling, and certainly he's likely to be more up on what's new in the worlds of technology and style. But you still have the edge when it comes to experience, and that makes you an important resource for your child.

Still, it can be very disconcerting to deal with the fact that your child is now at the borders of adulthood. For many women, having a child reach adulthood can be the first time they confront the fact that *they* are getting older. You can find yourself suddenly facing the realization that the years have been steadily marching on, when to you life had for so long seemed almost timeless. Don't let it get you down—as the cliche puts it, "You're not getting older, you're getting better!"

Forging a New Relationship with Your Child

Young adults are, by definition, inexperienced adults. They are still in need of your guidance and support as they learn to negotiate the wide world of independent life. What's best about this time is that, with independence, your child is likely to leave behind the old rebelliousness of her earlier, teenage years. And this means that she's much more capable of accepting your insights.

Being There

It's easy to think your mothering job is done when your child looks and acts so much like a grown up. But inside that six-foot-tall frame is a young person who still has a lot of maturing to do. You know this from your own early experiences with independence—you wanted to try things for yourself, but you made a lot of mistakes while you were learning the ropes of adult responsibility. You know that it took some time to develop the emotional maturity you needed to stand completely on your own.

And this is just as true for your child as it was for you. In fact, her inexperience can provide you with the foundation upon which to begin building your new relationship with your adult child. If you provide opportunities for her to come to you for advice, and share with her some of your own memories of being on your own for the first time, you can forge a comfortable new bond.

Mom Alert!

The surest way to derail the opportunity of forging a new, strong relationship with your adult child is to try to force him into a role more suited to an earlier age. Holding on to the reins too tightly will only make him push you away.

Counsel with Care

But you'll need to step carefully as you offer advice and support. Think back, once again, to your own early years of independence. You might have been glad to have your mom to help you figure out how to handle day-to-day problems, but you certainly didn't want to *regress* into the restrictions and rules you lived with as a dependent child. This will be true for your newly adult son or daughter, as well.

Remember: Your job as mother does not stop just because your child has reached the age of majority. It just changes in certain fundamental ways. When your child was 16, he probably saw you as out of touch, a little silly, and mostly an embarrassment. But now, with new adult independence and responsibilities, he will begin to have experiences that may help him understand where you've been coming from, all these years.

Creating a Healthy New Dynamic with Your Child

So, how do you go about building a new, more mature relationship with your child? One good way is to bond through shared experience. Here's a partial list of things you can bond with your child over:

➤ Living within a budget

➤ Coping with pressures on the job

➤ Finding and decorating that first apartment

➤ Dealing with roommates

➤ Dealing with a landlord

Sharing Your Experience

Using these experiences as a basis for communication and for forming a new bond with your child has a distinct advantage. They all involve practical skills in which it's only natural that you'd have more expertise, so there's a good chance that the two of you can discuss them with little risk of challenging his or her newfound sense of independence.

Momma Said There'd Be Days Like This

Teenagers can be very dismissive of your opinions and advice, but as they approach independence, things change, as one mother learned. For the last six years or so, she couldn't offer the slightest opinion without getting shot down by her teenage daughter, usually with the comment: "Oh, Mom! You just *don't know!*" But one day shortly after the daughter's nineteenth birthday, the two were sharing brunch. Out of the blue, the daughter observed: "You know, Mom, it's amazing how much smarter you've gotten, now that I'm older...."

Best of all, these practical issues of day-to-day living can provide you with a nonthreatening rationale for staying closely involved in your child's life. And who knows? While you're sharing your hard-won insights on getting a landlord to make apartment repairs, you just might move on to more personal subjects—like your child's hopes, dreams, and plans.

And Sometimes a Little TLC Is Welcome

While it's important that you respect your adult child's newfound independence, sometimes your more conventional Mom identity will still be welcome. Your child will quickly come to see that independence isn't always the grand adventure he thought it would be. Don't be surprised to find that your nurturing skills are actively sought every once in awhile, just as they were when he was much younger.

The key is to let your child come to you, instead of imposing your nurturing urges on him. When life in the real world gets tough, or when he's feeling under the weather, a child naturally turns to the person who represents security and love— and that's you, Mom.

Adjusting Your Mothering Style Once Again

Have you noticed the pattern, yet? At every new stage of your child's life, you face the challenge of reevaluating your mothering style and adjusting it to suit the new conditions. This time in your child's life is the final, and potentially most rewarding, adjustment you'll make. If you manage to make the change gracefully, you open the door to a lifelong relationship with a fine young adult—who just happens also to be your child. There are few relationships more rewarding than this one can be, so you want to do everything you can to make it a strong one.

The Dos and Don'ts of Mothering an Adult

The secrets of handling this transition gracefully are pretty basic. Here's a quick overview of how to manage it:

Do	Don't
Be available with advice and counsel when it's requested.	Rush in and impose your way of doing things on your child without being asked.
Be willing to share stories of your own early days of independence.	Badger your child with comparisons of how you handled things better when you were her age.
Make it clear that your child is still a vital part of your family, even if she is living independently now.	Close the doors to your child if she needs to come home for a little mother love when the going gets tough in the grown-up world.

The essential message is this: You can't be so smothering that you undermine your adult child's sense of independence, but you want to avoid being so completely accepting of her independent status that you give the impression that you don't care about her anymore. Your goal as parent at this stage in your child's life is to help her to feel empowered to take charge, and that's best accomplished if you make it clear that she always has a home and family to turn to when life gets tough.

Some things you can do to build a strong dynamic in your new relationship:

➤ Make it clear that you still hold to your rules and values, and that you expect your child to respect them.

Womanly Wisdom

At this age, communication with your child is crucial. While she's more self-reliant, she's also more vulnerable to making dangerous errors in judgment. Now more than ever she needs to know that she has your support and love, no matter what.

➤ Keep the lines of communication open. Make it clear that you welcome an opportunity to contribute to your child's life, and that your child is still a part of your life, too.

➤ Be willing to let your adult child turn to you for comfort when the responsibilities of independent living get a little overwhelming. Make it clear that you believe in her ability to cope with her life, but that you can empathize when she expresses a need to admit weakness every once in a while.

➤ Be receptive if your child is willing to talk about his plans, goals, and dreams. And, if he's open to your input, offer guidance to help him create a strategy to achieve them.

Evaluating Your New Role

Mothers do not know what to do when their children come of age. After 18 years or more of being at the core of our children's lives, it's hard to find that they've moved on to build a life of their own. It's easy to feel rejected and lonely, and to express those feelings by interfering in the life they're trying to build for themselves. But resist that urge as strongly as you can—your child needs your support, not your control.

Your adult child can become your buddy. For the first time in her life, she's beginning to confront adult problems that she's never had to recognize. As she does so, she will begin to develop an understanding of many of your actions and priorities that previously were inexplicable to her. This gives you both new ground on which to build a bond.

Staying Connected

Keep in mind that even though your child has achieved young adulthood, there will still be plenty of opportunities for you to do some good mothering. You may even find that this is the age when you do some of your best work. Your goal is to find a way to provide that gentle push your child might need in order to successfully leave the nest, while still extending a hand for support when she needs it. You want to help your newly matured child to feel secure and loved, and to know she always has a place in your home, while encouraging her to step further and further into full adult autonomy.

This requires that you strike a very delicate balance. As your child is moving off into his own life, you too are beginning to build a life—one that is no longer centered on his needs. And, however mature he may think he is, he will be sensitive to this change in you.

Preparing Your Child for Your Own Independence

You see, you're not the only one who has to adjust to a newly independent person in your mother-child relationship. Your child will be dealing with *your* own newfound independence, and this may be a little frightening. He may perceive the changes in your life as a rejection of *him*.

However much a child strives for the chance to be on his or her own, it's a rare child indeed who doesn't harbor some hope that Mom will stay just as he remembers her from his preschool days. You want to make your own changes gradually, sharing what you're doing with your child every step of the way. Just as you want them to make space to include you in their new lives, so will your children want to continue to be made part of yours.

Mom Alert!

Be alert to the possible messages your child may be picking up from you. At this age they're quick to perceive, and rebel against, any sense of judgment and rejection—even if none is intended.

Striking Just the Right Balance

This time in your child's life calls for you to loosen the reins while simultaneously making sure your child knows you are not going to let go of them completely. Your young adult needs to reassure herself that even though she has moved off into her own life, she still has a home to come back to, where she'll always be welcome and cherished.

During this transitional time for both you and your young adult child, it will often be difficult to know how much to let go. You may sometimes be tempted to use controlling behavior—become more demanding or intrusive in your child's life just because you're not ready to trust her to fly safely and well on her own.

But don't do it. Young adults are especially vulnerable to criticism from their parents. They need to feel that their dignity as independent actors will be respected. Try shifting your perspective about your child—viewing him as you would anyone of his age that you don't share a mother-child bond with. Would you speak to a young person at your office the way you speak to your child? The best present you can give your child at this stage in his life is to accord him the respect you would give to *any* independent young person of his age, and to resist the impulse to indulge in relating styles that were appropriate when he was much younger.

Spreading Your Own Wings

Now that your children have grown into adulthood, you'll have much more time for yourself. This can be extremely disconcerting, especially if you've spent the last 18 years pretty much exclusively centered on raising your child.

If you still have a few younger children who aren't yet ready to leave the nest, your life will not change much with the independence of this one child. But once all your children have left the nest, you'll discover that you need to develop a new routine for yourself—one that, this time, can focus on your own development and interests.

Getting to Know... You!

So now what? Well, go back to the drawing board. Who are you? What do you like? What interests do you have? Don't be surprised if the answers to these questions don't come quickly—you've just spent the better part of two decades (at least) immersed in the interests of your children, and it's not at all uncommon for mothers to lose track of their own goals when they're busy tending to the needs of their families.

Of course, some women manage to keep a full, well-developed life of their own going throughout their childrearing years. If that's you, that's great. But for the rest of us, this is the time we need to start thinking of new ways to bring interest and fulfillment into our lives, now that the children are grown. It doesn't have to be anything earth-shaking. It just has to be something that gives us a reason to get up in the morning and get engaged in living.

Here are some things you can do to help you "get a life" when your children need you less:

➤ Make a list of subjects that you have always been interested in but never had time to study.

➤ Make another list of hobbies or crafts you think you might enjoy.

➤ Sign up for an exercise class.

➤ Reconnect with your spouse—both romantically and otherwise—and see if you can't rediscover the relationship you enjoyed before the children were born.

Womanly Wisdom

While exploring your options for ways to fill your newly freed-up time, take it slow and easy. There's no rush, and you want to make this new phase in your life enjoyable—you don't want to spoil it by introducing unnecessary pressures.

When You Just Can't Seem to Move On

Some moms become so immersed in their childrearing role that, when the children are grown, they can't seem to let go and build a new set of interests. If this is where you find yourself, consider counseling or therapy. Sometimes an outsider can help us make adjustments in our lives that we just can't manage on our own. The fact is that when our children need us less, we need ourselves more. But where do we begin to find that self after years of nurturing everyone else? The task of finding yourself can seem daunting, but with diligence, humor, and patience, it can be done.

And remember: Your job as mother will never really be over. If you've done your job well, you'll always have a place in your children's lives. What you have now is just a generous portion of extra time that you haven't had for a long time. It is perfectly acceptable and unselfish for you to take that time for yourself—you've earned it.

The Least You Need to Know

➤ When your child reaches young adulthood, it's time to renegotiate your mothering style once again.

➤ Adult children still need their moms; they just need a lot more autonomy then ever before.

➤ You can build a strong new relationship with your adult child by respecting his new, adult identity.

➤ New bonds can be forged by sharing your own practical expertise with your child.

➤ With your child now flown from the nest, it's time to rediscover who you are and to put some energy into nurturing yourself.

Chapter 16

Varsity Blues: Helping Your Child Prepare for College

If you are preparing your child for college, then your child must be close to the age of majority. This is a tricky stage of transition for him. But in choosing to go to college, your child is at least giving you one last stage between home and real world. So *you* get a little time to get used to the idea that your "little" one (who may by now be taller than you are) is really growing up. And for many children, going off to college is their first taste of real freedom, so you want to help them approach it with some goals in mind.

In this chapter, you'll learn how to handle your child's transition from dependent child to independent college student. And along the way, you'll learn how to use this time to forge a strong new relationship with the young adult your child is now becoming.

Matriculation into Maturity

When a child is on his own for the first time there is a tendency for him to want to mimic what he believes is adult behavior. The problem is, he's still young enough to believe he can have the privileges of adulthood without the accompanying responsibilities. College-age kids, in other words, often view this time as a sort of glorified childhood, only the toys are more interesting.

This can be troubling for you as a mom. Whatever fool stunts he may have tried during high school were done under your watchful eye, but when he goes off to college your child suddenly finds himself far from home, facing adult situations with the expectation that he will be making the decisions on his own.

Well, the most you can do is hope you gave your child enough information to guide him in his choices, and that life doesn't give him enough rope to hang himself. You have to trust that your years of teaching right from wrong, wise from foolish, can now serve as a kind of guardian angel that will keep your child from doing anything *too* stupid.

Mom-isms

To **matriculate** is to enroll in something, usually a college or university. Your child is matriculating into college. You, at this time, are matriculating into a new group, too—the elite group of mothers-of-adult-children.

Womanly Wisdom

The sooner you start saving for your child's college education, the better—colleges cost...a *lot*. If you can, set aside a little each month while your kids are still small. Properly invested, that little bit will grow into a hefty sum, and you'll have a good head start on covering tuition costs.

Containing the High Cost of College

When your child approaches college age you need to start thinking about a lot of things. Close to the top of the list is the very real issue of how you are going to pay for it. If you do not already have a plan in place you need to come up with one, fast—especially if your child has unrealistic expectations and no chance for a scholarship. College today is very expensive, and middle-income families have few options for financial aid, unless your child can qualify for an academic scholarship.

Considering Your Child's Contribution

You need to think about how much you want your child to contribute to the financial aspects of her education. If you are going to handle the whole tuition cost, make sure that you nonetheless provide parameters that will eventually help your child achieve financial independence. One of the biggest mistakes a parent can make is to do everything for a child, and then throw her out of the nest without any experience of financial responsibility. That is a sure way to maintain a dependent child for a lot longer than you would ever expect. You need to start treating your college-age child as a maturing young adult, even if you are going to take care of most of her needs during school.

Should Your Child Get a Job?

There are many compelling reasons for not expecting a child to pay for school or hold a job during college. An education has value, and some children are unable to balance schoolwork and employment. You do not want to diminish your child's ability to concentrate on learning. Colleges typically assume that students concentrate most, if not all, their energies on their class work and on building a rewarding extracurricular life.

On the other hand, all schools assume that there will be some student contribution to tuition costs. This contribution is usually assumed to come from seasonal and summer employment. This is not a bad thing: You definitely want your children to understand how much work goes into earning a dollar. And you want to give them an object lesson that they do not want to be limited to the types of jobs available to people without an education.

Keep in mind that many children do succeed in putting themselves through college. Juggling work and school is highly stressful, but it builds character. There is a downside to this, however: Some children who carry too heavy a burden of responsibility at too young an age may later need to cut loose to make up for the fun they think they might have missed.

Mom Alert!

Summer and seasonal jobs are hard to come by—unless your child plans ahead. If he or she doesn't look for a summer job until vacation has actually begun, your child may find that all the good or interesting ones are already taken. Spring break is a good time for your child to start scouting around for a summer job.

The Social Side of Education

Of course, your children are going to want to have active social lives in addition to pursuing their studies, and there is a lot of benefit to allowing your children the freedom to pursue their personhood in addition to their academic goals. They are going to learn a lot about themselves in the process and are going to lay the groundwork for their future. This is the time for them to experiment with different interests before they lock themselves into a set path.

Such weighty thoughts aside, college is just plain cool. And the social side of college is an education in its own right, as much as any course work. College is where children learn to fly on their own, socially as well as academically. They'll make mistakes and probably do a lot of things you'd rather not know about. But mistakes are opportunities for learning, and most children come through their college years intact.

Goal Setting: Theirs, Not Yours

College students are treated very differently than they were in high school. The entire system is geared toward making them responsible for their choices and actions. They are expected to really *want* to grow up. If they resist too much they are going to wind up confused, depressed, or out of touch with their peers. And the school will let them know if they aren't making the grade. So if you've prepared your child to appreciate the importance of college, you can expect him to do the right things. And the best preparation is to help your child set goals.

And the Award for Best Supporting Mom Goes to...

The best way for you to help your child set goals for college is to do a lot of listening. Your role at this point in your child's life is supportive, rather than directive. It's good to offer suggestions, but they should help expand an idea your child has, not undermine it.

Momma Said There'd Be Days Like This

God bless my mother, but to this day she says she should have handled my choice of college major differently. From the moment I was born I was creative and very artistic. Mom, however, was practical: "You need to earn a living." I liked to gab, so I went to law school—not a place terrifically supportive of artistic desires. It wasn't long before I realized that I didn't like studying law. But I did start writing. When I realized I could actually make a career out of something I enjoyed I was ecstatic—and that was the end of my law career.

Helping Resolve the "Major" Dilemma

One of the biggest challenges your college-age child will face is selecting a major. While you may have opinions on the subject, this really has to be left up to her. You can help best by working with your child to identify her likes and dislikes, and help her set goals that are geared to her interests. This approach pretty much guarantees that you are going to have a motivated, happy, and very likely successful student. Children should be taught to look inside themselves for guidance as to where to take their lives. Their lives are not meant to be sacrificed to boredom and misery at the altar of a guaranteed paycheck.

If your child is primarily interested in studying an area that will ultimately make him a lot of money, that's just fine. At least that is an honest goal. But make sure the choice is his. The most difficult aspect of helping your child set goals at this stage is keeping yourself from overly influencing the outcome. Even a young adult wants his mother's approval. Even without uttering a word, if you give that look of nose-in-the-air disapproval, you will have a negative impact on your child's decisions. You want to be involved in your child's life, and you want to offer guidance if you're asked for it. But you do not want to cause your child to think you disapprove of anything that will really make him happy.

Modulating Your Mothering Style

The difficulty in finding a way to be supportive without pushing your *own* agenda is that it seems you have to learn this trick practically overnight. One minute you have a teenager with whom you're still doing the mommy drill at bedtime: Did you brush your teeth? Did you do your homework? Did you set your alarm? Then, suddenly, your child goes off to college, and you're supposed to be able to switch all those mom-worries off. That's hard to do: You can't stop mothering just because your child hits a certain age. And, in fact, you don't really have to. You just have to be more subtle about it.

Self-Reliance: the Gift That Keeps on Giving

You give your child a wonderful gift when you allow her to come to her own conclusions about her future. Let her do her own research on what is available in certain fields and what kinds of majors will take her in the right direction. But encourage her to keep her options open for a while: You don't want your child to feel locked into anything. Help her learn to make the kinds of decisions that will influence her future.

Above all, make sure your child takes her time in making important choices. Most schools don't even require students to choose a major until the start of the third year. The first two years are intended as a time of exploration, when students are encouraged to try different things and see what interests them most.

The most important thing you can do at this stage in your child's life is to help her see that making choices in life begins on an internal level and works its way out, instead of the other way around.

And It's Not All About You

This time in your child's life is not the time for you to relive or fulfill your own unfulfilled ambitions. You are helping your child set his *own* goals. However well-meaning you may be, if you impose your needs and dreams on your child, you're requiring him to sacrifice his own. We *all* have a path that's right for us, and although you can guide your child in his search for his own proper path, in the end he has to walk it alone.

Womanly Wisdom

When you're making major decisions, the question you start with makes a big difference in the outcome. If you begin with the question, "What should I do with my life?" you are going to end up very confused. If you start with the questions, "What do I enjoy?," "Who am I?" and "How can I create a life that best reflects me?," you are going to build a foundation that can last a lifetime.

Checking Out the Campus

When your child explores which college to choose, you'll have the chance to experience the great adventure of campus visits. When your child has narrowed down the possibilities you should definitely take the time to go and see the schools. You make these trips for a practical reason—to evaluate the prospective schools and find the one best suited to your child's interests and personality, but there's an additional benefit: These college visits with your child are a special time for bonding.

Get to Know the New Town, Too

When you're checking out the schools, check out the towns they're in, too. Some are more student-friendly than others. Remember that, in addition to attending school, your child will be a member of the local community. You're a mom, so you're going to be worried about your child's safety and happiness in her new surroundings. You want to make sure the area offers enough in the way of transportation, activities, and security. If you check out the place and it lives up to your standards, you'll spend a lot less time worrying about your child while she's away at school.

Advise, Don't Command

Visiting the schools makes it easier to give guidance without seeming to impose your own agenda on your child. You have concrete examples and experiences to use to explain your position, and since your child made the campus visit with you, she can relate directly to the opinions you express. You can say, for example, "Little Town U. looked great, but did you notice there's no bus service into town? You're looking at a two-mile walk whenever you need to go buy toothpaste...." With examples to back up your suggestions or advice, you'll sound less arbitrary, and your child is more likely to listen to what you have to say.

Mom Alert!

When you're visiting college campuses, don't bring along younger siblings. They are likely to become bored and disruptive because the trip has very little to do with them. But this is a very big event in your college-age child's life and he deserves to be the center of attention.

You are helping your child make a very important decision. Although you are the final arbiter, you want to encourage your child's participation in every step of the process. If you feel a particular school is a bad choice, allow your child to know how you feel. You may find that your child has the same reservations.

Last-Chance Lectures

It is the summer after high school graduation and you are trying to mentally prepare yourself for the changes that are ahead. You have to get in some last mothering fixes before your baby leaves your nest and comes back a changed person. How do you get your almost-in-college child to sit still for your last-minute lectures?

Money Talks

One of the best things you can talk about is money. It's certainly likely to be high on your child's list of concerns, so he'll be receptive to a conversation. At the same time, while you're talking about finances, you'll find lots of openings for bringing up all the other issues that might be worrying you. For example, talking about how much money your child needs for transportation costs gives you a natural opening for a little lecture on security on campus after dark. Talking about money for snacks or junk food opens the door for a refresher lecture on good nutrition. The possibilities are endless.

So, begin with the budget. You want to make sure your child has the skills to live on his or her own. Make it very clear to your child what your expectations are and what his or her expectations should be. If you're planning to give your child money at regular intervals—say at the beginning of each month—you want to make it clear that a frantic phone call asking for more at the end of the first two weeks will not be appreciated.

When setting up a budget for your child, there are basic items you'll want to account for. You pay the dorm and meal-plan costs up front with the tuition, so the money you send your child during the school year will largely be spent on incidentals and entertainment. Here's what that allowance will probably be spent on:

➤ Books and supplies

➤ Personal care products or cosmetics

➤ Snacks to eat in the dorm

➤ The occasional pizza and movie

➤ Clothes

➤ Music CDs or cassettes

None of these items is crucial to your child's survival, but they may make a big difference in her enjoyment of her college years.

> **Womanly Wisdom**
>
> Figure out a realistic budget for your child and stick with it. Keep it consistent: If you give a certain amount one month, you should give the same amount the next. You could set up an emergency account with a cushion in case your child needs something extraordinary.

Putting Together a Payment Plan

You may want to make deposits into a checking account twice a month to help your child budget. That is a lot like the real world. Children do not have a lot of discipline, especially as college freshmen. When they realize how far the money will stretch, they will learn to comparison-shop or do without certain things.

Keep Listening to and Loving Your Child

Once you've gotten a few of those last-minute lectures out of your system, remember this: The best thing you can do with your child right now is to be open to his questions. Now's the time he just might be ready to share with you his own fears and worries, and you want to be ready with encouragement and support.

Moving On Up—to the Dorm

When I went moved into the dorm at college I made the mistake of packing everything I owned. I was so excited to be moving out of the house that I decided to bring my house with me. When I got to college, though, I realized my mistake—once I'd un-packed, there was no room left for *me!*

Keep in mind that your child will have less space than ever before. A typical dorm room is the size of a glorified closet. Some are larger, but there is certainly not room for massive amounts of junk. The simpler the better.

Decorator Mom

In the summer months just before your child goes off to college for the first time, you're going to need something to keep the going-away blues at bay. One way to keep the time fun and light is to get involved in helping your child pick the things she'll need to decorate her room. This lets you share in her excitement, and helps you feel that you're still an active part of her life.

Dorm Room Necessities

There are all kinds of matching bins and wastebaskets so your child can keep her stuff separate from her roommate's.

Mom Alert!

When you shop for dorm supplies, let your child make the choices if you can. College fads and fashions change so quickly that no mere mom can ever hope to keep up with what's "in." What you think is cool could stigmatize your child for life.

A good reading lamp is important, as is *anything* that will encourage organization—from a file cabinet to index cards. But keep in mind that the key concept is simplicity. The more stuff, the more difficult it will be for your child to keep things clean. And you don't want your child to overwhelm any roommates with too much stuff.

Posters or decorative items are a definite must, but this is a choice you *really* must leave to your child. Those puppies you think are so charming will just not cut it for your newly grown-up child's collegiate tastes—she'll probably replace it with something that looks like a cross between a monster and musical instrument. Think of it this way—at least *you* won't have to look at it every day.

Letting Them Go, a Little at a Time

Girls and boys are certainly different when it comes to packing them up and taking them to school. Depending on the child, you may find that you have to do a lot of things on the sidelines. You may just be asked to dump stuff and leave. Do not take it personally. You *want* your child to prefer the company of other college-age kids to yours. You are still loved and needed—just in a different way.

Save Him a Place to Come Home to

But no matter how proud you are of your child's newfound adulthood, you will be sad when you first send him to college. Give it time. You will soon adjust to having one less person in the house. You may even consider renting out his room. But don't be hasty. College kids can still be very territorial. It is probably better if you leave everything exactly as it was left, sort of a shrine. It will reassure your child to know that his room still waits for him, and it will reassure you as well—the room will be a constant reminder that he will, sometimes, come home.

Surviving the First Visit Home

When your child comes home for Thanksgiving break during the freshman year, be prepared for some attitude. Your new young adult is going to expect special treatment commensurate with his or her new status. Play along where you can. Make it clear that certain rules are to be abided by, but try not to resort to the mothering tone—that's a sure-fire way to spark a revolution. Make your house rules clear—explain that you are, after all, still a mom. You have a right to certain expectations of behavior, even from a grown-up college kid.

Most of all, don't take the new college persona too seriously. Your child is working out a whole new identity now, and that sometimes means that you bear the brunt of judgment: You're too uncool, too smothering, too protective…in a word, too much a Mom. Don't worry—your real child *will* return someday. You just have to hang in there until that day finally comes.

The Least You Need to Know

➤ The values you instill in your child as he grows up will help him set his adult goals.

➤ Avoid trying to overly influence your child's choice of schools and courses of study.

➤ Take the opportunity to visit prospective colleges with your child—it's a wonderful opportunity to build a new, adult bond with one another.

➤ College is expensive—it's best to begin saving for it when your child is very young.

➤ Expect your child to come home with attitude, at first, but don't let it worry you—it's only a temporary phase.

Part 5

Special Issues on the Motherhood Trail

Raising our children can be challenging under the best of circumstances. When you add in some of the extra complications that life can toss your way, you can expect to really be put to the test. In this part of the book we'll explore some of the special problems some mothers face, from coping with the special needs child to surviving as a single mom.

Sometimes the challenges we face are daunting, but mothers are a special breed—we always seem able to reach deep within ourselves to find the strength and humor to make it through, no matter what. And, as a member of the powerful sisterhood of moms, rest assured that you will make it, too.

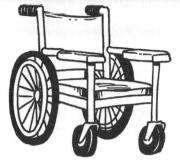

Chapter 17

Living with a Special Needs Child

In This Chapter

➤ The challenge and creativity of the special needs child

➤ Identifying your special child's needs

➤ Finding strength and hope together

➤ The power of being proactive

The first thing most mothers do when handed their newborn is check all the fingers and toes. When all outward signs of health are accounted for, we breathe a sigh of relief.

But many children are born with recognizable differences. Political correctness aside, we will immediately think "defect" or "handicap" and be terrified. No one really questions the idea of loving the baby. There is just an innate understanding that life is not going to go according to plan. Few mothers who discover "defects" in their children will react in a rational, enlightened way.

In this chapter, you'll learn that as the mother of a special needs child you are indeed facing a daunting challenge, but one that carries its own special rewards as well.

When Your Child Has Special Needs

Of course, many problems are not immediately discernible at birth. And even if you got an instruction sheet with your baby as you would with a new toy it would probably be incomprehensible. It would be great if all babies came with computer printouts of every potential physical, mental, and learning problem they are going to face. If you could know ahead of time that a child would develop cancer or have a mood disorder or some kind of disability, you could prepare yourself a little. But no. You have to wait like everyone else to see what unfolds. All you can count on is that raising a child, no matter what the circumstances you are given, is going to be a shared journey of survival and discovery.

There is a good cosmic reason for being left to our own devices. Although it seems infinitely unfair, responding to the unexpected needs of your offspring will bring out skills, talents, wit, and fortitude you would never believe you possess.

Having a child with special needs—and what child doesn't have them, to some extent—is part of your journey. It will bring out the best and worst in you and ultimately it will give you a tremendous opportunity for self-realization and spiritual growth.

There are no clear-cut answers for dealing with a child with special needs. Many times, as in cases of attention deficit hyperactivity disorder (ADHD), you may have no idea what is going on with your child. All you know is that your child seems more difficult than other children do, and you don't know why.

It's No Reflection on You

What is the first thing you are going to do when something doesn't seem right? You are going to blame yourself. If you are self-actualized enough not to blame yourself, don't worry—almost everyone else will do so. You will be blamed when your child acts up, shows poor impulse control, gets in trouble, acts like a barbarian, or does any number of things that seem intended to humiliate you.

Momma Said There'd Be Days Like This

If your child is hyperactive, I do not have to tell you what it's like to take her to a restaurant. And one hyper child is capable of accelerating all the others to higher speed. One night my husband was going to meet my three children and me at a family restaurant. He got stuck at the office and was late. By the time he arrived, the kids at our table were completely out of control. I was wild-eyed, and everyone else in the restaurant had signed a petition for us to get our food to go.

When the Problems Are Severe

There are many special needs challenges you may be faced with. Some are so devastating that there must be a very special reward awaiting mothers and children who suffer such hardships. There is nothing more painful to consider than coping with a child with terminal illness.

Children with blindness, deafness, developmental disabilities, or paralysis have special needs that are frustrating and disheartening, and the experience must be lonely at times.

It Is OK to Fantasize

What is worse, the mothers of special needs children not only blame themselves for their child's struggles, but also become guilt-ridden if they are not always thrilled with the challenges and sacrifices involved. All mothers fantasize about being childless on a tropical island somewhere—no cellulite—sipping frozen fruity drinks. At least I do. Throw in a few body builders on the beach in European bathing suits—hmmm.

When you are a mother of a special needs child you may feel very guilty when you slip into these fantasies. Instead of viewing fantasies as something all mothers experience, you may see them as somehow abandoning your child. All mothers want a break, and special needs mothers especially deserve one!

Mom-isms

You and your professionals (i.e. psychologist, pediatric psychiatrist) will want to be conservative in labeling a child too soon. What matters is there is a set of symptoms that interfere with your child's functioning. Your approach needs to be to address the symptoms without ruling out several possibilities.

The Quest for Answers

My own experience with special needs has been learning to cope with *attention deficit hyperactivity disorder* (ADHD). My older daughter was always different from other children her age. Of course, as her mom, I always viewed her as being interesting, creative, and more fun than other children. I still do. But all the while, she was coping with undiagnosed ADHD. Actually, as of the writing of this book we are still in the throes of solving the puzzle of accurate diagnosis. Sometimes special needs are not only one thing and must be approached from several perspectives.

The Creative Side of ADHD

All her life, my daughter kept unusual collections of things and enjoyed exploring topics that were not typical for a child her age. Instead of fairy tales she would beg for books on dinosaurs. Instead of dollies she would ask for lizards and snakes. Not only did she ask for them, she knew all about them and could tell any grown-up a thing or two about their care.

During her early years my daughter was shuttled between her "earth mother's" farm environment—50 acres of frogs, snakes, and other assorted creatures—and her father's immaculate home in the center of an upscale, closely knit community. It was a difficult time for us in the sense that I felt ostracized and my daughter was constantly put in the middle of some fairly rigorous parental competition.

The First Signs Become Apparent

Then, in addition to all this parental strife, my daughter became a difficult child. She was showing early signs of ADHD, but because she was not hyperactive, it was very difficult to pinpoint any set of symptoms as being caused by anything other than the stress of being from a divorced home. She could be a very unpleasant child. Other people might say she could be a little monster, but since she is my beloved child I will only say she could get on your nerves. She was demanding, easily agitated, and often very argumentative.

As she got older we tried different things—but nothing seemed to help. She did a slow crash and burn, developed extreme performance anxiety in school, and started to do poorly. The more the blame was focused in my direction, the more protective I became of her and of myself, and the more the vicious cycle continued.

Looking for Clues

I knew something was wrong with my child as soon as she started exhibiting signs of anxiety. I thought it was because her father was so critical and I did not admit that it might not be completely his fault. I now know that a biochemical disorder can be exacerbated by certain environmental factors, but those factors don't cause the condition. Attention deficit disorder (ADD) and other biochemical disorders are inborn, not cultivated. So there's no point in laying blame. The focus should be on how to help the child. And the greater the cooperation between the parents, the better for the child.

The problem with our situation—and it's a very common problem—was that there were enough external factors confusing the issue that no one thought to check our daughter's biochemistry. I had testing done on her through the school but the outcome was inconclusive. Still, the test results contained a lot of the information we could have used to arrive at a proper diagnosis, if only we had been looking in that direction. Instead, we continued the futile argument about which environment would be better for her, my creative one or her father's more controlled household.

Although I felt very frustrated and often depressed about the situation, I didn't give up the search for answers. That old mother's intuition thing would nag at me to always look for something else to explain things.

The Clues Mount Up

This child had a special spark, but something inside her was preventing her from reaching her potential. Although she wanted a more relaxed environment, and it was having a positive effect, it was not changing her

Mom Alert!

Be vigilant in seeking solutions, instead of looking to place blame, when your child shows serious problems in school. Too often a real disability is left undiagnosed because teachers—and parents—are too quick to assume the child just isn't trying hard enough.

performance in school. That remained consistently awful. Every time there would be a teacher conference I would hear the same dreaded comment: This child is not working to her potential.

One day I realized that the issue was not just her environment—it was now a serious issue of her health. I felt it my mission to discover what would help her to simply be a happy, functioning kid. Under the circumstances, I was very alone. The child, at twelve, was refusing to go to school, and I was accused of coddling her. I tried everything to get her to school short of calling in a police officer. I tried to tell people that I thought her extreme phobia had to indicate a serious problem, but all I was told was to get her to school.

Spiraling Downward

By this point, my daughter was having trouble keeping track of assignments and would fib about doing them. Her grades plummeted, and now she began having asthma attacks and became prone to illnesses that would keep her out of school. Again I would be blamed, because when she was at her father's he was able to get her to go to school.

I really thought I was losing my mind when my daughter started to slip into depression. I was being told she was fine at her father's, but then at my house she would fall apart. I have since learned that a child can pull it together in certain environments if he feels he has to. When a child is with his mother he most likely feels emotionally safe enough to let everything out. The problem is I was beginning to feel as though I was hallucinating.

Pinpointing the Problem, at Last

When my daughter reached adolescence she fell further apart, but in some ways she was also beginning to pull herself together. She finally realized that something wasn't right and she became very cooperative when I was finally able to get her a preliminary (good) diagnosis of clinical depression and then attention deficit disorder. These are serious conditions, and she's likely to be dealing with them for a long time—possibly all her life. And yet, just having a starting point and some names for what was bothering her brought us all relief. Especially my daughter, who had been convinced that her troubles were all her own fault because she was stupid and lazy.

After conservatively experimenting with various medications we finally found a combination that seemed to work. Medication is extremely important for these mood disorders and for ADHD, and can in fact be miraculous. After only a few days on Ritalin my daughter came home with an A+ on a language arts exam—a class in which, prior to diagnosis and medication, she had been earning a consistent D+. Neither of us could believe it. I practically alerted the media. I felt so validated and I knew that she did, too. I could see her self-esteem expand before my eyes.

Womanly Wisdom

Sometimes just getting validation that there are children with similar symptoms who fit within certain diagnoses (a diagnosis) can make a huge difference in your special needs child's self-esteem. With a name to put on her condition, she can finally stop blaming herself for the limitations she has been laboring under all along.

Vindication and Jubilation

Of course, medication did not magically solve all her problems overnight. She is still in the throes of medicinal experimentation but I am confident we are on the right track. She had fallen pretty far behind, and a simple increase in her ability to concentrate was unlikely to overcome her disadvantage in that regard.

It had been and still is a very difficult journey trying to find answers that would help my daughter just be herself with whatever potential she has. She has been fighting a constant struggle that is really from within. It has been very confusing for all of us. During some very crucial developmental stages she was learning not to trust herself, no matter how hard she tried. It is devastating for a child to feel that no matter what she does she can't succeed.

When in Doubt, *Ask!*

The most frustrating thing about conditions like ADHD is that you just can't always know which questions to ask. I had never heard of ADHD, and, in fact, it is common for the condition to go undiagnosed in many of its sufferers. But the difficulty of diagnosis is not matched by a difficulty in treatment. The effects of appropriate medication combined with counseling and support can be so profound as to seem almost magical.

Dealing with the Fallout in the Family

A special needs child can influence the harmony of the entire family. When you have a child with an undiagnosed disorder you can be sure you will have conflict between husband and wife and constant struggle between siblings. Different rules apply to special needs children. For the first time in years, now that my daughter is on the right track and I have a sense of what I am dealing with we argue less and get along much better. I am much less exasperated because I can see things from her perspective and I know I am a good mother and that she is not purposely trying to drive me bananas. I can often ask her to do something without getting much argument in return— something I could never do before.

Of course, not all behavior problems are caused by faulty biochemistry. Some children are just plain bratty and spoiled. They present a parenting challenge, but the problems they cause are simply not in the same ballpark as having a child who can't respond to whatever discipline method you use. For example, ADHD children have difficulty understanding the consequences of some of their choices. If you try to discipline them by consequences, you need to make sure the consequences are immediate enough that the kids will care about them.

The Importance of Being Proactive

Whatever your child's special need may be, it is important for you to continue seeking answers until you are satisfied that you have the information you need. As much as we might wish it were otherwise, most situations are not clear-cut. You can't walk into a doctor's office and expect to get all the answers. You have to be far more proactive than you would like to be, because otherwise you will not get the answers you need. You can't give up.

We were fortunate because we found professionals who were able to give us some of the answers we needed. We are now getting help with the school issues and are learning how to work behaviorally with some of the issues related to having ADHD or whatever my daughter's ultimate diagnosis might be. We are always looking at ways to improve our lives, but we are doing it together and from a basis of strength and confidence. When you know what you are dealing with you can become a problem solver instead of merely reacting to situations. You can't control many things but at least you can alleviate your confusion about them.

A Mother's Crusade

Motherhood is a type of hero's journey, even under the best of circumstances. When you have a special needs child you have a special mission to fulfill on behalf of your child and yourself. Special needs force you to look inside yourself for the answers you can't find anywhere else. You need to avoid developing a victim mentality and learn to truly believe that you can make the difference. Pray for help and listen for the answers. Have enough faith in yourself and in your personal truth.

Mom Alert!

Although medication can make a major difference in your ADHD child's social and academic performance, remember that he *is* still going to need all the support you can give him. Don't forget that he has likely got a lot of issues to resolve from when he was struggling without a diagnosis. Seek counseling if you can so he can have even more support in working through those issues. A trained counselor can also give you the support you need. Sometimes mothers need help too.

Living with the Solutions

When you know what your child's limitations are, you can create in your home an atmosphere in which limitations need not be seen as obstacles. Attitude is the most important aspect of learning to live with an illness, injury, or anything that makes your child need something out of the ordinary. Some people insist on pigeonholing others, and pass judgment on anyone who doesn't fit into one of their neat categories of "normal" behavior. It is important to teach all children that being different is a blessing, not a curse.

If a child feels he is defective, he will have more difficulty believing in his own progress. If a child believes he can't do the same things his friends can do or can't accomplish his goals, he will live up to that negative expectation. The best gift you can give a special needs child is the confidence that will ultimately lead to independence. One way to do that is to teach your special needs child to recognize the need for keeping up his prescribed treatment. But remember, this is so he can be the best and healthiest he can be, not so he is in competition with others.

Compliance

A very important issue for children with mental illness, such as mood disorders or ADHD, is to make sure you give them enough understanding that they will always be in compliance with their treatment. As children grow into adolescence and young adulthood there is a great risk that they will decide they no longer need their medication. Some of the medications have such remarkable effects that they give the young person a false sense of security. He might decide to try to go it alone without the medicine in an effort to feel more like his peers. No one wants to think of himself as having something wrong with him that will never go away.

Womanly Wisdom

Start early in indoctrinating your child into understanding what is happening to her brain when she has problems concentrating or is having a stable mood. If you bring your child into the process of recovery as much as possible now, you have a greater likelihood of later compliance.

The best thing you can do is stress how important it is to keep to a regular medical regimen. When a child is younger you can literally put the pills in his mouth to ensure that he is following doctor's orders. But there will come a time in your child's life when he takes over the responsibility for treatment, and then you can only pray for compliance.

Speak the Truth

It is equally important that you tell your child the truth about things. There is nothing that can bring about denial as much as a diagnosis of something categorized as a mental illness. I believe mental illness is a misnomer when you understand the process of a chemical imbalance, but at this point in history, we cannot overcome pervasive ignorance on the subject. The minute you say "mental illness," you encounter a great deal of fear.

We don't need to label people according to disorders that are manageable with medication. If we need to label our children, we should do so only to understand what we can do to help them and what appropriate treatment might be. We want to start by helping them to see what is special and wonderful about them.

Share Your Experiences with Your Child

The most important thing you can do for a child who is going to need to rely on medication for the stability he has achieved, is to reinforce and then reinforce again the necessity for taking the medication and for avoiding recreational drug and alcohol use. One way to do this is to be open about your own struggles—if any—with a similar problem.

I was very honest with my daughter about my own history with manic depression and medication. I have always explained, in age-appropriate terms, why I take medication and what may happen if I don't. Many families with children who take medication for mood disorders have a family history of those disorders, due to the strong genetic link. Don't dismiss the opportunity for education by saying dismissive things like, "You used to have a crazy aunt." Children will respond to your attitude about their illness, and they need to learn to accept that you can have a disorder of any kind and still be OK.

Share the Experience of Others, Too

One thing that was very helpful for my daughter when she was still untreated was to see a website I had found about ADHD. It had a chat board where teenagers wrote to each other about how they felt before treatment and how much better they feel now. There is only so much a parent can explain to a child before the child tunes out. When peers who have experienced similar things convey those experiences, the impact is much greater.

Now that my daughter has the right professionals on board and is following a pre-scribed regimen (a proper diagnosis and medication) it is up to her to follow through on her life goals. A mother can be a support system and can help provide all the necessary resources to help the child find the answers, but there comes a time when the child has to make some very important decisions for herself.

Recognize Your Own Limits

This is why it is important for you as a mother to understand your limitations. Your child may have a disorder or disability that makes him or her different from other children, but unless your child lacks a certain reasoning ability and will need to be under your perpetual care, you must respect that he has free will. It is important that he be expected to exercise this free will for his own benefit or his own burden.

Knowing When to Let Go

You have a hero's journey tied up with helping your child find whatever solutions he needs but that is where your paths may split. Your child must then decide the kind of life he wants. No one can force your child to be healthy and happy unless he wants to be. After you have helped him find resources to make his path manageable, you have to step aside. Otherwise, his path will have no meaning for him.

The most difficult thing for a mother to do is let go. And doing so is 10 times more difficult when you have a child with special needs. In many ways the child becomes your focal point and you lose a bit of your own identity as you try to help the child fit in or be well. But remember that your goal is to help your child fly on his own. You are never going to stop worrying, but at some point you have to have faith in your child and trust that you have done the best you can.

The Least You Need to Know

➤ Laying blame for special needs problems is a waste of time and energy better expended on your child.

➤ Aggressively seek the information you need to secure a diagnosis for your child.

➤ Share your experiences with your special needs child—it will reassure them that they are not alone.

Chapter 18

Dealing with Divorce

Even in the best of marriages, there are going to be pressures that pull spouses away from one another. As time passes and you move into the business of running a life together, you can have marital problems based simply on boredom. Sometimes it is simply a matter of a temporary feeling: "You get on my nerves," or "I hate your face!" But sometimes the feelings are more serious. If you have overwhelming hostile thoughts and these feelings do not pass, you may have some marital difficulties that need professional attention.

In this chapter, you'll read about how to spot problems and try to fix them before they escalate to an actual rupture, how to handle the situation when a divorce is inevitable, and how you, as a mother, can help your child cope with the changes that divorce brings.

Giving Your Marriage Your Best Shot

If you are in the early phases of getting on each other's nerves you may just be shifting your focus from yourself to your husband. You may be legitimately dissatisfied with your life, and you may be looking to your husband to make you happy and fulfill your needs. This is a tall order, even for the most sensitive of husbands, particularly if you have not made your needs clear. Too often we expect our husbands to know instinctively what we want. We are gravely disappointed when they walk around with what appears to be a big question mark over their heads.

We may be dissatisfied with our lives and blame that dissatisfaction on the fact that he doesn't bring us flowers anymore. If you look at it realistically, he probably never brought flowers. But in the early phases of the relationship you wouldn't have cared. There was the excitement of something new, sexual tension, and all your dreams somewhere off into the future.

The Deadliness of Living in a Relationship Rut

If it can be avoided, do not let your marriage unravel due to lack of interest. Falling into a routine is natural. Unless you live in a city where there is a lot to do or are the great-outdoors type, you might find your time alone with your husband limited to dinner and a movie. When you let your relationship devolve to this level of routine, it is perfectly understandable that you will wonder whether this is all there is.

Or perhaps you finally get a night alone without the children and then find you have nothing to talk about. You may even wind up talking about the children. It is easy for a couple to define themselves as parents and lose sight of what they need from each other. It is also easy to define yourself as a mother and to forget your needs as a woman.

Womanly Wisdom

The secret to a happy relationship is to build on what you have, instead of focusing on what you do not have. Comparisons lead to envy, which is very destructive. If you were to switch places with the friend who "has it all," you might just find her problems are even worse than yours are.

Fantasy versus Reality—Reality Loses

Many women retreat into the world of fantasy. Romance novels and chick flicks are great entertainment. But if your relationship is already a little shaky, make sure you do not compare your husband to the fantasy hunks. You're only setting yourself up for disappointment. We can't all marry long-haired swarthy muscle men or bodice-ripping Civil War heroes. Fantasy men say what we want and behave the way we dream our mates will— and for good reason. Most romance novels are written by women, for women. The heroes are everything we want our stereotypical heroes to be. Real husbands, who sometimes wake up looking like the undead and take pride in how bad they can smell, simply can't measure up.

Beware the Grass-Is-Greener Syndrome

At one point or another, just about every woman looks at other women's husbands as if they might somehow be more perfect than her own. Tread carefully on this count. This is not a reason to change your life by changing your relationship. When you start the process of uncoupling you may find there is no turning back—even if you want to.

Breaking Out of Your Rut

If your life is not going the way you would like it to, it may just be time to reevaluate things. You have to be objective about the situation. Begin by being honest with yourself about your own role in the relationship. After all, you're not the only one with fantasies that aren't being fulfilled. Sweats and T-shirts may be comfortable and functional but they will not put us on the cover of any magazines. We may find ourselves in a rut and may be just as boring to our husbands as they are to us. Consider making a change in your routine. Even if it is a night of dress up, or attendance at a lecture, anything that says, "You are special. I want to be with you" is a good thing for the relationship.

Here are some things you can do to change your relationship routine:

➤ Make a date for a trip to a "no-tell" motel. If you do not know what this is, I am not going to tell you.

➤ Get away for a weekend alone and agree not to talk about the children.

➤ Attend a lecture that is not above either of your heads and that will give you something to talk about.

➤ Turn off the television for at least an hour at night.

➤ Take long walks alone together.

➤ Talk about the early days of your relationship.

➤ Talk about dreams and goals for the future and do not laugh at or belittle each other's fantasies.

➤ Spend an evening kissing each other with no sex allowed.

➤ Ask questions of each other and listen to the answers. Sometimes couples need to become reacquainted.

➤ Think of five things you like about each other and repeat them to yourselves when you feel restless.

➤ Write a list of what you love about your husband and give it to him. Reinforce what he does right.

Mom Alert!

Now you have children, bills, plugged toilets, and too many things to do. If you are not careful, you may have a marriage where no one shows up. At the end of the day you may not even have the enthusiasm to have a good argument.

Take a Reality Check

Some of your efforts at breaking your routine may feel artificial but they will go a long way toward preventing you from becoming hypercritical of your marriage. If the marriage becomes a monster of infinite proportions you will find yourself in an endless cycle of frustration. It may seem as though it would be fun to get back into the single world after you have heard all your husband's jokes for the 100th time, but it is really not worth the backlash of breaking up a family. It can be very lonely outside the safe world of the ordinary. And it is never going to be easy for your children.

Just a Phase?

If you can weather this boredom and familiarity phase with your husband, you just might find yourself coming out on the other side of it with new resolve and a refreshing new relationship. Treat it as a period of renegotiation. When you have been together for a while your needs change. Instead of using these changes to tear down what already exists, and moving on to something and someone else, you can tear down what is obsolete and create something new together. This will usher in a new phase of love that gives security to your children and a solid foundation for you. It requires effort to do this, of course, but in the end it is all a question of attitude. You need a sense of acceptance of each other to find this level of intimacy.

Spicing Up Your Sex Life

Sex with the same partner after years of getting to know each other can be wonderful. You don't need to seek excitement outside your marriage. You may just need to try a few new things.

For example, there are many wonderful videos about sex, eroticism, and fantasy that you can explore with your husband. You want to be sure to select tapes that you will both enjoy—if one of you is uncomfortable with graphic images of sex it won't be good for either of you. But if you find tapes that are more instructional and are based on improving the quality of lovemaking in a monogamous relationship you might find ways to achieve levels of intimacy you could never have imagined.

The Payoff

It is not frivolous for you to put so much energy into maintaining a sexual relationship with your husband. At the very least you want to make sure there is affection in the relationship. Human beings need physical contact. Studies have shown that infants do not thrive in situations where there is no one to hold and cuddle them. I am convinced that adults also need to be held and cuddled. Hugging is like a miracle cure.

Often, people turn to others outside their marriage to fulfill their need for closeness and intimacy when they don't feel they're getting what they need from their spouse. An affair is a way to distract yourself from the

Womanly Wisdom

The best way to hug your husband is heart to heart. Even if you have to stand on a chair, you want to align yourself so you are completely open to the transfer of love. It is very difficult to maintain anger or negative feelings when you are generating such a positive connection.

real issues of your relationship and is like a sugar rush. You feel great at the time but later comes the big letdown. Aside from any moral implications, when you become obsessed with an affair you are avoiding your true feelings and merely postponing dealing with the real issues.

Counseling Can Help

Counseling can help couples who have a good foundation. A good counselor can help you see things from each other's point of view and can help you develop strategies for bringing the relationship back on track. It is really worth doing if you can. Many aspects of your life will be negatively affected by the experience of divorce. Although divorce is now commonplace and is often the only solution to a bad relationship, many marriages can be made stronger by adversity if the couple makes the heart-and-soul commitment to stay together through whatever life throws in their path.

Mom Alert!

Divorce is not good for children or other living things. If you can't maintain a healthy marriage and need to uncouple, try to separate with kindness, keeping your eyes toward the needs of your children.

Uncoupling

Sometimes relationships cannot be salvaged. There are problems that cannot be resolved with therapy and an effort at better communication. Some people are incompatible at their core. Some relationships are violent and contaminated by drugs or alcohol, and some relationships have such a serious lack of trust that they cannot be restored. In these situations there is no choice but to divorce. Although divorce is difficult for children in any situation, it is worse to stay in a marriage that is destructive to your mental, physical, and spiritual well-being.

When Breaking Up Is Bravery, Not Cowardice

This is one of the most difficult decisions a woman can make. If you are the one having to decide whether your marriage is healthy for you and your children, I pray that you have the internal guidance, wisdom, and strength to make this decision wholeheartedly. If you have to make a difficult choice you should not beat yourself up over it. You are not a failure or a bad mother for choosing to end a destructive marriage. If you make the decision with thoughtfulness and an eye toward the larger implications, you should be considered brave. It is one of the most difficult situations you will ever face. It may seem as though your world is coming to an end, but you can survive and create a new and better life.

The most important thing you need is faith in yourself. Endurance doesn't hurt either. Divorce is an internal emotional battle as well as a conflict between two people. A strong support system is a blessing. So is faith in something higher than yourself.

Some married partners manage to "uncouple" by mutual agreement—they manage to make the break amicably. When it is done this way you can present it to your children in a united way and there will be less stress in the way you work out the details of your ultimate separation.

In reality, however, divorce tends not to be friendly. Even when both people eventually come to agree that divorce is the right thing to do, most divorces are instigated by one partner against the other.

Emotions will flare and blame and accusation will become the order of the day. Once the decision to separate has been made, human nature requires some kind of emotional distancing. This is why former lovers often become the bitterest of enemies. If one person is the so-called "wronged" party, he or she is going to have a particularly strong need to depersonalize the relationship and make the former partner an adversary.

Deciding to Make the Break

People can become very dysfunctional when their marriage is in trouble. My first husband and I tried therapy and were literally fired by our therapist. We definitely could not communicate. To make it worse, we were both trained litigators. We were not married very long—only four years—but it was long enough to make an impression on me. And we also had a child together.

I've been married twice. Neither marriage had any real chance for permanence. Each time I married, I lacked the self-awareness to know that what I was doing was not right for me. My first marriage was so unsuccessful that I tried everything possible to keep the second marriage alive long after I should have thrown in the towel. I slowly realized, however, that I had once again chosen my marriage partner poorly.

Deciding to end this relationship was one of the healthiest things I have ever done. It gave me a chance to use what I had learned to create a life that would sustain my emotional, mental, and spiritual needs. Even though I had two difficult experiences, I would always recommend marriage if you find the right person.

Divorce is not the easiest way to cope with dissatisfaction with your marriage. It comes with a high price, particularly when there are children involved. Unless your marriage threatens you physically, mentally, or spiritually in a significant way, you and your husband should try everything possible to keep your family together.

Womanly Wisdom

Before you even think about tying the knot, get to know yourself. Then, any decision you make about a partner is not going to reflect what you need to learn the hard way; rather, it will create a foundation from which you can build your dreams.

Early Steps to Separate Lives

When you decide to end a marriage you are going to feel temporarily insane. You may need some psychological help because divorce is one of the most stressful situations you will ever experience. You have to get used to the reality that someone you loved is no longer even a friend. When you first split up you will be amazed at the amount of anger involved. You might not have a conversation with your estranged husband except through lawyers. You might be facing a war over things that otherwise would not seem important. Divorcing couples fight over the division of property. And, most important, they fight over how to care for the children.

Consider the Children

It's best to approach uncoupling as reasonably as possible. If you can avoid a battle over custody you stand a greater chance of moving ahead with your life in a healthy way. Most important, the more vicious the divorce, the more it will hurt the emotional growth of your children.

The single most damaging factor for children of divorce is the continued conflict between the parents. If the parents have a bloodbath and vent their emotions through the court system, the children are the victims. They feel like rubber bands pulled between the two most important people in their lives. They have an inherent loyalty to each parent and should never be made to choose.

Working Through the Visitation Worries

When your children spend time with their father you are sure going to feel a sense of helplessness, and you will want to know what goes on at his house. It is only natural. In many situations the children have not been away from you, their mother, for any length of time. When you divorce, unless the court finds strong reasons to prevent this, you are going to have to send your children to their father's house while you stay home and worry.

Mom Alert!

Perhaps the cruelest thing a parent can do to a child is to put him or her in the middle of a divorce. Children are not property to be awarded as a prize. Although you might not think it could happen to you, most divorcing couples lose sight of the impact the divorce has on their children.

Womanly Wisdom

Divorce is so unnatural when children are involved. Think of it from their perspective. They are in a home—and now they have two homes. If you are having a war with your ex-husband, both homes become battlegrounds. The children do not feel safe and secure anywhere.

Shared Custody Works Best for Kids

What divorcing parents frequently forget is that the child loves both of them and doesn't want to have to pick sides. The child will want to maintain a relationship with both his mother and his father. Even in cases of violence and abuse. Unfortunately, in some situations the court has to limit the involvement of one parent. The children who have the most difficult time adjusting are those who are prevented from seeing and having a relationship with one parent. When a parent is suddenly absent from their lives children frequently think it is because of something *they* have done wrong.

Momma Said There'd Be Days Like This

Even though you would like to make your ex-husband disappear, you have to accept that your child wants a relationship with him. You may think he is an untrustworthy person, but you should not say so to your child. By bad-mouthing your ex you only hurt the child and potentially damage his trust in you. You do not want to force your child to choose between the two of you. And you do not want to diminish your ex in the eyes of his children. Eventually, your child will figure out his parents' merits and faults for himself.

Your Child Needs the Two of You

In typical circumstances your child will adjust best if he or she is permitted to have a relationship with both parents. That is to say, your child should feel neither your interference nor your disapproval when she builds a relationship with your ex. Even if your ex is not as supportive of this philosophy as you are, do not be pulled into an ongoing battle. Your children are able to learn by example.

Your child will have issues with her father that are separate from your relationship with her. Although it is very difficult to do, you should let them resolve their own issues. Be supportive but do not get in the middle; if you do, you will be the one to get burned. Children of divorce learn the art of manipulation. Do not be played as a pawn.

Calming Down the Combativeness

The actual process of divorce can be a nightmare. Otherwise reasonable and intelligent people have been known to slash their spouse's clothing and throw it out a window. People will wipe out bank accounts, leaving the other person with nothing. Some people even resort to violence. Divorce touches everyone at the core of their sense of security. There is a process of anger and grieving much like the one that occurs in a death.

Moving Through Mediation

You can prolong and accentuate the agony or you can try to approach divorce through mediation. Mediation is a fairly new system that is being adopted in most states. It is a wonderful alternative to standard divorce proceedings because the mediator, a neutral third party with certain education and certification, helps couples dissolve their marriages with the least amount of conflict. The conflict is resolved in a setting that is intended to balance the power between the parties so that both can express themselves and reach mutual agreement.

Both parties typically receive advice from individual attorneys so that they are aware of their rights, but in a mediation there are no lawyers present. The mediator may be a lawyer but he or she does not work as an advocate for either side. This gives the parties much more control in determining their own destinies and ultimately leads to greater cooperation between the parties as they continue to be parents to their children.

Mom-isms

Mediation is a process in which a third party helps couples negotiate a divorce settlement with the least amount of conflict.

Keeping Children's Interests Paramount

One of the nicer aspects of mediation is that it strives to keep the interests of the child at the center of the process, and separates the issues of child custody and property. In standard divorces custody issues often are used as leverage to influence the property settlement. People can be vicious when money is involved.

When the custody portion of mediation is complete, mediators often suggest bringing the children into the process so they can understand the changes that are going to occur. It is important to stress to a child that although Mom and Dad are divorcing each other neither of them is divorcing the child. Mediated agreements can even reflect statements of intention, as if the couple were substituting for the marriage vows a vow to continue to parent together.

Momma Said There'd Be Days Like This

Mediation is not for everyone. When I tried mediation with my first husband we made a little progress, and quickly reached an impasse. Mediation is impossible when two people are unyielding in their positions. It is successful only when the mediator can move the parties to a compromise position they can both live with.

There is no doubt that children with this kind of divorce experience adjust much more readily than children who are used as pawns in a dysfunctional adult chess game.

Custody Concerns

There are many ways to arrange custody of the children. It is not always necessary to divide time equally. Different schedules can accommodate the goal of fostering a relationship in both households. For example, not all ex-husbands are interested in having any custody at all. If your ex *is* interested, it is good to provide for access to school information and notices as well as to communicate about health matters. With the help of your mediator, you'll want to structure an agreement that enables each parent to be a parent while not causing too much interaction between the divorced couple.

If both of you know what is expected of you and such things as schedules are clear, there is very little reason for you to have to interact with your ex. What you want is a cordial relationship with your ex after the divorce. You do not want to be best friends if you can help it because that would send too many mixed signals to your children—they'll never give up the dream that someday you and their dad will get back together. It will also prevent you from moving on with your life. You will always have some emotional attachment to the father of your children but you should not put yourself in a position of hanging onto the past. With a little emotional distance, the past can look very rosy—and forgetting why the decisions were made can pull you into a great deal of internal turmoil.

Momma Said There'd Be Days Like This

When I separated from my first husband, I knew it was the right thing to do. But after a while of living on my own I started to doubt myself. He and I went out to dinner and we were on our best behavior. We sustained it for a while, but it wasn't long before we fell back into our former pattern of argument and hostility. That cured me of any ideas I might have had about getting back together.

Helping Children Cope with Divorce

When your decision has been made and the details have been ironed out you have to deal with the *real* issues of the divorce. Your children are going to need special attention to help them adjust to the changes in their lives.

Here are a few of the things to watch out for with children of divorce:

➤ Children of divorce often become skilled manipulators. Do not fall into the "buy-me-this" trap because you feel guilty.

➤ Children of divorce may have some backlash adjustments that do not appear until later. Just as you do, your children need to work through their feelings of loss and insecurity.

➤ Children of divorce may try to blame you for things because you feel you deserve it. This is a sure way to lose the balance of power in your home. You are the Mom, so you need to be in charge.

➤ Children of divorce may cling to you while they go through the adjustment to the new family structure. Don't be alarmed. It will pass. Just give a lot of hugs and reassurance that everything will work out, even if you are not sure it will.

Don't Toy with Toys

One of the biggest complaints children seem to have about divorce is going back and forth between households. Even if you are the most organized, color-coded woman in the world you will not be able to get through the visitation schedule without some lost articles of clothing or missing toys. As the children get older it is inevitable that homework that is due the next day will be at their father's while they are at your house.

These are the logistical facts of the divorced life. They are not overwhelming unless you allow them to be. Lower your standards of perfection and try to anticipate problems before they happen. You can create systems that can ease the burden on you, your ex, and your children.

It is important not to make a big fuss over missing items. Children see their clothing and toys as belonging to *them*, not to a particular house. If they are overly anxious about items left at either house, and feel they will be chastised, they may learn to omit the facts. It is difficult enough to raise children in an intact home to be open and honest. You do not want to paint them into a corner so they feel they have to hide the truth.

If you are concerned about items being returned, work it out with the ex, not through the child. Make it the parents' responsibility or treat it as a matter of organization for the child—not "my house versus his house." Children are perfectly capable of keeping track of things. It is fine to encourage them to organize their things the night before a transition. Just don't make it seem like a big deal. You can mark items you buy so that it's easier for the ex to send things back.

Womanly Wisdom

You can try sharing between your house and your ex's and not worrying about where items are, but get used to the idea: eventually one house will have all your child's socks and the other will have all the underwear.

The Kids Are Wiser Than You Know

Kids are much more resilient than you might imagine. The mother of a nine-year-old at my son's school approached me and thanked me over and over for my son's help. She explained that she was in the middle of a divorce and that my son had been instrumental in helping her son cope. I had no idea, of course. My son isn't even a big talker. Evidently he had talked all about it and had shown his friend the ropes. His behavior proves my point: If children are given love and support, a broken marriage does not mean a broken child.

Don't Forget Yourself

Although you are going to be focused on your children during a divorce, do not forget what *you* need. It can take at least two years to recover some sense of balance after a divorce. It can take even longer to be able to trust anyone again in an intimate way.

New Relationships

Many women need immediate reassurance that they are still desirable, so they jump into relationships to ease the pain of transition. You have to watch out for this. It can be fun for you but it can also rip your emotions to shreds. You want to give yourself time to heal from an unhealthy situation so you will be ready to handle a healthy one.

Mom Alert!

Rebounding is difficult at any time in life, but rebounding into ill-considered relationships when you have children is dangerous. Give yourself time, post-divorce, to get over your marriage and develop a clear idea of what's right for you before you jump into a new affair.

Besides, it can be very confusing for children if you bring a lot of new men into their lives. If your ex-husband has a regular visitation schedule, use this guilt-free baby-sitter to enable you to get out and explore new options. In this way you can have some social life without causing too much disruption for your family. Your children are used to seeing you as a mommy and might feel threatened by seeing you in flirting mode. When the time is right and you feel you have a relationship with potential, *then* you can introduce everyone.

Just remember to be good to yourself. Divorce is a difficult process but it can give you the opportunity to have the wonderful life you deserve. Don't be frightened. Change can be unsettling but it is also filled with endless possibilities. You have already seen a path that has not worked out for you. This new path may be just what you were looking for.

Going Back for a Little Mothering Yourself

When you divorce resist the temptation to run home to your own Mama. It is wonderful to receive support and love and assistance from your parents but you do not want to give up your autonomy. Families have a way of smothering the newly divorced.

Accept what you need but realize that the womb is only a temporary residence. You don't want to prolong the labor pains that are necessary to your rebirth. Nor do you want to give up the authority you have over your children. It is difficult for them to maintain respect for you when you are answering to an even higher authority—your own mom and dad.

You and your children can get through this time and can create a new kind of family. Today, unlike in previous generations, the nuclear family is not the only acceptable permutation. You can create a family in any form you like. This can be a very special time for you and your children as you bond together as a team.

Getting Peer Support

Be aware of your limitations and stress levels. If you have difficulty coping, get help or join a support group. You will feel awful if you take it out on your children. You need to know that there are common experiences for all women experiencing divorce. You are not a failure and your life is not over; it is only beginning. Remember to do some nice things for yourself.

When you are newly divorced here are a few suggestions of ways to be nice to yourself:

➤ On your nights without children do not feel compelled to go out. Get to know yourself again.

➤ On your nights without children make plans with positive people so you can develop a new social life.

➤ If you have time, take a class you have always wanted to take.

➤ If you need to be sad don't fight it. Just don't dwell on things that bring you down.

The Least You Need to Know

➤ If you can keep your marriage together it is worth it—divorce is a major trauma and is not always the best answer.

➤ Sometimes a marriage fails because of simple boredom. If you can get past that phase you can possibly have a wonderful life together.

➤ If you must divorce and do not have extraordinary circumstances, mediation is much better than a slugfest in court.

➤ Your children do not want to be caught up in a parental tug of war. They need to be free to love both of you.

Single Mom Survival

In the best of all possible worlds, no mother would have to go through the breakup of a family. But the reality is that many of us have marriages that are so dysfunctional we do not have the support we need, anyway. When a relationship breaks down the conflict can be unbearable. You will find yourselves arguing about the most ridiculous things.

At the end of my second marriage I could predict my husband with ease. I knew that if I said one thing, my husband would have to say the opposite. And if for example, one of the children spilled something right next to my husband, I would hear the bellowing sound of "De-bo-rah, so-and-so spilled on the floor"—as though somehow I had put the kid up to spilling in the first place.

When You Know It's Over

There is a point in the death throes of a marriage when something inside you breaks. When this happens you no longer feel anger, you no longer feel quiet desperation, you actually feel indifference. It is like waking from a deep sleep and finding that you have been dreaming the wrong dream. It really is a point of no return. You suddenly develop a perspective that you've never had. You finally recognize how hard you've been beating your head against a wall to perpetuate a relationship that doesn't even exist any more.

If you reach a point of certainty—as opposed to ambivalence—about your choice of divorce it is much easier to handle your new role as a single parent. You need to devote a lot of energy to your own healing but you also have an awesome responsibility to help your children navigate the waters of childhood. Even though their father is active in your children's life, *you* will still be providing them with an environment that has to become their anchor.

Dealing with the Initial Shock

Get used to this one simple fact: You are not going to feel much like doing anything for a while. It may be difficult for you to find the energy or emotional resources to do even the simplest of tasks. You may be hit with economic hardships and will certainly feel you have lost a certain level of status in the community. Even though there are many single mothers in the world today, you will still feel as though you are the only one. You will feel that people are staring at you, feeling sorry for you, or seeing you as damaged goods. You are no longer a married woman with the protection that status offers in our society.

But never fear—you'll get over it. When you realize that you have your freedom and that you have the inner strength to move forward into a life that fulfills you and suits your needs, you will no longer feel so frightened. You are much stronger than you would ever have believed.

Womanly Wisdom

We all have hidden resources that we can draw upon when put to the task. You can fix a toilet and kill a bug without a man around the house. And you can handle whatever it takes to manage your life.

If you feel like falling apart, don't hide it from your children (well, maybe a little). But make sure they know *they* have done nothing wrong. Tell them you are just feeling sad or even frightened but that you will all learn to do what needs to be done. Children are perceptive enough that you can't tell them everything is rosy when it is not. But you need to show them that even though you are scared you will never leave them. They need to see that you work hard to overcome obstacles and do not give up. This is the message you want to send them, even when you feel like hiding under the covers with a pillow over your head.

Learning Independent Mothering

When you are divorced you do not want to look to your ex-husband to do husbandly things for you. You need to develop your independence, and your children need to see that there is a clean break. This does not mean you should not be nice and friendly when there are transitions or situations involving the children. It means that you should go out and buy a tool kit. Ask neighbors or friends for help before you turn to your ex for the things he used to do around the house. You need to learn to rely on your own resources. Even though you may have been basically on your own during the marriage, it can feel surprisingly weird not to have another adult in the house. It takes some adjustment.

Handling Economic Issues

Many newly single women experience a loss of economic status. Instead of living in a house as you did when you were married, you may be living in an apartment. You may need to live with a relative. You may even need financial assistance. Do not feel embarrassed or ashamed if you need to ask for help from relatives or from the government. Even if you are blessed with a good financial settlement you may still need time to get on your feet and get used to managing on your own.

Negotiating the New Rules

If you need to turn to neighbors or friends for help around the house be aware that there is now a different set of rules. As a newly single woman you may now pose a threat to even the closest of your female friends. If you need to borrow someone's husband or boyfriend make sure you do not appear too flirtatious. You would be surprised to see how territorial females are about their men. You may be thinking, "You can have him! I don't want anyone in my life at the moment." But they are thinking, "Now she is single again and my mate is going to find her more exciting." Just don't allow things to move in that direction. Be aware that everyone needs to adjust to your new status.

Mom Alert!

Do not be alarmed if your female friends are territorial around you and their mates. Give everyone time to adjust to your new status, and even though flirtation is the last thing on your mind, be careful not to flirt with your friends' men. You need support, not suspicion.

Creating a New Identity

Whether you stay in the house or apartment of your marriage, or end up moving to a new location, you should make every effort to make your home your own. It is very good for your morale to redecorate to suit your tastes. When I divorced my first husband I got an apartment for my daughter and me. Because I had just ended my marriage to a real stick-in-the-mud, I went wild with decorating. I was reacting to the staid practicality of the home we had lived in together, all done up in earth tones. Although I had a shoestring budget I decorated my new place with so many flowers and so much lace it could have passed for a Victorian bordello.

You, too, can revel in creating your new, post-divorce identity. If you like purple with pink polka dots you can decorate in it. Express yourself in any way you want.

Celebrating Your Freedom

By the time a marriage fails, chances are it had begun to feel oppressive. In my case, I treated my new single status as the equivalent of having been paroled. I had a newfound appreciation for the simple things in life, like having my personal autonomy back. And I enjoyed the luxurious sense of freedom that comes when you realize that you can put your things anywhere you want without anyone saying a word about it.

There is a downside, of course—you will probably miss sex. But if you were in a dysfunctional marriage there probably wasn't much good sex anyway. Certainly it wasn't a good enough reason to stay in a bad marriage. If you need to work off some of that excess physical tension, try joining a gym. If it is a coed gym you can look at the buff behinds. If not, working out is a great stress reliever and can help you curb your libido so you don't think of doing something unproductive like jumping back into the frying pan.

Constructive Choices for the Single Mom

Here are a few other things to do when you are newly single:

➤ Buy a tool kit. Repairs are not brain surgery.

➤ Cultivate some helpful neighbors or friends.

➤ Ask for help when you need it.

➤ Redecorate to reflect your true and perhaps formerly suppressed personality.

➤ Revel in your freedom and appreciate the little things, like quiet.

Kid Crazies

When you have yourself in reasonable balance you'll need to pay particular attention to the way your children are handling things. I have never known of a child who has not had some emotional reaction to divorce. It changes their concept of reality. Even if the marriage was a constant battleground, it is the devil they know. Children have difficulty expressing their thoughts and fears directly so you need to be aware of subtle cues. I believe in talking to children at their level, no matter what the age. There are ways of explaining the changes in a truthful manner without giving them too much unnecessary detail or complicating things.

Momma Said There'd Be Days Like This

Children will look to your nonverbal cues to establish their reality. If you are upset each time they have to make the transition to their father's house they are going to think there is something to be upset about. If you are overly fearful about certain situations the children will internalize that fear, even if to them it has no rational basis.

Establishing a Visitation Routine

Try to establish a routine of visits to the father that leaves little to chance. If you can keep things consistent you make it much easier for your child to adjust. Flexibility is a good thing when there are special occasions, but those occasions should be deviations from a standard schedule. The child wants to know where he or she will be on a given night. Even though he may have only a vague sense of time and of days, he will like knowing that Wednesday is always Daddy day.

Your time as a single parent can be precious. While you are a single parent, despite the many struggles, it is a time when you really have your children all to yourself.

Building a Better Balance

There is a fine line between enjoying a healthy relationship with your children and making them the center of your universe so you can avoid getting back into the adult world. If you make your children the center of your world to the exclusion of everything else, you and they will have a much harder time if you find a new mate in the future. You limit your options and may create an emotional dependence that is not good for your child. If you are a single parent you do not want to create a situation that stifles growth and independence.

A child can never get too much love and support. One of the fun parts of being a mother is the chance to develop a whole new relationship with your child. You may have more time to spend with your child as a single parent because you do not have the distraction and demands of a mate, but you want to avoid leaning too heavily on your child for emotional support.

When I was a single mother and my older daughter was three years old I loved taking her places with me. It was a wonderful time that both of us still remember. She was great company and I was grateful that I was not so distracted by conflict to have missed out on the bonding that took place. I made special efforts to go to fun places because it was good for both of us.

Learning to Say No

I did, however, get into some bad habits that you would do well to avoid. My daughter and I had a little *too* much fun accumulating things. It is very hard to say no to a child when it is just the two of you. You want to overcompensate for so many things. There is nothing terminally wrong with it, but habits are difficult to break.

As the child grows older and develops more expensive tastes you will probably not have the budget to keep up the pace. You also don't want to send the message that your child is entitled to compensation because something's wrong with her. I have had to undo some of my earlier choices. It is easier to set better limits from the beginning. Single moms sometimes have trouble with the "n" word. We are afraid that somehow our children will stop loving us.

223

Maneuvering Around Manipulation

Discipline works with divorced children as well as it works with children from intact homes. It is just a bit more difficult to administer because of all the mixed emotions involved. You don't want to lose your temper, as is perfectly normal under the stress of a divorce. But you do not want to be afraid to be firm.

Just keep this in mind: Children in single-parent homes are master manipulators. Unless you are a clinical child psychologist you will never fully know when you are being played. Your children don't do it with malice. They just learn how to get what they want by playing all sides toward the middle. They have instincts to create equilibrium in any way they can—sometimes by manipulating parents to buy this and buy that.

Keeping the Peace with Your Ex

Your children's manipulation can also extend to the creation and maintenance of conflict between you and your ex. Children sometimes create situations to keep their divorced parents battling. It is a mechanism to maintain security with the emotions that are already known. Conflict has a type of comfort zone if it is what the child knows.

Be aware that your child may be the mastermind of some pretty intricate schemes. You don't want to be overly paranoid. You do not have demon possession in your midst. You just need to stay focused on what you know is right for your family unit. Do not get pulled in directions where you do not want to go.

Working on Your Single Mom Skills

Raising children is complicated enough without having the added factors of a divorce. Do the best you can. Pray for help, and love yourself and your children. Children have within them the mechanism to adjust to any situation. They will find ways to cope throughout their lives. Having a divorce in their personal history will not doom them to failure or to life as a sociopath. If you are supportive, loving, and understanding, you can allow nature to take its course. Your children have lives and decisions to make just as you do. You can't protect them from every potential trauma.

Keeping an Eye on Your Child's Reactions

One thing you *can* do for your child is to be observant. In some children the residual effects of divorce will not go away or balance out without some kind of professional help. You may notice problems in school or problems with relating to other children. You may see delayed development or unusual behavior, such as being overly withdrawn.

Momma Said There'd Be Days Like This

When I was separating from my second husband, our home was filled with conflict. My highly sensitive son had always seemed to be a quiet child by nature—we even briefly entertained the fear that he was slightly autistic. After our divorce, however, my son suddenly came out of his shell, talking about all kinds of things, including God and the planets. It was as though the floodgates had been opened. Evidently it took the divorce—and the end of parental conflict—to make him feel safe enough to cope with his surroundings.

The Many Flavors of Coping Mechanisms

Children find many different ways to survive situations they perceive as threatening. My son responded to my conflict-ridden marriage by creating an internal world to protect himself from the chaos around him. Although I watch him closely for signs of trouble in school or in other areas, he seems to have adjusted well to the positive changes in all our lives. His father is much happier out of our marriage and has a good relationship with his children.

Delayed Reactions

Sometimes a child's reaction to the stress of divorce will be delayed. You may not find out for years that your children have fears or resentment related to the break up. You can help them, but you need to realize that you are not directly responsible for their ability to heal. Realistically, all you can do is provide the resources for them so they can grow and develop in a healthy way. Eventually they will have to pick up the reins of their own lives. Many children of divorce use this event as a reason for not taking responsibility for their own growth. If you have been supportive of them, do not buy into this and guilt-trip yourself throughout eternity. We are all part of a web of interaction. You were a catalyst for certain events in your child's life but you can't control every outcome.

Fitting In

Things change when you are newly single. You may begin to feel somewhat alienated from your married friends, in part because it seems clear to you that you're coping with more problems than they are. And you'll be tempted to judge yourself harshly. You will feel you can't accomplish as much as you think you should. For certain, you'll often be tired. You are going to be adjusting your attitude to a new reality. Your new life will have many exciting aspects to it but you will need to learn your limitations and set your priorities.

Facing Up to Finances

If you have to go to work and have never worked outside the home, you are going to have to adjust to the demands of employment. If you have been out of the workforce for a while it is not easy to change your mindset into one that is income-producing. There are demands of the job that take some getting used to. You may even resent having to struggle if motherhood has been your sole job. You will also feel frustrated about not having the time to do things you were able to do when you were at home with your children full-time.

Mom Alert!

Nonpayment of child support by "deadbeat" dads is a widespread problem. If you do nothing else in your divorce settlement, make certain that your child's interests are protected—child support is, after all, for *his* benefit.

If you were a working mother you will not have to adjust to the working world but you *will* very likely have to adjust to a lower standard of living. Courts are not likely to award any kind of alimony, and child support typically does not cover more than the basics. At any economic level it is unlikely that you will stay exactly where you were before the divorce. You may be happy to be out of the relationship but you will have to adjust to your new economic life.

You're No Slacker, So Cut Yourself Some Slack

You need to develop thick skin as a single mother. People are not always understanding of how complicated your situation can be. Even if you are fortunate enough to have an ex who does not drive you crazy and to have children who are well-adjusted, you are doing more in a day than you probably ever expected. You may be tired.

Let yourself off the hook and do not hold yourself to the standards of the mythical supermom. Even mothers in good marriages cannot possibly measure up to those standards. The biggest problem for women who are divorced single mothers is that they constantly feel inadequate about something. Life is too short to spend it beating yourself up over every little thing.

You might find it helpful to carry around the following permission slip in your purse. When someone wants to criticize your performance as a mom, just hand it over for them to read.

I am a single mother and I have permission:

➤ To take care of my own needs—even if that means not being able to be all things to all people.

➤ To have a messy house within the limits of the health code.

➤ To not volunteer for everything at my child's school.

➤ To not have to contribute to every gift or party fund if I can't afford it.

➤ To be part of the world even though I do not have a husband.

➤ To be treated with dignity and respect even though I am not always able to do things as well as I would like.

➤ To be free from unwarranted judgment and criticism.

Life Is Not on Hold

As a single mother you do not want to live your life as though it will begin again only when you remarry. If you are blessed to find a suitable mate who will be compatible with your life vision, that is wonderful. But you owe it to yourself and to your children to have a life that is not based on any future conditions. If you do not have expectations you will find that your decisions are made with a clear mind and are not clouded by what you think you and your children need. It is nice for children to have a father figure in the house but any child would be just as thrilled with a stable and happy mother.

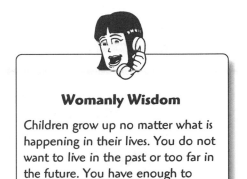

Womanly Wisdom

Children grow up no matter what is happening in their lives. You do not want to live in the past or too far in the future. You have enough to keep you busy right now.

Seeking Solace in Ritual

Make a good life for yourselves that includes spiritual connection if that is important to you. Most churches, synagogues, and religious communities can offer tremendous support for single mothers. These communities can also help stabilize your children's lives.

Family ritual is as important for a single-mother home as it is for a nuclear family. Do what you can handle and what will be special for all of you. Make it a bowling night once a month or have spaghetti for dinner on Tuesdays. Children do not have complicated needs. They just see what is special in life and enjoy celebrating simple things. Board games are great and offer inexpensive entertainment.

What you don't want is a family where each member does his or her own thing away from the unit. As the children grow this can enhance the alienation that comes from the experience of divorce. Even though you do not have a father in the home you should have a family unit whose members interact and are involved in each other's lives. Make birthdays special, even if they are simple. Make each member of the family feel important.

You may have had a divorce but you are blessed with children. The love you have for and receive from children is like nothing else. It is unconditional. Your children will truly accept you despite whatever limitations you think you have and will be a source of joy and love for you throughout your life. You will have tough times, as everyone does, and may even need outside help. But when you have children you have a richness of life that one who does not have them cannot possibly understand.

By working together you and your children can create a wonderful life that fulfills your dreams.

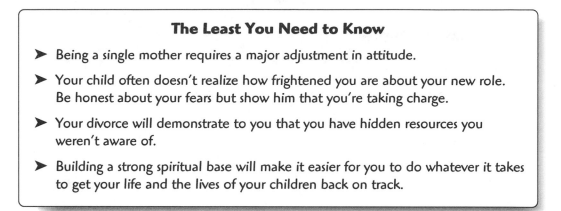

The Least You Need to Know

➤ Being a single mother requires a major adjustment in attitude.

➤ Your child often doesn't realize how frightened you are about your new role. Be honest about your fears but show him that you're taking charge.

➤ Your divorce will demonstrate to you that you have hidden resources you weren't aware of.

➤ Building a strong spiritual base will make it easier for you to do whatever it takes to get your life and the lives of your children back on track.

Chapter 20

Getting Back into the Dating Game

In This Chapter

➤ So you really want to date?

➤ Red-flagging the wrong kind of man

➤ Involving your children in your relationship

➤ When Mr. Right comes along

It has been a while. You have been building a new life for yourself and your children. You manage to take care of their needs and are settling into new routines. You spend Sundays at your parents' house and every other Saturday night alone. It has been fun renting all those movies you never used to be able to watch, and sometimes you don't get up and dressed on Sundays until the afternoon. Your television is almost always turned to the Lifetime channel and your closets are color-coded. Still, although you hate to admit it, on the weekends when your children are gone you are becoming bored.

Maybe it's time to bring some romance back into your life. If you feel you've given yourself enough time to recover from your divorce, now might be the time to rediscover the world of dating. In this chapter you'll learn the ins and outs of reentering the dating world.

Are You Dating-Ready?

Even though weekends when you were married were awful, with one crisis or another, those crises prevented you from having to think about yourself. Your main goal was to find a way to stop being miserable. Now you are faced with the even more daunting

Womanly Wisdom

Although it may seem impossible to you in the days immediately following your divorce, there will be love again in your life. Cultivate patience and faith and when the time is right you will meet someone to love.

task of discovering how to be happy. Many people can be happy all by themselves. They have hobbies or interests that fill their days with joy and satisfaction. Others, like me, do not particularly enjoy extended periods of solitude. Friends are wonderful and have always been an important part of my life but I have always been the type who wants male companionship.

Call me an incurable romantic, I happen to love men. I've never managed to rid myself of the desire to be around them. Men are cool. They are a challenge and in all honesty can make me feel positively spellbound. Maybe it is the yin and yang effect. A man and a woman create a certain energy that at its best makes a black-and-white world turn Technicolor.

Getting Started...Slowly

You need to be careful when post-divorce loneliness sets in. This is a very vulnerable time for a woman. You can easily be taken in by a handsome face and pumped pecs before you know what has hit you. This would be fine if all you were looking for was a fling. But for some reason many women are just not created that way. Even if we think all we want is sex, we have difficulty separating our emotions from the intimate act. Every time we have sex we share a part of ourselves. We feel diminished if the sex is part of something that has no emotional basis.

The Six-Month, No-Sex Rule

It is in recognition of the vulnerability of a just-divorced single mom that I recommend the six-month, no-sex rule. This rule is not sealed in stone. It is just a parameter you might find useful if you are divorced, lonely, and stepping into the dating scene after a long absence.

In essence, the six-month rule requires that you make an agreement with yourself that no matter what happens, you will not let a date proceed to the bedroom during your first six months back in the dating world.

Think of this as a form of self-protection: With the six-month rule you will have a good reason to say "no" when your date is making your head spin with passion. As a formerly married woman you are used to having sanctioned sex in the context of marriage. This means that even though it may not have been good or frequent, you were permitted to enjoy it and go all the way any time you wanted to. When you go back into the dating world you almost have to go back to junior high school when just saying "no" was an easy thing to do.

Welcome to the Brave New World of Dating

The world has changed during the time you have been married. But even though there is a lot of talk about safe sex and abstinence, in some ways the world hasn't changed a bit. People still take sexual risks, even though the sexual scene of the 1970s and 80s taught us that the stakes are much higher now than they were during the free-love era of the 1960s.

But that's not the only change you're going to confront. The etiquette (and lack thereof, at times) of dating has also changed. You're going to need a refresher course in the dating scene.

Re-learning the Ropes

When you get back into the dating world you may not remember all the subtle ways a man has of trying to seduce you. You are emotionally vulnerable and will believe whatever you want to believe. You will want to believe that fate has now rewarded all your misery with the one-and-only soul mate you have been waiting for. Be careful. Men are as commitment-phobic today as they were the first time around. If you come on too strong or expect too much right away you are going to be hurt.

Mom Alert!

You have to protect yourself. Your feelings are fragile and no orgasm is worth setting back the progress toward self-realization that you have made since your divorce.

So, Just Who Are You Looking for?

Aside from your sexual desires, you are going to feel the loss of a partner in child rearing, and might look at all new men as potential fathers for your children. Nothing scares a man off faster than thinking he is wanted only to take care of a ready-made family. Although you want to let men know from the beginning that you have children, you want to get to know a person as a potential companion or partner for you and not as a parent for your children.

Now, how do you meet these new men in your life? You have been married for a while. You have children. Don't rule anything out. As you go about your daily business, you should always keep your radar in tune. It is a shame, but over fifty percent of marriages end in divorce. That means there are lots of single men—you may even meet some at the PTO meetings. Many men get involved in what previously has been viewed as a mother's job, simply so they do not get left out of the loop. It is not uncommon to see the ex-husbands at school functions right along with their ex-wives.

Checking Out the Dating Venues

There are obvious places to meet men, such as groups like Parents Without Partners. You need to be aware that many of the people who join these groups have the same issues to work out that you have and may be even less balanced than you are. You may find some friends, which is very important, or you may find someone who can share your path toward a new life.

You need to decide whether you are looking for dates or potential partners. You can always go to singles bars if you are looking for flirtation. You may find some nice people to date or you may find only the barflies. If you stick to your six-month rule and a no pick-up policy, it won't matter. You control the outcome by being cautious, not getting drunk, and only half listening to any lines sent in your direction.

There are also singles clubs that are wonderful in getting you back into circulation. Your church or synagogue very likely has an organization for singles, and there may even be fun activities to get you out of the house. It may seem a bit dorky, but at least you know that people who make the effort to join are seriously looking for new relationships and are not just interested in a one-night stand.

Here's a list of things you can do to get yourself back into circulation:

➤ Go about your business but keep your radar in tune for the men who are also divorced or single.

➤ Get involved with such groups as Parents Without Partners.

➤ Go to singles bars as long as you control the outcome by staying sober and avoiding pick-ups.

➤ Join singles clubs through churches or synagogues.

➤ Accept offers to "fix you up."

Womanly Wisdom

Don't ignore the well-meaning efforts of relatives and friends. Blind dates are the oldest form of matchmaking. Everyone wants to help bring people together. You never know. Although I believe fate will bring you and your soul mate together when you are both ready, I also believe that sometimes fate needs all the help it can get.

Attitude Check, Please!

Dating after divorce depends a great deal on your attitude. If you are extremely angry at men for the actions of the one man you divorced, you are going to send out signals to stay away from you. You may want some therapy before you reenter the dating life. Even if you are able to date again, you are not going to be OK. A divorce is a trauma that will influence how well you are able to handle a new relationship. There is a difference between needing time to learn to trust a person again so you can establish an intimate relationship and being able to go out in a casual way without wanting to punch out someone's lights.

Don't feel guilty about wanting to go out and have a good time, but you might want to save your dates for your children's visitation times with their father. Simply put, you don't want to involve your children in your dating life until you've had time to get an accurate sense of the man you're dating.

If you are like some mothers who do not have any relief because of an absent ex-husband who is not involved with his children, it is still best for you to meet your date somewhere away from home and keep your social life your personal business.

When you are dating, your children might find you more obviously sexualized than if you were just interacting with their father, and they may begin to feel threatened. Dating is a much smoother process when the children are not made to feel insecure about their position in the family hierarchy. Children are threatened by change. You do not want to start involving them until you are sure it is worth the effort. Inevitably, you may have extended relationships that do not work out. You just need to gauge the potential for the relationship to be long term before you all make the effort to work at it together with your children.

Getting back into dating after having been married may seem a frustrating and impossible prospect. There will be disappointments, but you also have all the potential in the world to find the relationship that will be right for you. In a bad marriage you know that you are only going to have more of the same. When you are single and dating you have infinite possibilities.

Mom Alert!

Never bring a new date to your home—that can endanger not only you, but also your children. Until you've had time to really get to know one another, meet in public venues.

Will History Repeat Itself?

Well, you managed to escape your unhappy marriage and all the emotional pain it caused. You are free but want a new companion to help you pick up where you should have left off. You have many dating options and feel pretty good about yourself. Your self-esteem has risen and you feel you are a catch for any man with half a brain. Time to let down your guard? No way.

Unless you have gone through therapy or have had some type of religious awakening, you run the risk of choosing the same kind of man you just got rid of. This may seem like a cruel joke but it is the absolute truth—it happens all the time. Even if you think you are choosing someone who is the exact opposite of your ex-husband you run a statistical risk of choosing someone who will ultimately lead you to the same kind of dysfunctional relationship.

But don't give up hope. You can prevent this travesty of romantic justice. How? Pray a lot and keep your eyes and ears open. Trust your intuition and do not ignore any misgivings you might have about the new man in your life.

Meeting Mr. Right

My first marriage was filled with loud, obvious conflict. I perceived my husband to be a highly controlling and explosive personality. The last thing I wanted now was someone else just like him. When I was single again I dated as much as I could and had a

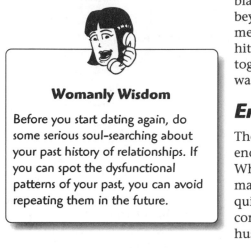

Womanly Wisdom

Before you start dating again, do some serious soul-searching about your past history of relationships. If you can spot the dysfunctional patterns of your past, you can avoid repeating them in the future.

blast. But I kept to my own six-month rule and well beyond, because I was feeling a little gun shy. Then I met a wonderful man who lived in a different state. We hit it off, had a lot in common, and were going to get together in a month in my home state. By this time I was feeling ready to look for future prospects.

Enter Mr. Wrong

The only major problem is that I hadn't really learned enough about myself since my first marriage broke up. While I was waiting for my new friend to visit I met the man who was to become my second husband. He was a quiet and soft-spoken man—seemingly a complete contrast to the loud, argumentative style of my first husband. I thought our relationship was fate.

After we spent some time together, I began to get a weird feeling of déja vu when I was around him, but I dismissed it because he didn't seem as though he would have a harsh word to say about anything. As our relationship escalated quickly into something more serious I remember praying that this was not another lesson for me. I was sure that, this time, I was making the right choice. I told my out-of-state friend to still visit, but also told him that I was now serious about someone else.

Of course, you can see how this was going to end. My second husband was very much like the first, he just wasn't as obvious about it. For some reason, I was somehow still looking for a controlling, difficult partner—I was not yet psychologically ready to be married to someone who would actually give me the love and acceptance I needed. Unknowingly, I had chosen for the second time someone who essentially was emotionally absent.

Breaking the Patterns

The good news is this: None of us are fated to repeat our mistakes for the rest of our lives. All it takes is gaining a little maturity. Apparently, when my second marriage finally, mercifully, ended, I must have at last been ready for real love.

Can you guess the happy ending? As if to right a wrong, the universe conspired to bring my out-of-state friend back into my life—as my third husband. It is amazing to be in a marriage that is supportive, loving, and also based on friendship. I am grateful that fate stepped in because I might have continued the cycle of unhappy marriages until I felt enough love for myself to know that we all deserve better than that.

Taking Inventory

As you are reentering the dating life you need to take an inventory of yourself. Look objectively at the lessons you have needed to learn about yourself and about love. We all have to learn these seven lessons on our path to self-realization:

Courage	Ego
Tolerance	Love of humanity
Self-protection	Love of God
Self-love	

Many situations in our lives can be defined in one or more of these categories. Each of us learns these lessons in individual ways. As you take an inventory of your life and of your relationships, try to put events in the context of the relevant lessons:

➤ It takes a great deal of **courage** to look at a situation in your life and say it is not working. When we do so we often are going against the grain of traditions our society holds dear. It is not easy to leave a marriage and to have the courage to give relationships another chance.

➤ To have **tolerance** is not only to understand and accept the limitations of other people. It is also to give yourself a chance to grow without too much self-criticism. Do not feel stupid if you seem to keep choosing the same kind of man. It is just nature's way of sensitizing you to your own vulnerabilities. Just don't jump into marriage until you fully evaluate your choice. Time is the best way to test your judgment. Tolerance enables you to see your life in a bigger context. Every decision you make is just a part of your journey. Sometimes it is necessary to make bad decisions so that you have an opportunity to move on.

➤ As a single mother you need to learn to **protect** yourself. You only have your better judgment to prevent you from making a choice that leads you in the wrong direction. I believe you will eventually get where you need to go but it may be the hard way. The more you learn to protect yourself the better your chances of not having to repeat difficult lessons.

➤ **Self-love** is one of the most important lessons and is particularly apparent in matters of relationships. We often choose partners as a reflection of how we feel about ourselves. If I had had more self-esteem and had felt more worthy of love I never would have allowed myself to stay in such destructive relationships. In a way I am grateful to both of my previous marriages for intensely threatening my self-identity and thereby giving me a way to learn to love myself.

The remaining lessons will be discussed in Chapter 23.

If you use these lessons to help you create an objective perspective of yourself you will see why you may be repeating certain lessons through your choice of mates. If you have a sense of what you are doing maybe you can stop it before it happens.

Red-Flagging Your Dates

You can also watch out for some obvious danger signals that you can spot by taking your time to get to know someone. The following scenarios should raise red flags all over the place:

➤ If your date talks about himself and doesn't ask anything about you, this is not a good sign.

➤ If your date belches at the table and shows other outward signs of being disgusting before you have even had a second date, expect more of the same.

➤ If your date becomes sullen if you refuse to see the movie he has chosen, you can bet he is a manipulator.

➤ If your date makes critical remarks about you, such as "You would look so much prettier with shorter hair," run so fast he won't know what hit him.

➤ If your date whines about the check at a restaurant on your first date or is rude to the waitress, think about how he would be at bill-paying time.

➤ If your date talks about his mother more than to mention he has one, cross him off your list.

➤ If you are attracted to your date but have to dig for things to talk about, think about how long it would take for you to go insane if the physical attraction wore off.

Keeping Your Eye on the Prize

You have had a marriage that has not worked out. You have children to think about and have had to start your life over. You deserve to improve your life, not take it back into chains.

Mom Alert!

If you never learned to be on your own, you may be panicked by single parenting into accepting a new partner who is as bad as or worse than the one you left behind.

But maybe you're frightened of being alone. That may inspire you to try to change your dreams to fit what you've found, even if it's an unsuitable relationship. But you deserve more than that.

Do not sell yourself short in this way. Sometimes patience and soul searching are what you need to bring the right relationship into your life. You do not need to settle. Your children do not need a father so badly that you should sacrifice your happiness. Instead of making a checklist of what you think you want in a mate, try just being open to meeting the people that fate sends your way. Then take a good long time to get to know them. You're more likely to find a suitable mate that way.

Life has a way of balancing things out, if we give it a chance. Patience and trust are necessary and will be greatly rewarded in the end. Look at me—until my perception changed I never even imagined that my life mate was right under my nose. I was no longer willing to accept the scraps of life. You shouldn't be willing to either. You want a life mate who reflects who you are at your best or who is able to help you bring out your greatest potential. If you choose someone who only dampens your flame, you are not in the right relationship.

Involving Your Children in Your Relationship

When you find someone you care about who seems to have some future potential for you, you are going to want to bring your children into the picture. Of course, you want your significant other to already know that you have children. Otherwise, you may find a situation on your hands. Not every man is capable of accepting children that he perceives as belonging to another man. And some men may be frightened of the responsibilities children represent.

As soon as you are officially dating or can find an appropriate moment to mention it, you should get it out into the open. You don't want to get involved with a man who has negative feelings about children. All men will have some reaction that may seem a bit odd, but that is not the same as having them say they hate rugrats and would never have them in their home.

Preparing for Initial Resistance

Your children are going to figure out that you have a relationship going with some-one—probably long before you are ready to bring the parties together for their initial check-each-other-out session. Older children will have the most difficulty assimilating a new person into your familiar life together. They would often prefer to have you all to themselves because they will likely have the most vivid memory of the life you had with their father. Even though they know that relationship is over, they will find it difficult to visualize you with another man. It becomes an issue of loyalty.

Problems of Premature Attachment

The risk you run with younger children is that they will form an immediate attach-ment. This is why you want to be pretty sure your relationship has some potential before you allow your younger children to bond. Even though you cannot always predict the outcome of a relationship, it is easier on a child not to have to experience too many unnecessary losses.

Managing a Slow Merge

Once you have introduced your new man to your children you do not want to imme-diately become a surrogate family. You do not want to have overnight visits until the children become comfortable with the prospect that your boyfriend is someone who may be here to stay. You can certainly choose whatever is comfortable for you, but if you take this slowly you lower the risk of emotional backlash from your children as they adjust to your new life. Keep in mind that they may feel threatened, fearful that they could lose you to this new suitor or that the new man will change the rules of the family.

Keep Some Private Family Time at First

You also want to avoid including this new man in too many of your family days at first. You are developing a relationship that has to have at its basis a strong bond between you and your new man. If your time is spent focused on becoming a family unit you are not going to be able to keep things in balance. You may be forced to skip some important stages of your relationship on the course toward greater involvement and commitment.

At the same time, you are also building a whole new family configuration as a single mom with your kids. They, too, deserve your attention and your time while they work through the change in their lives that divorce has brought.

Time Is on Your Side

You don't need to rush anything. You can take your time to allow everyone to get used to each other and for you to decide whether you really want to create a new family. If you have any reservations you should listen to your intuition and wait until either the feelings are resolved or you understand clearly that the relationship is not right for you. This is your chance at a new and happy life. If important aspects are missing, wait for another situation to come along. Do not settle because you are lonely or think you will never have the right opportunity.

Preparing to Take the Plunge

If you are sure you have met the right guy, give your children time to get to know him on their own terms. Give them space and do not insist that they do anything that is not comfortable for them, such as hugging him or giving him goodnight kisses, until they are ready.

Here are a few warning signs that your new man could be wrong for you:

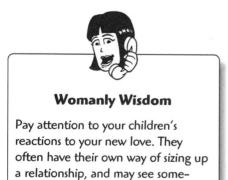

Womanly Wisdom

Pay attention to your children's reactions to your new love. They often have their own way of sizing up a relationship, and may see something you don't but in fact, should.

➤ Your children run screaming to the neighbors whenever he arrives.

➤ He has no past and vaguely mentions something about witness protection.

➤ Your dog's hackles rise whenever he is in the room.

➤ Whenever the doorbell rings he reaches for his gun.

If none of these occur, and you have eliminated the possibility that your new man is the one they featured on "America's Most Wanted" last week, you may be on the road to many new and exciting adventures together.

Remember to constantly reassure your children that you still love them and that no new relationship will change that. Tell them that you are all going to form a family and ask for their input. The more they feel a part of things the less frightened they will feel. You may be surprised. If this is the right man for you your children may be as happy about things as you are.

The Least You Need to Know

➤ Wait six months after your divorce before having sex with a new man—for the sake of your own emotional health.

➤ Don't rule out singles clubs or the help of family and friends when you're looking to meet someone new.

➤ Be cautious, to avoid repeating the mistakes of your past relationships—get in touch with your true needs and find someone who fits them.

➤ Don't rush into involving your children with your new relationship.

239

Chapter 21

Blended Families

In This Chapter

➤ Getting to know each other

➤ Avoiding conflicts with the exes

➤ Helping everyone feel at home

➤ Creating a family forum

You have met someone really cool. You have evaluated him very objectively on the scale of how badly he could drive you crazy. You have developed a friendship and have spent enough time together to know you are pretty serious about him. Remember the six-month rule. Take your time before becoming intimate and becoming serious.

Even if it has been five years since your divorce, your first very serious relationship will still be on the rebound. Your old issues will rear their ugly heads and you may be more vulnerable than you think. Choose some period of time that suits you and do not allow yourself to get hooked until you are sure it is what you want.

But then, after you've given yourself a real chance to get to know this new person, you may find yourself looking at the prospect of merging your household with his. In this chapter you'll learn all about blending families.

Meeting Each Other with Love

If you believe you are in love with someone and are willing to give marriage another try, then by all means go for it. There will be some unique challenges, but you could wind up with a very happy life. Just because you have been divorced doesn't mean you can never have a good, nourishing, and healthy relationship. You might have a bit more stress in your life than some people, but it can be well worth it. As long as you have your eyes open and are aware of the obstacles, you can make everything work out well for you, your future husband, and your children.

Making the Introductions All Around

When you find that special someone, the first obstacle you are going to face is introducing him to your children. You will be amazed at how much influence your children's perspective has on your ultimate decision. You are going to try to avoid giving your children that much power over you, but you know that in the early stages of the relationship (especially), you will be monitoring your children's reactions to your potential mate and giving them more weight than his reaction to them. You have needs as a woman, but if you have been head of the household in a unit with your children for any length of time, you are going to be very territorial.

Momma Said There'd Be Days Like This

When my daughter was 12 we were talking about our past and the fact that I divorced my incompatible second husband. She looked at me and said matter-of-factly, "I could have told you not to marry him, Mom. You just should have slept with him."

Kids Are People, Too

Of course, there are situations in which mothers bring in mates who are not good with their children. These situations are unfortunate and very unhealthy, especially if they lead to abuse by the stepfather. If a woman and a man look only to their own relationship and view the children as merely an inconvenience, they are creating a potentially explosive situation. It is good for a mother to be protective of her children, particularly when she is bringing in another man to fill the role of father figure. The children should be her first priority and then great efforts should be made to create a new and thriving family unit.

Love is very important, but it is not the only glue that will hold together a blended family. Many issues need to be addressed from the beginning. Children need security, and when you remarry you run the risk of putting your children in another situation that potentially could lead to a traumatic loss.

Coping with Children's Issues

Take your time getting to know someone before you jump into another marriage or serious relationship. You have to keep in mind that when children are involved things are not so easy. If you are thinking about settling down with someone who argues with you a lot and has no patience with children, you are going to have a very tough time maneuvering through the normal issues of raising a blended family. If you know that you are really in love and do not mind constant conflict, this could be a good choice for you. I just know that being in a nurturing environment now with my third husband has made it one million times easier to have a life.

When you feel you have made a good choice and are ready to move on to the next step, there are several things you can do. If you have young children, under the age of 14, bribery works to get things off to a good start.

Here are a few good ways to introduce your prospective husband or significant other to your children:

➤ Invite him for dinner at your home but make sure he brings your children gifts of something relatively forbidden (like candy) as well as a desired toy.

➤ Plan to have dinner together at some kid-friendly restaurant, and definitely let them have dessert at his request.

➤ Have him come over for an evening to watch cartoons or play video games.

➤ Take a trip to the zoo or some other favorite kid hangout.

Let your children get to know him in small doses until they begin to ask about him on their own. Patience now can be a great asset later.

When you introduce a new person to a child the child is always going to be cautious. When you introduce a boyfriend, your child will sense a difference in the relationship and may feel threatened. There are definitely things your significant friend should not do the first time he meets your children. The same things apply when you meet *his* kids, if he has any.

Here are several things to warn your boyfriend about when he first meets your children:

➤ Avoid trying to show any immediate signs of affection. Even an enthusiastic high five can be greeted by a suspicious icy stare.

➤ Do not call any child over the age of two by any condescending names. If you call a child a baby you might as well expect to set back your cause by several points.

Mom Alert!

Statistically, 50 percent of all second marriages end in divorce. This is not a good statistic.

➤ Never try to be overly fatherly. Even very young children have loyalty to their biological father, even when that father is no longer in the picture. Take things slowly and give the child time to adjust.

➤ Never discipline the child in a harsh manner, particularly if it appears to contradict the methods used in the household. A new man in the house has to earn his status in the eyes of the child. If the child is a nasty little heathen let his mother handle it. He is just testing you anyway.

➤ Don't argue about anything with the mother in front of the children. A child is very leery of new people and will see even minor bickering as a threat. When trust has been established you are free to go at it as any normal couple would do.

➤ Don't be overly affectionate with the mother when the children are around. The children may still have fantasies of their biological parents getting together. Too much in-their-face smooching will make them feel edged out of the relationship. They'll react by acting out to gain more attention.

Reading the Reactions

When I first got together with my husband we looked for every opportunity to slobber over each other. We had been best friends for more than eight years, so when the passion hit it was volcanic. Inevitably we would be caught kissing by my youngest, who would literally get between us. She wasn't trying to break it up—she wanted to be kissed too. Even the dog would get in the middle of things. I guess they were happy to see me so happy.

The Fierce Tug of Loyalty

My son, on the other hand, was not so sure at first. He liked my husband a lot but was fiercely loyal to his own father. He was a little older and tended to be very protective. If he caught us kissing or holding hands he would give us a funny look. Not quite disapproving but very unnerving. We did our best to play it cool, which helped him and my husband develop a bond that worked for them.

Everyone Reacts in His Own Way

Each child adjusts to a new relationship in his or her own way. In any situation it is best to give the new relationships time to grow at a pace that works for each person involved. You can't force harmony. At first, when you begin a new relationship involving your children and a new man in your life, expect everyone to be at odds. You are likely to be excited about starting a new life while your children will be desperately trying to cling to the old. It will be a little crazy for a while, but with patience, understanding, and a lot of love, it can work out just fine.

Avoiding Cat Fights

There is another situation you may find yourself in. You may fall for a guy who has children of his own. This would be fine if you could become the only mother in their life or if you had some measure of control over your destiny in this regard. But remember, with a stepchild comes the fact that you become a stepmother, and there is usually an ex-wife to contend with. For some reason, although there can be great rivalry between fathers and stepfathers, the issue seems to become greater when you are dealing with two mothers who have an influence in the lives of the same children.

Momma Said There'd Be Days Like This

My ex's new wife is a perfect match for him, right down to waging all-out war on dust bunnies. When she first moved into the home my ex shared with our daughter and her reptiles the new wife hired a housekeeper and went on a cleaning rampage. One day my daughter heard two bloodcurdling screams. The housekeeper ran out the back door, never to return. My daughter and her father found the new stepmom standing by the newly cleaned freezer, gingerly holding a bag of frozen mice—snake food. God has such a sense of humor.

Several of my friends have husbands who have been married before and have one or more children. All I have to do to get one friend rattled is to mention her stepson's mother. My friend will go on and on about what a rotten person that woman is and how they could never get along. She has no respect for her whatsoever. The happiest time for her came when her stepson came to live full time with her and her husband. Although he was already a preteen it was worth it to her to be able to have some kind of family unit that would include this child in their lives.

Many times stepmothers remain relatively out of the picture. It depends greatly on how involved the father is with his children. In cases of the typical father who visits with his children and a mother who raises them, it's quite likely that the

Womanly Wisdom

It's wisest to remain above the fray if your ex's new wife gets hostile. As long as she is not interfering with your child's safety or self-esteem, she need not be more than a visitation pick-up blip on your household radar.

stepmother will stay uninvolved except as relates to her own household. Or, if the stepmother has her own child to keep her occupied, she won't be tempted to interfere in the mother's childrearing in any overbearing way.

Mom Alert!

Children are quite proficient relationship saboteurs when they want to be. All the more reason to take it slow as you build a relationship with your stepchildren.

Slow and Steady Wins the Race

If you are in a situation where *you* are going to be a stepmother, it is best to establish a friendship first with the child. If you want to have any authority in your own home you definitely do not want to come on so strong that you give the child no choice but to resist. You can have better luck if you view yourself as an additional person who can add to the quality of the child's life. If you have trouble knowing where to put yourself, concentrate on the signals you get from the child. You don't have to hold back love, but you do not want to give it so fast and so much that the child can't trust it.

Taking the Household Reins, Gently

On the other hand, a woman in the house becomes the person in charge. You will have a lot of conflict on your hands if you lead the child to feel pushed aside and overlooked. Children are very good at maintaining their position in their homes. To them it is a matter of emotional survival. You would not believe how much a child, even one of average intelligence, can manipulate a situation in order to maintain a sense of security. If you cause the child to feel threatened, do not be surprised to find some very subtle efforts at sabotage.

Manipulation is not necessarily evil and mean-spirited. Children may not be conscious of why they are doing something. They are only looking at the immediate result they want to achieve. If they are worried that Daddy loves the new wife more than he loves them and will abandon them, children look for ways to survive—maybe by developing an illness with real symptoms. Maybe, through naughty behavior, the child will find ways to pit one parent against the other. A child can be aware of exactly what will upset everyone and will not hesitate to use this primitive form of intuition.

Take the Children's Worldview into Account

The problem can be avoided when the stepparents and biological parents become more aware of what the blended family world looks like to a child. You can tell yourself that, as the adults in the situation, your needs and decisions override everything else. But this would be very shortsighted. If you put your child's feelings and worldview into the equation, you are going to be able to avoid problems before they happen.

All children really want is love and security. They don't care if they have two parents who love them or four parents. The more the better if they feel valued and loved. It is when children feel threatened or pushed aside that the problems develop. It is more difficult to reassure children in blended families; their history has proven that things don't always work out according to plan. Although it is difficult to think about the children when everything seems a mess, doing so really goes a long way toward straightening everything out.

Brady-Bunching It

Stepparents have legitimate frustrations and concerns. When you think of marriage you think of a nuclear family where there is a daddy, a mommy, and the children. You imagine yourself with some kind of "normal" life, like what you have seen on TV. Nothing too fancy. A few million dollars would be nice, but after a divorce, being able to go through a day without palpitations would be nice, too.

When you blend a family, whether it is a divorced mom with a man with no children, a divorced father with a woman with no children, or a man and woman who are both divorced with children, you are going to have some simple logistical problems. You have a lot of personalities to contend with. You also have:

➤ Clothing that gets lost

➤ Books that are at one house when they should be at the other

➤ Schedules that collide with vacations

➤ Illnesses that now pass through two homes

➤ Resentment, and people to appease

➤ Petty jealousies and competitiveness

Womanly Wisdom

A family cannot be said to be truly blended until all members—both parents and all the children—fully accept one another as part of the unit.

I am only familiar with my own situation with two ex-husbands, three children, and my new husband. Thank God my husband and I know each other well enough not to have to deal with many of the conflicts newlyweds have.

Striking a Balance: The Chocolate Incident

When you have a blended family it is vital that the parents create a united front. You have to decide ahead of time how you are going to handle situations. If you don't, the children will try to pull you away from each other so that they can be in control.

Stepdad in the Shadows

For example, my husband stayed in the background for a long time while I tried to be the strong one. I am not the most consistent disciplinarian and at times the children can run rings around me. I was also overprotective of my children because I had not yet learned to let go of a certain level of authority over them.

Mom Alert!

A common point of contention between partners in a blended family is that one parent resists granting to the other a reasonable level of authority over the children. Children quickly learn to take advantage of this situation, and discipline becomes difficult, if not impossible.

Well, you can't run a house when one parent's hands are tied behind his back. My husband tends to be a gentle person who is not explosive. But he can do a slow burn. When we first got married the children were wild. They were reacting to all the changes and could not be contained. They tested the limits at every opportunity. Even though I trusted my husband with my heart, I didn't trust him with my children. The children are with us most of the time and so he is essentially the most consistent father figure they have. I didn't realize it at the time, but whenever he tried to step in and take over some authority in the home I would run interference. We would get into a head-butting routine—and the child would get away with murder.

The Battle of the Van

One day, we had just driven our brand-new minivan to my brother's wedding. My husband had asked the children nicely not to eat in the new van because we are notorious for being very hard on our vehicles.

My younger daughter, who does not always believe rules apply to her, was warned several times not to eat her piece of chocolate in the new van. Sure enough, every time we turned around she had a piece of it in her mouth. We gave her the benefit of the doubt but took the chocolate away from her. When we pulled up to the reception we saw that she had another piece of chocolate and was dropping crumbs on the seat. Somehow, my husband had an epiphany, and at that very moment decided to become a father.

Shadow Stepdad No More

He got out of the van, calmly opened her door, took the chocolate out of her hand and—to the utter amazement of all three children—threw it to the ground and stomped on it. He looked like a crazed man and I truly worried that somehow we had driven him right over the edge. He went on for what seemed like hours, jumping up and down on the chocolate, grinding it into the pavement, and shouting, "Do you want it now? Huh? Do you want it now?"

He had never even so much as raised his voice to the children. My youngest cried as she watched her precious treat being smashed to smithereens, but in all honesty the other children cracked up laughing. I have always been frightened by outbursts of temper, but it was cool to see him blow his stack. We really had been pushing him around and he had been patient beyond the point of reason. He cooled off quickly and joined in the laughter, even though the youngest didn't see the humor in the situation.

Achieving the True Blend at Last

The chocolate incident, which is one of our favorite stories in our new family history, marked a significant turning point. I had to learn to let go and to trust him enough to share the job of running a household. This is a common issue for couples in this situation. You do not start out on the same footing as couples who marry and have children together. You have a lot of history to overcome. You need a lot of love, patience, and insight to get through some of the rough spots. I didn't like having to look at how I was contributing to the stalemate in my family. But when I was able to be honest with myself, growth became easier.

We have really tried to talk about the children so that we both have a say in matters. One of my husband's biggest complaints was that he felt he had no real authority in the house. He didn't until we worked it out together and I stopped resisting his desire to be involved. It is not easy to allow someone into your life when you have had a marriage fail. You will see this in yourself as you try to repair the damage in your soul. You can love to your heart's content, but you have to be willing to learn to trust again.

Helping Everyone Feel at Home

To make a blended family work you need to try to create something new that works for you, your husband, and your children. You can't play by the old rules, but you do not want to settle for just being people who share the same house but don't get involved in each other's lives. This can be painful at times. You start with the commitment to each other and the children. Then you build from the premise that you want everyone to be safe, loved, and nurtured. Everyone is important to the family unit. It is not "your" child or "my" child, but *our* child. Children do not get caught up in labels like step-this and step-that and half this or half that. What is half a relationship, anyway? I think it is best for a blended family to view itself as a family: Nothing more, nothing less.

If you each have children from earlier marriages living under one roof, you are going to have some complicated issues to address. It is going to get tricky, especially when the children become teenagers. Do not hesitate to get family counseling if the road is rough. You can't be expected to know all the answers.

If you look at it from the children's perspective, the most important thing to them is to have a sense of belonging. If you make your house a home for all the children and do not show overt favoritism to one set of children over another, you should be OK. It will not be easy for you, and you should be commended for your courage. When you make your blended house a home you will be amazed at how totally "normal" it can be. You will always need to be on your toes. But you can have a life filled with as much love and fulfillment as anyone else's is.

Creating a Family Forum

In any family, especially a blended family, it is important to create some type of family identity. In my family one of my children has one last name, two of my children have another last name, and they all have a different last name than I do. There isn't much we can do about it. We have tried some fun ways to create a family identity that unites us under one theme.

I created a family newsletter that featured what was going on with each child. I probably had more fun than they did, but it helped us see that we are not just a conglomeration of bodies. It is great when you can do things together. Road trips are a pain, but they do provide togetherness.

One thing we do, which is strictly for my sanity, is to have the occasional trial. When the children are fighting about something and try to drag me into the middle of it, I hold a family trial. I act as judge and have them present their cases. (At least my years of law school aren't completely going to waste.) It gets them to focus on the situation more rationally and has defused more than one difficult situation.

Womanly Wisdom

One really effective way to defuse conflict among children is what I call the "you hurt your sister now you have to hug her" ploy. It really does work. By the time they get to the hug they are usually laughing.

Just because you come from different places does not mean you can't create a family identity and forum. Although it may seem artificial, we actually try to have family meetings. If you don't take the time to find out what is on everyone's mind, especially when you have children who have been influenced by another household, you will be buried under the weight of the confusion.

It is interesting to see how children will pull together over certain issues. I highly recommend informal family meetings—other than at the dinner table—to go over things that are on *their* agenda as well as things that are on yours. The one thing a blended family needs in the extreme is order. Whatever I can do to maintain that order brings us a step closer to keeping the peace.

At times, the challenge of living in a blended family may feel as though it is too much for you. Sometimes it is not destined to work out, and it just won't. But often it is the best possible opportunity for you to learn the lessons that will ultimately give you the balance and peace you deserve from life. As you approach your everyday challenges try to do so with a total commitment to the marriage. You have many levels of healing to do. If you are feeling the threat of another loss you are going to get caught up in that stage of the relationship. It is too much of a distraction and you have more important work to do.

Make a pact with your husband that you are going to work things out in whatever way you can. Be compassionate toward each other and give each other a lot of praise, appreciation, and support. Your children need you to be steady and solid for them. You deserve the support a stable marriage can provide. But you will be doing a lot of things all at once.

Aside from turning to each other for support and turning to professionals to help you through any of the crises beyond your realm of understanding, you always can turn to God for help and guidance. Whatever connects you to your spiritual center can be a lifeline for your family. I truly believe that members of blended families have priority treatment when they ask for help. Why not? So much good can come out of a new family unit that is built by people who have learned from past mistakes and who understand the importance and blessedness of a stable home.

The Least You Need to Know

➤ Blended families have a set of challenges unique to them.

➤ It is important to establish a means for both parents to have authority in the home. The parents need to create a united front as they try to raise their children.

➤ Children have a way of taking control of a situation if they're not given firm limits by parents who are both involved.

➤ Seek out creative ways to build family unity, including a formal family council.

Part 6
Getting to Know You

You've spent a lifetime getting to this point—the place where your children are finally grown and you can build new relationships in your life. First and foremost you'll be looking for a new foundation for your relationship with your child—one firmly founded on friendship. But most of all, this is your time to turn your attention to your own spiritual growth, and in these chapters you'll find the insight you need to develop a spiritual strength that will enrich your life and the lives of those around you.

Chapter 22

Friends at Last

In This Chapter

➤ Moving out into the real world: Your child leaves the nest

➤ Moving back into the nest: The prodigal returns

➤ Making friends at last

As you learned in Chapter 15, "Loosening the Reins Without Letting Go," once your child reaches the age of majority, your relationship is going to change. The world recognizes him as a full adult and he is going to want to be treated as such. But you can still have some influence and involvement in your child's life, if you've taken the time to build a strong relationship and are able to recognize your child's new status in the adult world. One thing is certain: You are once again going to have to renegotiate your motherhood style to suit this new situation. In this chapter you will learn how to take the relationship you've built with your child over the years and nurture it into one that suits your shared adult status. You'll discover that you never stop being a mom, and that mothering an adult child can be a truly rewarding phase in your ongoing parent-child relationship.

When Your Child Leaves the Nest...

When a child turns 21, the law removes any remaining status limitations, such as drinking alcohol. Your child is now grown up enough to make all the bad decisions she chooses. She may herself be fully convinced of her adult status and instant impeccable judgment. But as you well know, this is a time when big mistakes can be made, and as a parent you *will* worry. Especially because this is also a time when young people can be held the most accountable. No one is going to cut them the same breaks they might have received at a younger age. So the consequences of your child's mistakes are significantly higher than at any earlier time in her life.

Dangerous Behaviors

Your child will face some significant temptations as she tests her new independence. And for some reason drinking is the most common rite of passage into this stage of adulthood. Perhaps this is because of the pervasiveness of advertising that presents drinking as an essential component of "good times." Drinking lends itself to the image of carefree sophistication that is so seductive to someone this age.

Momma Said There'd Be Days Like This

I observed an interesting scene recently at one of my favorite restaurants. A family seated near us was celebrating the oldest daughter's 21st birthday. The birthday girl declared that it was her night to drink, and her mother ordered one of each of several types of drinks she mentioned. The mother said, "Drink it all if you want to. Maybe tomorrow when you wake up with a big hangover, you'll realize how stupid it is to drink too much."

You will worry about your adult child, but you can only hope that your children aren't interested in drinking to excess or indulging in any other dangerous behaviors, because you are no longer legally in a position to stop them. You can tell them you do not approve because of the health risks, the safety risks, and the fact that drinking makes people behave foolishly, but if you do so in too preachy a manner you run the risk of alienating your child. As difficult as it may be, you probably want to avoid making too big a deal of it.

Remember, your 18- to 21-year-old is still in many ways an adolescent in adult's clothing. This is one of the most difficult transition times in your life and the life of your child. You will find that you often have to bite your tongue and let your child take some risks. Or at least find ways to suggest rather than command when you want to influence his or her behavior. This is, in other words, the time when the lifeline between the two of you is stretched to its fullest extent, ultimately to snap and permit two separate, adult identities to form where once there was the joined parent-child unit.

You will feel the tension. You may even have some power struggles as the two of you negotiate a new relationship based on parity as adults. At times, you may feel you will never again have a good relationship with your child. But don't fret—you're just feeling a little disoriented as you leave behind your old style of mothering and set about developing a new one. You have gotten this far. All the pangs you feel now are nature's way of beginning the process of finally pushing your child out of the nest.

You will be reviewing what you have learned, your child will be reviewing what she has learned, and you will both need to establish a new relationship on new terms.

Support, Don't Control

It is difficult to mother a young adult but, however much he may resist, he still needs to know you're there for him. The early twenties is such an age of insecurity for most people that you'll be hard-pressed to find ways of directly helping your child that he will accept. There is not much a mother can do during this time except lend support. You can't take away the pain of broken relationships, disappointments, failures, and disillusionment, no matter how much you might wish to do so. You can offer support and advice but you do not want to come across as overbearing.

You have to encourage your children to dare to go out and risk failure. But this is hard. You don't want them to fail, and you don't want them to think they will fail. But you *do* want them to know that the only real failure is not trying at all. If there is something they want badly enough, they have to be willing to take the risks and make the effort to try to achieve it. You are not doing your child a favor if you try so hard to protect him that you remove the need for him to try things on his own.

But you're a mom, no matter how old your child may be. It is easy to be overprotective. It is much more difficult to hold back and watch from the sidelines. You can still keep your radar and intuition finely attuned, but do not make it obvious.

Womanly Wisdom

You'll find it hard, but you must try to refrain from sharing your opinions when you see your child in situations that you can recall going through in your own youth. If you stay too involved in decisions or continue to parent too long after your child should move on, you risk reinforcing whatever insecurities your child may be trying to overcome.

...And Builds a Nest of Her Own

A very difficult part of letting go, now that your child is an adult, is to reserve judgment when you're faced with the way your child chooses to live. There is no way your child is going to maintain the same standard of living you have provided. But if your child is ready and able to set up an apartment or share a house with friends and wants to be out on his or her own, it is a good idea to encourage such a move at this age.

There are limits, of course. You do not want to stand by silently as your child moves into an area with the highest crime rate of the city. If there are real safety issues that you absolutely must raise, you will have to find a tactful way to make your point. You might try an appeal to logic by actually getting the crime statistics to prove your point. Try to offer alternatives in the same rental range, but do this all in the spirit of rational discussion—if you let yourself become argumentative or controlling you may simply confirm your child's need to go with her original choices.

Momma Said There'd Be Days Like This

A person's first home away from home is a very special thing. My first foray out of university housing was into a turn-of-the-century house that I shared with two other girls. I will never forget the look on my mother's face when she and my housemates' mothers first walked through the dilapidated old house. She was clearly appalled—and she told me years later that she never stopped worrying that the house would fall in on our heads. But to her credit she did not try to stop me.

Your Child's Home Is Where the Bonding Can Be Done

My first apartment on my own was a shoebox I shared with my cat. I had mason brick bookshelves and a thimble-sized kitchen I decorated with contact paper, but it was home. It boosted my self-confidence and made me very happy. I certainly could have had more luxurious digs at home with my parents—but at what price? At this age, both the mother and the child are working through such serious identity crises that they are best off in separate quarters until at least some of the issues are resolved.

By letting your child build her own nest you are saying, in effect, "I respect your maturity and your need for independence." On the other hand, when you are asked to help her find a place of her own, by all means help your child if you can—it's a wonderful opportunity to forge the early terms of your new relationship.

Mom Alert!

Don't make it too easy for your adult child to stay in your nest. At the same time, be careful that your nudges to encourage him to try his own wings aren't construed as rejection. You want him to fly out into the world with confidence, secure in the knowledge that he always has a place in your life.

When You Need to Nudge a Little

Your child may not be ready for fully independent living at exactly the age of 18 to 21, but when he has the desire and confidence to move on, he'll go.

Some technically adult offspring, however, take a little longer than even you can handle—you may run out of patience while you wait for your child to be ready to make the move. This is no great sin.

If this is true in your family, I wouldn't suggest packing his things and renting out his room, but you can drop subtle hints. And if your child is the type who wants to be taken care of long after it is appropriate for you to do so, you're fully justified in moving on to dropping not-so-subtle hints. You're not being mean. Your goal is to help your child develop the tools to know when it is time to move on, as well as the tools to do so.

Bringing a Few Feathers for the New Nest

If your relationship with your child is such that he welcomes your help in setting up his new house, it can be a wonderful rite of passage for both of you. You can even create ritual around it to mark the moment.

First, however, you want to help your child put together the basic necessities. Even if it means a trip to the Salvation Army, you can share in the fun of helping your child pick out his or her first couch, coffee table, dinette, and bed frame. You can throw in some extra things from your own home, if you have anything suitable. This is a very good opportunity for bonding and for building a new relationship based on the visible recognition that you respect your child's status as an adult.

There is no reason you can't help your child buy other necessities like sheets, dishes, glasses, and silverware if you have the money and like doing that sort of thing. Just be sure to set a budget and allow your child to pick out the items according to his or her taste. It is too easy to succumb to the temptation to shop on your own and present your purchases (and your taste) without reference to your child's preferences.

Womanly Wisdom

If you can't help your child outfit her apartment with no strings attached, do not get involved at all. This is a time to help your child cut the dependency strings, not attach new ones.

This should be a shared experience, if at all possible. Make it clear ahead of time what the budget is so the spending does not become an issue. If your child knows ahead of time what to expect, he or she is given the adult option of planning and budgeting. Another benefit of this method is that your child should not feel any guilt about accepting your gift.

Cutting the Ties That Bind

While it's important that you help your child break free of his or her child status, you also have to cut your own strings—the ties that bind you into your earlier mothering role and inspire you to try to control in an effort to stay connected. Old habits die hard.

Can't Buy Me Love

Money is one of the most commonly misused tools with which parents attempt to maintain control over their adult children. It's important to avoid the temptation to buy your child's continued attention or his compliance with your wishes.

If you are worried about losing your child or not having any attention or companionship after your child is on his own, tell him how you feel. Direct discussion is far more effective than second-hand manipulation will ever be. You want to be able to love your child and to know that your child loves you for who you are, not for what you can buy.

So, if you can't afford to help your child set up house, be honest about that, too. Tell your child that you would like to share the experience when he or she has saved enough money to make the trip to the store. It is the time you share that is important. For all you know your child may want to buy everything on his or her own, for that feeling of personal accomplishment.

Bless This Home

After the new place has been set up, you and your child might find it fun to create a ritual to bless it and make it a home. Do whatever makes your child comfortable. Here are some ideas for a blessing ritual:

➤ Bring bread, salt, and honey to the new home. They symbolize happiness, prosperity, and protection.

Mom Alert!

Whatever you do, do *not* let a first apartment or house pass by without some recognition. These ritual markers serve an important purpose in helping everyone adjust to different stages of life. They also simply make life fun.

➤ Use Native American smudge sticks made up of cedar, sage, and wheat grass. (They're available at many herbal or natural food stores.) You light the end of the stick and let the smoke line the perimeter of the rooms. This ritual is done to cleanse and purify the home and can also be done to bring prosperity.

➤ Drink a toast to the new home—anything from sparkling cider to champagne will do.

➤ Light candles and carry them from room to room, to celebrate your child's moving in. This is a purifying ritual, and can also be done to summon joy into the home.

➤ Go ahead, be conventional: Hold a housewarming party.

When Your Child Flies Back Home

You may have a young adult child who moves back into your home after college or never leaves. This is frequently a difficult situation to handle well. If you expect to exercise the same control you had before your child turned into a young adult, forget it. Your child may make decisions with which you heartily disagree, but you are going to be living in a war zone if you expect to change things through force or intimidation.

If you have an adult child living in your house, you need to set firm rules that must be accepted as a condition of his or her continued right to remain. This is, after all, your home, and you have a right to expect that your standards of civility and family life are respected. Explain to your child, if need be, that in his own home he will have the right to set the rules, but here in your household, you and your spouse have ultimate authority.

Setting Expectations

If your child is legally considered an adult (over 21) you may need to hold him to responsibilities you would not have expected of a younger child. You want to reinforce the idea that you have a family system that only functions when every member participates. There is, in other words, no free lunch.

If your adult child is not willing to contribute to the betterment of the family, you have a problem that must be dealt with before it gets completely out of control. You do your child no favors by indulging such behavior.

Working Through Conflicts

If your adult child moves back in with you after being away at school, serving in the military, or even after a divorce, you may find it awkward at first. When a person has been on his own for any length of time he is not going to want to step backward into the "rule zone." And you may well have come to truly enjoy your own freedom from day-to-day parental responsibility.

Womanly Wisdom

Expect some conflicts. Don't feel guilty if you find yourself feeling a bit territorial, and don't be surprised if your returning child doesn't appreciate your having converted his old room into a walk-in closet.

Breaking the Old Motherhood Mold

You are going to be tempted in one of two ways. Either you'll want to overmother your returnee, or you'll want to drop the whole idea of mothering. If you choose the latter you might find a young adult trying to guilt-trip you into giving her the attention she thinks she deserves. Every child, regardless of age, expects a mother to nurture and nurture until the end of time. They often find it difficult to accept the possibility that you might want to actually have a life that isn't centered around their needs.

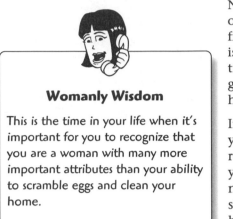

Now be honest with yourself. If you have never been one to show any desire for an individual identity distinct from your role as mother prior to your child's return, it is partially your fault if everyone expects you to continue in your established role forever. You have laid the ground rules and then changed them. You are going to have to give everyone time to adjust to the new you.

If you do not want to get back to the grind, do not let your adult child pull you back into the pampering routine. Fight that impulse to cook breakfast and ask your son whether he remembered to brush his teeth. Do not even *think* of doing your daughter's laundry unless she is willing to do yours in return. There is a limit to how much you have to devote yourself to the caretaking of people who are perfectly capable of taking care of themselves.

You Reap What You Have Sown

Maybe you were one of the smart mothers who started your children taking care of themselves from an early age. But if you are like most of us your children probably are used to having things magically taken care of for them. It is a part of the expectations associated with our role as mothers that we should take on more than our share of domestic duties. Even though you may have made it your personal crusade to break free of this stereotype, don't be surprised to find that you are still expected to be the one in charge of managing the home. If you don't mind having this expectation thrust upon you, that's fine. But it is too easy to simply accept such a role assignment, even when it is contrary to what you personally would find fulfilling.

Insisting on Assistance

If your child wants the status of an adult, then he or she has to behave like one. That means helping out and taking care of things for himself. Any adult child is fully capable of opening a can or operating a microwave—there is no reason that he or she cannot handle the basic necessities of life. Emancipate yourself so you can enjoy the presence of your child rather than enduring her presence in your home as a burden.

Your House, Your Rules

If your adult child moves home you may also have conflict about choices like overnight guests. As much as we don't like to think about the things our children choose to do, we know what we might have chosen to do at the same age. If your child is living with you, you have to decide how comfortable you are with his having an overnight guest. This is a question that is best decided *before* it becomes an issue. In the end, this, like every other issue of your adult child's behavior and participation, is up to you. If your child cannot accept your preferences, he or she is free to move away.

Ultimately, having an adult child in the house means you are going to have to establish some kind of pecking order. You want to work toward mutual respect, but in the end, it is your wishes and those of your spouse that must be respected.

Making Friends with Your Adult Child

If you establish parameters of respect, you can really start to have fun. You can let your guard down and relate to your child as a person. You may find you actually like him or her now that you are no longer charged with the constant responsibility of active mothering.

There is a certain stage when you start to see that your child understands things about life in much the same way that you do. You can tell an off-color joke and not worry about offending your child's sensibilities or corrupting her future. You can enjoy each other's company and talk about things on a much more heart-to-heart level. This is the good stuff of life.

Momma Said There'd Be Days Like This

Although my children are not adults, I see how wonderful the relationship can be. We can spend time with each other now without the tension of her wanting to parent me and me wanting to resist the feelings of vulnerability. We even talk about our men and the funny things they do. I love having a relationship with someone who also knows me almost better than I know myself.

There is a point in your relationship with your child when you can really talk heart to heart. This is a wonderful gift. It is important to share thoughts and feelings in an open and loving fashion. And when your child is an adult, there is truly no need to keep things hidden. A child has a right to know the stories of his or her family history.

Most of us have come through several generations who had many tribulations to overcome. When you have developed a good relationship with your child and have gotten past your need to mother, you can become more of a good friend. You can bring together the legacy of your past, whether good or bad, and create something good for future generations.

Mothers and their children help each other learn lessons and heal their souls. There are so many missed opportunities where this special relationship is not acknowledged and this task not carried out. In my opinion, this is the next step in your role as mother. You are always a mother—but as a friend you now become equal to your disciple. You are able to honor who your child has become as an adult and to share in his or her happiness. Your love, support, and friendship will enrich each other's lives.

The Least You Need to Know

➤ After a child reaches the age of majority (21) your relationship will change to one of greater equality and mutual respect.

➤ Some children want to move out on their own and some, after being out on their own, want to move right back into the nest.

➤ If your child moves back into your nest, remember that you and your spouse have the final say in the house rules to be followed.

➤ When your child becomes an adult, you can stop mothering in the traditional sense and work instead toward creating a relationship that more closely resembles true friendship, only deeper.

Chapter 23

Reclaiming Your Nest

In This Chapter

➤ When your children have all grown

➤ Spiritual growth: Creating a whole new you

➤ The new life

Can you believe it? Your children have grown up and left the nest. They come home for visits and on holidays. They have careers and one of them is even thinking of getting married. There are so many wonderful things to look forward to.

My, but the house stays clean these days. You can take out your expensive antique collection of perfume bottles, the ones with the fragile stoppers, that have been hidden behind glass with a kid latch all these years. Even when the children were old enough not to break things you still didn't trust them to live down their past misdeeds.

The house is so quiet. You play the kind of music you enjoy. You sit at the table in the middle of the day and sip a cup of decaf. You look back at the years and ask yourself, "Where did they all go? How did I live through them? How am I going to live without them?"

In this chapter you'll explore the possibilities that arise after your children have all grown up. You'll discover that there is a whole new world ahead of you, one in which you're still a mother (you always will be one), but in which you have as well an opportunity for personal, spiritual, and marital growth.

Finding Yourself When the Children Have Gone

It is tough to begin to redefine yourself after years of being centered on your children. You know you are not going to see them as much as you did when they lived under your roof. Now you feel guilty because of all the times you calculated exactly how long it would be before the last one would move out. You started thinking about it when your five-year-old jumped on your bed and broke the frame. You thought about it when your son rigged up a sled to go sliding down the staircase. You thought about it when your daughter stole your favorite sweater and ripped a big hole in it.

Taking Stock

Now those awful but wonderful days are gone forever. They live only in your memory and in the photographs and movies you had the foresight to take. So it's OK to sit down at your table and have a nostalgic cry into your coffee. It is sad that life is so short and that the moments of our lives seem mere flashes of light.

But don't despair for too long. There is still a lot of life ahead of you. You need to remember that being a mother is only one part of your path. You are a woman with many more journeys ahead of you. You have helped to bring life into this world and, with your love and nurturing, you've helped make things better.

Womanly Wisdom

Remember that your memories of your children's early years are filtered through the rose-colored lenses of nostalgia. They were indeed good, fulfilling times, but don't let false comparisons between those memories and what you have in the now blind you to today's joys.

You'll Always Be a Mom

You will always have your children. They will always be a part of you and you a part of them. Now it is their turn to walk their path and use what they have learned to stretch their own boundaries. Believe me, they are not going to forget you. They couldn't if they wanted to. It just doesn't work that way. Try to let them go with love and unconditional acceptance of their choices. It is now up to them to continue the path chosen for them and which they have chosen.

Creating a New Life for Yourself

Now that the children are out of the house, there are many things you can do to make it easier on yourself. If you have friends, surround yourself with them. If you do not have friends you'll want to go out and find some. If you make it a priority and follow up, there are many places to meet people in the same stage of life as you. Here are a few ideas for getting started in building a new circle of interests and friends:

➤ Check into your local community college or the continuing education extension of your state university for courses that might interest you.

➤ Sign up for an exercise class at the local gym.

➤ Get into the habit of long walks—visit neighborhoods outside your own.

If you need to, change your home environment. You do not need to keep it as a shrine to your children. If it makes you too depressed to be constantly reminded of their absence, ask them to claim their important possessions—then use the empty room to build that home office you have always wanted. If you approach it with love and explain to your children why you are changing the home when all their memories are tied up in it as well, they will most likely understand. You can make it a family event to go through all the funny accumulated possessions.

You can redecorate a house on a shoe string if you have a bit of creativity and a lot of chutzpah. It can be a lot of fun to try different things. You are now going to decorate your home for *your* lifestyle. You may want to keep one room available for future grandchildren or guests, but if not, go to town. If you can afford it, put in that Jacuzzi™ you have always wanted. If you can't afford anything so elaborate, get an easy chair, a reading lamp, and a boom box. A place to call your own. You deserve it.

Get involved with things you have always wanted to do. If you are physical, challenge your body with courses in yoga or T'ai Chi. If you are intellectual, challenge your mind. If you are social, have a lot of fun. And if you are all of these, the more the better. If you work, enjoy the extra money now that you have no children to support. If you don't work, look into starting a career that you would enjoy.

Life does not end when our children leave home. In fact, their departure is often just the beginning of a new life. You are not filling time, you are just getting on your own path without any other passengers. You are going to see what destiny puts before you. If you are blessed to be in a good marriage that has sustained the travails of child-rearing, you can rekindle the relationship that was divvied up long ago between everyone's competing needs.

Mom Alert!

Be careful to not take on so many activities and projects that you are overwhelmed. You want this to be a growth experience, not a frantic effort to avoid acknowledging an empty nest.

Momma Said There'd Be Days Like This

When I used to visit the country fairs I was always happy to see the older couples square dancing together. They were very serious about it and enjoyed it. Square dancing is not for everyone, but couples can learn all kinds of things they enjoy doing together.

Creating a New You

When my siblings and I had all left home for good and were settled into our own lives, my father made a career switch. He opened a company of his own that became very successful. When my mother got tired of not mothering and not doing anything very interesting she joined the company and became an integral part of it. I can't say they didn't argue a lot—they actually enjoy doing that. But when my father went into semiretirement because of health concerns, my mother took over the business. Now, when I want to hang out with her I have to make an appointment! It is a pleasure to see her blossom into a dynamic businesswoman at an age when many women are winding down.

Womanly Wisdom

What you choose to do at this point in your life need not be fancy or someone's idea of prestigious—it only needs to be satisfying.

There is really nothing wrong with choosing not to start a dynamic career when your children grow up. The beauty of life is that when you cover your basic needs of food, shelter, and clothing you can do whatever you want to do. If you don't want to go back to school, write a novel, become an astronaut or a congresswoman, then don't do it. Your life and your path have more to do with what is going on inside you than with how you spend your time.

Discovering Your Spiritual Path

People think the spiritual path or life's path is measured by how much you do and what you accomplish. It is really measured by how much you give and receive love. Anything else is just a product of time and space. Our souls grow in ways that we cannot consciously influence. We are given potential spiritual lessons in every moment of every day. The way we respond to them is what guides our future.

As I mentioned in Chapter 20, "Getting Back into the Dating Game," everyone is given the spiritual lessons of:

➤ Courage

➤ Tolerance

➤ Self-protection

➤ Self-love

➤ Ego

➤ Love of Humanity

➤ Love of God

These lessons have importance in our day-to-day lives but are most relevant on a spiritual level.

Spiritual Courage and Tolerance

The lesson of *spiritual courage* refers to the willingness of a person on a deep and nonconscious level to accept the possibility that what is found deep within the soul could be the truth even though other people might say otherwise. We were not created to be spiritual followers in the sense that our faith, no matter what our religion, must ultimately come from within. We have to be willing to go against the grain because true spirituality is a living and constant thing. It requires that we bring together all our own thoughts and feelings and merge them with the knowledge we have been formally taught. Each of us is a potential vessel for spiritual truth. The first lesson of courage is to accept that there is more to learn than we can ever possibly know.

Human beings want answers. To know spiritual courage is to accept that some things are unanswerable.

The lesson of *spiritual tolerance* is not what it might seem. Tolerance is equated with patience, which is certainly a virtue no matter how you look at it. But spiritual tolerance is more akin to an unconditional acceptance of the fact that all people have the right to come to their own truth in their own way. We can influence or advise when asked to do so, but we need to accept a person's choice to be right or to be wrong. If we deprive a person of the freedom to choose his own way we are essentially standing in the way of that person and God.

We always want those closest to us to see the truth as we see it. It is the greatest act of love to allow a person to come to the truth as he or she believes it on his or her own.

Self-Protection

This lesson has to do with knowing which people and situations to trust and which not to trust. It is noble to want to love everyone and everything, but there are people in this world who truly choose to be negative. As remarkable as it may seem, we are all made up of a dynamic energy. This energy is essentially positive if we are on a spiritual path, But it can be contaminated by the negativity that surrounds us. It is up to us to protect ourselves and our dynamic energy. This may mean setting limits and boundaries with people who may be energy vampires. It is one thing to be nice to people and quite another to throw away your own vital energy on people who will give nothing in return. The love of the world is supposed to be circulated. There are people who don't believe in it, and who want to see others wallow in the same misery they find themselves in.

Love is an infinite energy. Human beings are limited by our perceptions of life and our own choices. One thing you might want to do is to create a spiritual boundary like a force field around yourself. Visualize a mirror that reflects back anything a person might throw in your direction.

Mom Alert!

Be careful to accept yourself as you are, and avoid comparing yourself with others. Such comparisons lead nowhere.

You can receive and give love but you do not need to take on other people's confusion and pain. You can help those who sincerely ask for help but you do not have to deplete your life force to do it. Learning to protect yourself does not mean that you will become cold and unloving. Rather, it means that you will have more love to go around where it is truly appreciated.

Self-Love

Human beings typically do not love themselves. This is one of life's great tragedies, because God loves us. In fact, there is nothing a person can do to cause God not to love him or her. People can turn from God and basically pull the plug on themselves, but God is unconditional love. God expects human beings to be imperfect. We wouldn't be here if we didn't have to experiment to get it right. But we are more judgmental of ourselves and each other than God would ever be of us. We block the love of God and of others because we consider ourselves to be unworthy.

So many people have an abundance of love right under their noses and are afraid of it. We think we should be perfect, so instead of looking at what we do right, we focus on what we do wrong. We often have internal battles that destroy our self-confidence. We have distorted images of ourselves because we too often compare ourselves to everyone else. We are all in the same boat. The lessons are the same and we are not in competition with each other. Some people have more of a particular lesson to learn than others have, but it is all supposed to lead us to an understanding of how much we are already loved and of how wonderful and perfect we are by the simple fact of our existence. God does not make mistakes. If you are alive, even if you think you are the worst person in the world, you are important to God and to the grand scheme of things.

Womanly Wisdom

Understand that this point in your life is well-suited to embarking upon your own spiritual quest of self-fulfillment.

If you understand how unfathomable God is and you believe in miracles, doesn't it ever occur to you that everything you have ever done and everything you have ever thought is already known by God? Do you really think you can put anything over on anyone? God loves you anyway. It is you who can't forgive yourself your bad judgment or imperfections. There are consequences to your actions, but to require your own suffering is to block God's light. To block God's light is to take away from others and, essentially, to take away from God. You don't want to do that do you? If you look at it that way, it is a good deed for you to learn to love yourself. So what are you waiting for?

Spiritual Ego

The *spiritual ego* lesson is a difficult one. It is the difference between wanting to love and serve God and humanity and wanting to *be* God and be served and loved by humanity. There are many wonderfully spiritual people who couldn't get past this one. They see the love and illumination and they become blinded. Then they see the beauty in themselves and they forget about God and everyone else.

All people are subject to this lesson on one level or another. But when you get past it you will know that all people are part of God and have equal potential. When you reach this point you will want to start your day asking what you can do to serve the greater good rather than "What's in it for me?"

This does not mean you should not be good to yourself. It means you do not want to impose your will on other people and make them feel as though they're less in God's eyes.

Love of Humanity

When you learn the lesson of *love of humanity,* it's difficult not to smile all the time. You are aware of the people who don't get it and know that they will or at least can. You also will have an instant connection to those who do. You feel the positivity, love, and miracle of life and know that everything is going to be OK. We as mothers have a wonderful new generation of special children who will be loved and nurtured and who will carry forward the work of the spiritual pioneers.

Momma Said There'd Be Days Like This

When you learn this lesson it's difficult to see differences in people. Your heart shows you the sameness. You can't accept that some people are created less and others more. You know that some choose darkness in their hearts, but that has nothing to do with which vessel their souls were placed in.

When you learn this lesson you want to hug every child you see and you want to be a part of the bigger picture.

Love of God

No one can define God for you. But when you have learned to love God, no one can tell you that you don't know what God is. Enough said.

These lessons are for all people, especially women. We are coming into our own in this millennium. Our earth needs love, nurturing, and intuition.

Your Old Husband

As you begin to look at your life from the perspective of a woman's role in the millennium and in terms of the seven spiritual lessons, do not fall into the trap of assuming that your husband is a spiritual dunce. I have seen many marriages strained because a wife decides she is moving so quickly up the spiritual path that hubby can't keep up.

Remember, the spiritual path is one thing, and your marriage is another. You need to stay grounded in history and whatever loving relationships you have. You may be starting a new internal life but do not throw out the old one. Your husband is not required to embrace any of the new concepts or thoughts you might have. In fact, I think it is by design that women often go this route alone.

And you can't live in the spiritual world all the time if you are a person who also lives on Earth. People who lose sight of their mundane world are prone to going wacko. They jump from one new idea to the next and forget that the path is not about what you read or what you wear. It is about how you feel and how you live your daily life.

Remember, these lessons are described here just to help you put your life into the context of something higher than sparkling white laundry. If you think you can take this list and check each item off as it occurs, think again. You can't fudge self-realization. When you have learned the lessons you will know it by the serenity and the connection to God you feel.

Womanly Wisdom

Does spiritual growth mean life won't still have its problems? No, but you will see problems differently. They are part of the process. You may feel less helpless when you have to handle your problems, or you may just take them in stride.

Starting Your New Life

When you see the big picture of life, it is more difficult to mourn changes such as children moving out. You can't help but feel a renewed sense of adventure when you see that each individual's life has a purpose that does not end with a particular stage. You can renew your romance with your husband, you can try new things, or you can simply marvel at all the miracles that life brings to you every day if you watch for them. And with the right attitude, you can become a part of the miracles, just as you were when you helped bring a new life into the world. The world is a constant creation with infinite possibilities.

The Least You Need to Know

➤ When your children leave the nest, cry if you need to but then try to see the bigger picture.

➤ You still have a full life ahead of you that reflects your individual path.

➤ Women are an important force in the future of this world.

➤ Our lives are spent in understanding our role in the creation of our future.

Chapter 24

Celebrating a Job Well Done

In This Chapter

➤ Charting the course of your new life

➤ Looking back on your motherhood career

➤ Looking forward

In the final stage of your motherhood career your children will have grown into loving, caring adults raising children of their own. Your children are individuals with their own hopes and dreams. They have their ups and downs and sometimes they turn to you for advice and help. You never hesitate to give both. You never chastise or condemn. You remind your children that everything in life is a lesson and that they can handle anything thrown in their direction. In this chapter you will take the time to celebrate your successful navigation through the waters of a lifetime of mothering.

Charting Your Life's Course

Sometimes you may feel put upon. "Mom, can you watch the kids this weekend? I know you don't have anything much planned." Or "Mom, can you help us out with this or that material need?" You always want to say yes, but you know that that is not the solution. If you say yes to everything, no matter what you really feel, you are creating resentment within yourself and you are not really helping your children.

Setting Boundaries

You need to remember to set limits and boundaries, even with your grown children. Even though they have families of their own they are still going to see you as the "mom" and are going to lean on you at times when you might even need to do some leaning. As with every other stage of life, honesty is the best approach. Make your statements and responses reflect what you need and not be about how guilty your child should feel for having asked you for something. It is natural to ask. It is unnatural to say yes when you really need to say no.

Form the Supportive Center

Remember that no matter how old a child is, you are still at the center of his or her universe. What you do and say will always matter. So be kind to yourself and to your grown child by being uncritical and supportive. The world is already critical and competitive enough. There is nothing wrong with giving good advice if asked, but when your grown child brings a new idea or is excited by something, join in the excitement even if you think it is pure lunacy.

Mom Alert!

Guilt is never a good teaching tool.

You have already raised your children. You have a love bond and a history together, but you are not still raising this person. You have to take yourself out of that mode or you will find your children avoiding the kind of intimacy you crave. Now is the time to really appreciate your children as people. Trust them to accept the parameters that people have with each other. If you do not want to watch the grandkids, say no. If you want to help them out and you enjoy spending time with your grandkids, say yes and mean it. Learn to say what you mean and live with what you say.

Carving Out a New Role, One More Time

Don't allow grown children to manipulate you, and try not to manipulate them. Direct expressions of love are always the best. If you miss your children and want to see your grandchildren and feel you are being ignored, call your child and say, " I miss you and would enjoy spending time with you." Do not call and say, "Why haven't you called me?"

Momma Said There'd Be Days Like This

A grandmother is a very special member of a child's world. Strive for a warm, close relationship. This means communication if you do not live nearby and visits if you do. Remember important dates and show an unconditional acceptance of anything the child does. But recognize that your role is very different as grandmother than it was as mother.

At this stage of the game you do not want to alienate anyone by appearing to be overly critical. Your objective is to express your love, not to make someone feel guilty and bad about himself for not attending to your needs.

Approval Is Key

The greatest gift you can give your daughter or daughter-in-law is approval. If you start from the basis that you believe in her competence and mothering instincts, you will be given the opportunity to add your two cents when the going gets rough. If your daughter or daughter-in-law feels competitive with you in any way for the prize of supermotherhood, you are going to be left in the dust, no matter how valid and valuable your advice might be. If you want to have a good relationship with everyone, be diplomatic. It's time to pass the torch to this new generation of mothers and to offer support, not competition.

It is not good diplomacy to be uninvolved in the care and raising of grandchildren. This puts you in a no-win situation. If you seem disinterested in your grandchildren because you do not want to step on anyone's toes, you are going to be perceived as uncaring. So show your interest, but do so without challenging the judgment of your daughter or daughter-in-law.

Making Space for Everyone's Needs

It is amazing how quickly grown children can regress into the self-centered belief that they deserve all or most of your attention. Just remember who you are and how much you have already done for everyone. You have a right to do whatever you want to do with your life. If you do not want to be as involved as everyone wants you to be, decide on your limits ahead of time, make them known, and try to be attentive in ways that matter to you. If you let everyone know you love them and are there for the special times, no one can expect you to devote this time in your life to raising more children.

Grandmothering with Style

Sometimes you might find yourself in a situation where you are asked to take a more active role in the raising of a grandchild. You may have a child with special problems, or you may need to help a child after a difficult divorce. The family bond is strong and it is unlikely that you would turn away your child and grandchild, even though these responsibilities are not part of your plans.

If you decide to take on these responsibilities, wonderful. But you should never allow yourself to be taken for granted. If you are completely in

Womanly Wisdom

The privilege of being a grand-mother is that you do not have the full responsibility for the child, as you did the first time around. You do not have the same pressures or expectations. Enjoy it.

charge of your grandchild you will have less difficulty than if you have your own child in the house as well. If not, remember how you might have felt as a young mother or father in trouble. You want to be helpful but you also want to be sensitive to issues of territory. The grandchild might try to inadvertently pit you against your child. Try to anticipate the conflicts that can arise with two mothers or a mother and a grown son in the same house and focus your attention on helping to raise happy, healthy children.

Children are far more resilient than the adults in their lives. If a child is in a home where he or she is loved, it does not matter whether he's in the so-called nuclear family. There are so many different combinations now that I think anyone would have difficulty establishing a norm.

At this stage in your life you are most likely pretty settled about who you are and what your life is about. If you are fortunate you might have something you love to do, friends to keep you company, the love of a spouse, a few grandchildren to dote over, enough money for some fun, and good health to go along with it all. These are simple things that I wish for all of you. At this time in your life you will reflect on the past and consider the effect it had on you and your children and has now on your children's children.

Now would be a good time to take out the photo albums or make some if you have simply shoved your photos into boxes. You can take up scrapbooking and have fun creating keepsakes of family legends and history. Whether you know it or not you are still the glue that binds your family together. You make things special.

Applying Your Principles of Spiritual Growth

Now is the time to look back and see what you have learned, and to apply your points of spiritual growth to your life's career as a mother and a grandmother.

Courage

As a mother you were given many lessons of courage. Children do not come with instructions and there are many times no one can give you the answers you need to care for them. Sometimes what you know about your child is completely different from what everyone else says. You need courage to persist with what you know is true.

Momma Said There'd Be Days Like This

Mothers of special needs children especially have to learn lessons of courage. Sometimes you have so much information working against you that you have to brave to hold on to your own sanity. Obstacles are thrown in your path and you must hold on for dear life. Your child is the center of your universe and you will do whatever it takes to protect him.

Mothers throughout history have shown remarkable courage when it comes to their children. There is no greater force than a mother who is protecting her child. Many a mother would give her life for her child.

Time never stands still and attitudes change. Mothers of every generation need to have the courage to evolve with the times and not get caught up with outmoded methods. Mothers are a living part of the ongoing creation.

Tolerance

Mothers are faced with lessons of tolerance every day of their lives. How can you love a child so much and not want to smother it with overprotection. When you are aware of the potential dangers in the world, it is remarkable that children are not kept in sealed boxes and let out only for occasional romps in the sun. But mothers allow their children to grow and to create lives of their own.

The greatest gift of tolerance is to allow a child to make mistakes. A mother who accepts her child in spite of mistakes is acting as a teacher and guide. This kind of mother recognizes that each soul has a separate purpose and that each person has his or her highest obligation to God. Although we can guide our children through this world we can't stand in the way of their true destiny.

Self-Protection

Mothers are faced with decisions of discernment every single day. It is a mother's job to be responsible for a dependent life. And in managing or co-managing a household there are issues of self-protection every day. Aside from the obvious (watch out for danger or rip-off situations), a mother tries to create a sanctuary and safe haven for her entire family. A home is meant to be a protected environment that helps prepare its members for the world at large and the challenges of life.

Women are by nature very giving. This lesson is difficult because our motherly instinct is to take care of and overprotect our children throughout their lives. We have to learn to set limits and boundaries. After all, we too are souls whose path is connected to God. If we are always focused on everyone else we can never do what is in our own higher good. We can't possibly listen to our inner voice if we are always running to the aid of everyone else.

Think of a sunflower. It is large at the center and has many petals. If we as mothers live our lives moving from petal to petal we will never be the center of our own flower. If we are at the center we can meet our own needs and still participate in the lives of others—the petals of our bloom.

Self-Love

So much of mothering is thankless. You expect your children to be cuddly and loving all the time. But that's just not the way it usually works:

➤ When they are infants they spit up and pee on you.

➤ When they are toddlers they run away from you.

➤ When they are children they demand from you.

➤ When they are teenagers they push you.

➤ When they are young adults they leave you.

Being a mother can really affect your sense of self. It is something women are expected to know how to do, and it is one of the things we feel most inadequate about. We seldom feel that we are good mothers. We don't even allow ourselves to feel we are good enough mothers. We always feel judged and we take responsibility for everything.

We constantly give lessons of self-love because to truly love anyone else we have to love ourselves. Children help us learn these lessons because they make us see that we must be doing something right. Even if we have the lowest self-esteem, when a child says "I love you" it fills us with unconditional love. Children do not judge their mothers in the way we all think they do. They are rooting for us to believe in ourselves. We torture ourselves instead of receiving all the love that is available to us if we only open to it.

Mom Alert!

If you didn't understand the way things really are you could easily get an inferiority complex. Children do not always return love in visible ways.

Ego

It is hard for mothers to ask for help. If we are so unable to feel worthy, how could we ask God for help. So, in essence, we have to decide whether we want to serve God by allowing the energy to flow through us or whether we want to *be* God, believing we have to do everything ourselves.

The ego lesson is really about surrender. We, as mothers, need to transcend our own need to be completely in control. There are so many things in our lives that we will never be able to influence. We need to focus our attention on the things we can control, like ourselves.

Love of Humanity

When a mother fully accepts the love of herself, love of God, and the unconditional love and acceptance of her children she will see that we are really the mothers of all children. All children belong to us. If children are suffering without love and the basic necessities, we are responsible. If children are being abused, we are responsible. All children are precious and should be protected and loved. We, as mothers, need to work together to see that this becomes a reality in our lifetime. We can't judge the mothers who are unable to care for their young. We must focus on the children themselves, no matter how they are brought into the world.

Love of God

To be a mother is to have the greatest opportunity to know the love of God. Mothers can experience the unconditional nature of love, which is the definition of God. No child is perfect, and yet a mother is given the opportunity to love that child as God loves all people.

All people are given opportunities to learn these seven lessons but I believe their importance is more strongly relevant to the women of our time. Women, and mothers in particular, are going to lead the world toward peace in the new millennium. We need to recognize the big picture of our lives so we can cope with the day-to-day expectations. There is always a bigger picture than the one in front of our noses.

Whether you are just having a baby or are cuddling with your grandchildren, being a mother is a journey of self-discovery as much as it is anything else. You and your child share paths that are intertwined but always separate. You help give life to your child but the child also gives life to you.

The Least You Need to Know

➤ Celebrate your job well done.

➤ As you move through the cycles of motherhood do not forget to tell yourself how special and wonderful you are.

➤ Even if no one else remembers to mention the good job you've done, you will always know by the love you receive.

Bibliography

Some Mommy books that feel good to have around:

Beekman, Susan and Jeanne Holmes, *Battles, Hassles, Tantrums & Tears*. New York: Hearst Books, Good Housekeeping Parent Guides, 1993.

Faber, Adele and Elaine Mazlish, *How to Talk So Kids Will Listen & Listen So Kids Will Talk*. Avon Books, 1982.

Faber, Adele and Elaine Mazlish, *Siblings Without Rivalry: How to Help Your Children Live Together So You Can Live Too*. Avon Books, May 1998.

Ginott, Dr. Haim, *Between Parent & Child*. New York: The Macmillan Company, 1965.

Godfrey, Neale, *A Penny Saved*. New York: Simon & Schuster, 1995.

Gurian, Michael, *The Wonder of Boys*. New York: Putnam, 1997.

Jacobson, Michael F. and Bruce Maxwell, *What Are We Feeding Our Kids*. New York: Workman Publishing, 1994.

Katherine, Anne, *Boundaries: Where You End and I Begin*. Hazelden Foundation, 1994.

Lighter, Dawn, *Gentle Discipline*. New York: Meadowbrook Press, 1995.

Popkin, Michael, *Active Parenting*. San Francisco: Harper 1987.

Poretta, Vicki and Ericka Lutz, *Mom's Guide to Disciplining your Child*. Alpha Books, 1997.

Telushkin, Joseph, *Words that Hurt, Words that Heal*. New York: William Morrow & Company, 1996.

Wahlroos, Sven, *Family Communication*. Chicago: Contemporary Books, 1995.

Weinhaus, Evonne & Karen Friedman, *Stop Struggling With Your Child*. Harper Paperback, 1998.

Wolf, Anthony E., *Get Out of My Life: But First Could You Drive Me and Cheryl to the Mall?* New York: The Noonday Press, 1991.

Index

U–V

W–Z